"This brilliant book places the spirituality of the Tibhirine monks not only within the drama of the Algeria of their time, but also within the life and struggles of each of the monks. It is a marvellous introduction to monastic theology, and of the greatest pertinence to our own time of rising violence. I recommend it without reservation."

—Cardinal Timothy Radcliffe, OP

"A rare book, a profound study of the spirituality of the monks of Tibhirine, which shows us how to live out our faith together today, to the very limits of love, in friendship and respect."

—Dom Thomas Georgeon, postulator of the cause of the 19 martyrs of Algeria

CISTERCIAN STUDIES SERIES: NUMBER 305

Life Here Together

The Prophetic Gift of the Tibhirine Monks

Jane Foulcher

Cistercian Publications
cistercianpublications.org

LITURGICAL PRESS
Collegeville, Minnesota
litpress.org

A Cistercian Publications title published by Liturgical Press

Cistercian Publications
Editorial Offices
161 Grosvenor Street
Athens, Ohio 45701
cistercianpublications.org

Library of Congress Cataloging-in-Publication Data

Names: Foulcher, Jane author
Title: Life here together : the prophetic gift of the Tibhirine monks / Jane Foulcher.
Description: Collegeville, Minnesota : Cistercian Publications, [2026] | Series: Cistercian studies series ; number 305 | Includes bibliographical references. | Summary: "Life Here Together tells the story of the seven Tibhirine monks, kidnapped and murdered in 1996 during Algeria's "black decade," and speaks to the prophetic witness of the monks and what it meant to be deeply tethered-to each other, to their place, to their monastic tradition, and ultimately to the Christ they followed faithfully"-- Provided by publisher.
Identifiers: LCCN 2026016607 (print) | LCCN 2026016608 (ebook) | ISBN 9780879073992 trade paperback | ISBN 9780879074029 epub | ISBN 9780879073978 pdf
Subjects: LCSH: Trappists--Algeria--Tibehirine | Notre Dame de l'Atlas (Monastery : Tibehirine, Algeria) | Christian martyrs--Algeria--Tibehirine | Victims of terrorism--Algeria--Tibehirine | LCGFT: Biographies
Classification: LCC BX4155 .F68 2026 (print) | LCC BX4155 (ebook)
LC record available at https://lccn.loc.gov/2026016607
LC ebook record available at https://lccn.loc.gov/2026016608

For Freddie, Peggy, and Morris

May you know the love of learning
and the desire for God.

Contents

Abbreviations

CE	Common Era
CF	Cistercian Fathers series
CS	Cistercian Studies series
CSQ	*Cistercian Studies Quarterly*
CST	Constitutions and Statutes of the Cistercian Order of the Strict Observance
EG	*Evangelii Gaudium*
FIS	Front Islamique du Salut
FLN	Front de Libération Nationale
GIA	Group Islamic Armé
LG	*Lumen Gentium*
MW	Monastic Wisdom series
OCSO	Order of Cistercians of the Strict Observance
PCID	Pontifical Council for Interreligious Dialogue
RB	The Rule of Benedict
SAS	Sections Administratives Spécialisées
SUP	Statute on Unity and Pluralism
USMDA	Union des Supérieurs Majeurs d'Algeria

Peur de l'avenir ? Mais non, puisque seul l'amour a de l'avenir.
Afraid of the future? Why no, because only
love has a future.

—Christian de Chergé
(Letter to Maurice Borrmans, October 22, 1976)

Preface

The story of the seven Tibhirine monks, kidnapped and murdered in 1996 during Algeria's "black decade," is compelling. But it is their way of *living*—peacefully alongside their Muslim neighbors in the Atlas mountains—that challenges us.

After the monks' deaths in 1996 Pope John Paul II urged their Cistercian brothers and sisters to guard the monks' memory so that it might be "fruitful in the future of the Trappists and for the whole church." It is a heritage for all people of faith. In his message to the 2025 Meeting for Friendship Among Peoples held in Rimini, Italy, Pope Leo XIV drew attention to this heritage, inviting us to see in the Algerian martyrs our own call to "self-giving" and to a way of living that offers a prophetic witness to a world in peril. Pope Leo has challenged Christian leaders to build every community as "a 'house of peace,' where one learns how to defuse hostility through dialogue, where justice is practiced and forgiveness is cherished." And he observed, "Peace is not a spiritual utopia: it is a humble path, made up of daily gestures that interweave patience and courage, listening and action, and which demands today, more than ever, our vigilant and generative presence."[1] His words speak precisely to the prophetic witness of the Tibhirine monks.

There is much we can learn from the small monastic community of Notre-Dame de l'Atlas that might help us to navigate the challenges of contemporary life, and to offer hope in an increasingly fragile and dangerous world. The monastic

[1] https://www.vatican.va/content/leo-xiv/en/messages/pont-messages/2025/documents/20250811-messaggio-meeting-rimini.html.

way of life challenges contemporary individualism and, in the West particularly, versions of spirituality that have been increasingly untethered from their religious traditions. There is a danger in this untethering. As the Australian scholar David Tacey observes, contemporary secular spirituality is like "a lovely flower in a vase on the table, but, lacking any roots, it will fade quickly and vanish from view."[2] The Tibhirine monks show us what it meant to be deeply tethered—to each other, to their place, to their Cistercian monastic tradition, and ultimately to the Christ they followed—and yet to be open and hospitable to the other, to difference.

The monks' legacy, their gift to us, is to be found in their lives: in the way they lived out what is, in the end, our shared vocation to follow Christ. The aim of this book is to open that gift by listening to the monks' voices and by opening a window or two on their lives, so that the breath of the Spirit that infused their lives might inspire us too. Because while they inhabit a powerful and dramatic narrative, they are simply human, like us, "living here together"—"*vivre ici ensemble.*"[3]

[2] David Tacey, "Contemporary Spirituality," in *Oxford Textbook of Spirituality in Healthcare*, ed. Mark Cobb, Christina M. Puchalski, and Bruce Rumbold (Oxford: Oxford University Press, 2012), 473.

[3] "Comment, dans la situation présente, rejoignons-nous le charisme de notre Ordre? (21 novembre 1995)," in *Sept vies pour Dieu et l'Algérie*, ed. Bruno Chenu (Paris: Bayard, 1996), 180.

Acknowledgments

I first encountered the story of the Tibhirine monks as a doctoral student in 2008. A simple database search delivered an article by Edith Scholl, OCSO, introducing Christian de Chergé's chapter talks on humility—the focus of my research. I had hit gold. I keep returning to the monks of Tibhirine, and every time I do I am blessed.

I am not a monk, nor a Roman Catholic, nor indeed a French speaker. I live on the other side of the world from Algeria, in rural Australia. Nothing especially equips me to write about the monks of Tibhirine. But it is the fruitfulness of each return to the monks, especially to the writings of Christian de Chergé and Christophe Lebreton, that allows me to hope that this modest engagement with their lives might contribute to making the community of Notre-Dame de l'Atlas better known in the English-speaking world.

A warm thank you to the Association pour la protection des écrits des sept moines de l'Atlas and to Éditions de Bellefontaine and Éditions du Cerf for permission to reproduce the monks' writings, and with enormous thanks to Liturgical Press and Cistercian Publications for their generous funding of the permissions costs. I am most grateful to the mostly anonymous transcribers of the archival material held by the Abbaye Notre-Dame d'Aiguebelle—especially of Christian's chapter talks and homilies from his handwritten notes. A work of dedication. Similarly Marie-Dominique Minassian's extensive work in gathering the monks' writing for publication has been an extraordinary gift. I have pored over many of these texts at a *lectio*-like pace and found myself enriched.

In working with the French texts, I am deeply indebted to Kate Watson, who spent many hours combing through and improving my amateur attempts at translation, bringing to the table not only her fluent language skills but her first-hand experience of French Catholic spirituality. I could not have embarked on this project without Kate's support. Tim Watson periodically came to the rescue with his experience in translating French theology.

I am grateful to Charles Sturt University and St Mark's National Theological Centre in Canberra for access to their library and research resources. A special thanks to the Revd. Dr. Graeme Garrett for helping me clarify my priorities and to the Rt. Revd. Professor Stephen Pickard for reading draft chapters and encouraging me to press on. It has been a pleasure once more to work with Professor Marsha Dutton, whose keen editorial eye always results in a better book, and with the expert team from Liturgical Press.

Thanks to the good people of the Anglican parishes of Braidwood and Manuka, my Reidsdale neighbors and Canberra friends, and especially my family, who have all taken a warm interest in the project. My deepest thanks go to my husband, John Foulcher, for his tireless encouragement and for enduring my long absences, actual and virtual, while I focused on writing to a deadline.

Some material in this book has appeared in earlier forms. Part of the Introduction was published as "Living Hope: The Witness of the Tibhirine Monks," *St Mark's Review*, no. 266 (December 2024): 58–68. Chapter 1 draws on a few paragraphs from *Reclaiming Humility: Four Studies in the Monastic Tradition*, CS 255 (Collegeville, MN: Cistercian Publications, 2015). Chapters 3 and 8 draw on material published as "A Monastic School of Peace in Post-colonial Algeria: Christophe Lebreton's Tibhirine Journal," *Spiritus: A Journal of Christian Spirituality* 24, no. 1 (2024): 24–46.

A Note on Translation

Regardless of one's own capacities, the work of translation is never straightforward, and I am deeply grateful to those who have already offered English translations of some of

Christian de Chergé's and Christophe Lebreton's writings. The translator is a juggler, trying to be faithful to both the language of the original and the language of the translation. Franz Rosenzweig, one of the most important twentieth-century translators of the Hebrew Scriptures, said, "Translating means serving two masters. It follows that no one can do it."[4] The Italian phrase *traduttore, traditore* expresses this even more sharply: translation is betrayal. In the translations that I have risked I hope not to have entirely betrayed the Tibhirine monks. I have tended to stay close to what in Biblical translation is called a "formal equivalence" approach. I am not unhappy with the idea that the monks should still sound French in the way that they express themselves!

Language points towards rather than pinning down thought and experience—and perhaps this is even more so when it comes to theology, making translation across different languages and cultures particularly challenging. I hope that I have been able to signal at least some of the rich resonances that are often found in the written heritage of this monastic community. Their writing is not only deeply imprinted with Scripture, especially the gospels and the psalms, but also with the French Catholic spirituality of the mid- to late-twentieth century and the fresh winds of Vatican II.

Some elements of translation pose particular difficulties. Gendered language, such as the wide use of *l'homme* ('man') in Christian's writing, are problematic for contemporary English readers. However, I have chosen to translate *l'homme* directly as *man* rather than *human*.[5] These are texts of their time and culture. Occasionally I have offered the original French

[4] Quoted in John Barton, *The Word: On the Translation of the Bible* (London: Allen Lane, 2022), 18.

[5] Jennifer Rushworth and Matthew Cheung Salisbury rightly point out that French is a more gendered language than English. In their introduction to their translation of Christian de Chergé's late chapter talks they discuss this translation challenge and their somewhat different strategy (Christian de Chergé, *God for All Days: The Final Monastic Chapters of Christian de Chergé*, trans. Jennifer Rushworth, ed. Matthew Cheung

for particular words or phrases in brackets or longer texts in footnotes. Some key phrases do not translate easily, the prime example being *priants parmi d'autre priants,* which I render as "praying among others who pray" (discussed in chapter 6). I have retained the capitalization of whole words from the French texts, as the writers use it for emphasis. Similarly, the French texts often use an ellipsis (. . .) as an indication of an unfinished thought, or a thought that does not quite reach a full stop. I have retained these and therefore use brackets for ellipses [. . .] to indicate my omissions from quoted texts.

Quotations from the Bible generally use the New Revised Standard Version (NRSV), although it has been necessary in some instances to translate directly from the French in order to retain the sense of the interpretive comments being made by the text's author.

Psalms are numbered using Hebrew numbering with the Greek Septuagint number given in parentheses. The monks, in line with Roman Catholic liturgical practice of the time, used the Greek Septuagint numbering inherited via the Latin Vulgate. However, in line with *La Bible de Jérusalem* and with contemporary US Roman Catholic practice I place the Hebrew psalm number first (e.g., See Ps 73 [72]:9).

Salisbury, MW 73 [Collegeville, MN: Cistercian Publications, 2025], xxix–xxxi).

Introduction

The path has been marked out,
we have only to walk along it.
—Bernardo Olivera

In the early hours of March 27, 1996, seven French Cistercian monks were kidnapped by heavily armed insurgents from their monastery in the small Algerian village of Tibhirine, in the foothills of the Atlas Mountains. The monks would not have been surprised by their abduction, nor by their subsequent execution, which their captors announced was carried out two months later, on May 21. Each of them had anticipated this moment and its probable end.

The brutal deaths of the seven monks shocked Algerians and French alike. But such savage violence had become routine during Algeria's "black decade," the civil war that tore the country apart from the early 1990s to the early 2000s. Perhaps as many as two hundred thousand people, mostly Algerian Muslims, lost their lives.[6] Among them were nineteen priests and religious, including the seven Tibhirine monks: Fr. Christian de Chergé, Br. Luc Dochier, Fr. Christophe Lebreton, Fr. Bruno Lemarchand, Br. Michel Fleury, Fr. Célestin Ringeard, and Br. Paul Favre-Miville. Two of the community's monks survived, missed by the kidnappers: Fr. Amédée (Jean) Noto and Fr. Jean-Pierre Schumacher.

[6] Martin Evans and John Phillips, *Algeria: Anger of the Dispossessed* (New Haven, CT: Yale University Press, 2007), xv. Official estimates range between 100,000 and 150,000.

Their story begins with the establishment of a Cistercian monastery in French colonial Algeria in 1843 and weaves through their individual, often decisive, encounters with Algeria during or after the war of independence; their formation and profession as Cistercian monks; their evolving vocation living alongside their Muslim neighbors in Tibhirine; their particular place in the renewal of the small but faithful Algerian church seeking to contribute positively in a Muslim majority country; and finally, the shared agony of the Algerian civil war.

The small monastic community of Notre-Dame de l'Atlas had first been visited by armed insurgents, members of the Groupe Islamic Armé (GIA), on Christmas Eve 1993. This visit followed an ultimatum issued in October by the GIA warning foreigners to leave Algeria within a month. During December, as the ultimatum expired, four foreign nationals were assassinated in Algiers, and twelve Catholic Croatians had their throats cut at Tamesguida, a few kilometers from the monastery. The Christmas Eve visit by the local GIA leader Sayah Attiya and his men permanently marked the monks, both individually and as a community. Christian de Chergé's extraordinary *Testament* was completed at this time. Christophe Lebreton's prayer journal offers us an intimate window into its immediate and ongoing impact. The monks continued, by choice, to live alongside their Tibhirine neighbors in a situation of increasing insecurity and violence, until their abduction and execution just over two years later.

A Heritage "too big for us"

Why did they stay? How do we understand their witness? Do the lives and deaths of these seven monks have something to say to us, especially in a world of increasing violence and fragility?

The monks' abduction was widely reported and their fate anxiously watched by a horrified French church and nation. Prayers were offered around the world for their safe release.

The GIA demand that the French government negotiate the release of prisoners in Algeria and France in exchange for the monks was not met. The consequent GIA announcement of the execution of the seven monks on May 21 was reported internationally.[7] Church bells across the whole of France were tolled in their memory. Their story has been seared into the consciousness of both church and state in France. Their legacy began before their remains were buried.

Texts from and about the Tibhirine community began to be published almost immediately after the monks' deaths. A growing corpus of books, articles, films, and even music and theater, primarily in French, has been produced to honor the monks and explore their story.[8] And their own voices are being increasingly heard through the ambitious publishing program of the Association pour la protection des écrits des sept moines de l'Atlas. On December 8, 2018, after a process that began in 2006 to formally recognize the martyrdom of the nineteen religious and priests who were killed in Algeria between 1994 and 1996, the seven Tibhirine monks were beatified—in the Roman Catholic Church the first step toward sainthood. Fittingly, and with permission negotiated with the Algerian government, the ceremony was conducted in Oran, Algeria, the first ceremony of its kind to be held in a Muslim country.

In thinking about their legacy, we can begin in no better place than with Dom Bernardo Olivera's challenge to his Cistercian brothers and sisters on the first anniversary of the monks' deaths. Olivera was the abbot general of the Order of Cistercians of the Strict Observance (OCSO) from 1990 to 2008; he knew the Atlas community well. He had made an extended visit to the community in 1991 and flew to Algeria following the GIA announcement that the monks had been executed,

[7] The monks' deaths were the subject of a French judicial inquiry that commenced in 2004. The 2018 report cast doubt on the accounts of the monks' deaths proffered by both the Algerian government and the GIA.

[8] A bibliography is maintained by the research center dedicated to the Algerian martyrs, led by Marie-Dominique Minassian at the University of Fribourg. See https://projects.unifr.ch/tibhirine/fr/ .

arriving to the news that their remains had been discovered. He presided over their burial at Tibhirine on June 4, 1996. In his circular letter of May 21, 1997, the first anniversary of the monks' deaths, Olivera challenged his Cistercian brothers and sisters to keep their memory alive, not simply because these seven brothers deserved to be remembered, but because they had left a heritage to be shared. Pope John Paul II had already alluded to that heritage in a message to the general chapter of the Order, meeting in Rome in October 1996: "you are the custodians of this memory, guardians in prayer, in common discernment, and in the concrete directives which you decide upon, so that the memory of this event [may] be fruitful in the future for Trappists and for the whole Church."[9] Olivera comments,

> It is true. We are the heirs of the martyrdom suffered by our brothers. We have no doubt that they are the light of the world. A lamp is not lit and then put under a basket. It is set on a lampstand. What, then, can we do to have the memory of these events bear fruit for the order and for the entire Church?[10]

The first responsibility, Olivera appreciates, is to understand the nature of this legacy: what is this light that the Trappists are pressed to share? He articulates with "clarity and

[9] Bernardo Olivera, *How Far to Follow: The Martyrs of Atlas*, CS 197 (Kalamazoo, MI: Cistercian Publications, 1997), 107. For the Italian text see https://www.vatican.va/content/john-paul-ii/it/messages/pont_messages/1996/documents/hf_jp-ii_mes_19961010_monaci-trappisti.html. Members of the Order of the Cistercians of the Strict Observance (OCSO) were in the past widely known as Trappists, since the seventeenth-century reform of the Order was centered at the French abbey of La Trappe. Today members of this branch of the Cistercian family increasingly identify themselves simply as Cistercians or as members of the OCSO. Notre-Dame de l'Atlas and its motherhouse Notre-Dame d'Aiguebelle are members of the OCSO, so historically they were often known as Trappist communities.

[10] Olivera, *How Far to Follow*, 105.

conviction" what he believes is "the heart of the heritage" that the monks have left. Again, he begins with John Paul II's understanding of their gift:

> The *Testament* which Dom Christian de Chergé left behind contains the key for understanding the tragic event in which he and his confreres were involved, the final meaning of which is the gift in Christ of their life. "My life," he wrote, "was given to God and to this country."[11]

Olivera continues, "the inner key for understanding our brothers is the commitment of their lives to the following of Jesus."[12] This might sound self-evident, perhaps even trite—yet Olivera knows that following Jesus is by no means a given, even for monks. He understands discipleship as a subtle and ongoing process:

> The following of Christ implies a double reality. The first is dynamic, a movement. The second is static, remaining with him. Obviously remaining near Jesus depends on moving toward him. This double reality comes to form a single one made up of the dedication and gift of self. The person given to Jesus moves toward him so as to be transformed by him and in him. Unfortunately, and it is sad to say so, Christian and monastic life is full of persons who are "deeply moved," but hardly move at all.[13]

Olivera's thinking here is akin to the notion of "abiding" found in the Gospel of John, especially in the image of the vine, an image that offers the double sense of stability and movement (John 15:1-11). The connection to Christ gives life, and without this connection people wither. But being part of this vine also means being pruned to ensure fruitfulness: human

[11] Olivera, *How Far to Follow*, 106.
[12] Olivera, *How Far to Follow*, 106.
[13] Olivera, *How Far to Follow*, 106.

flourishing is not achieved without cost to the unruly self. Olivera's wry conclusion makes for uncomfortable reading: following Christ invites an openness to transformation, to change. After a day working in the monastery's vineyard, Christophe Lebreton reflected, in an entry in his prayer journal, on this "double reality" of discipleship: "Constancy, permanence, stability . . . and then: mobility, the road. Both 'Abide!' and 'Let's go forward!'" Christophe understood that it was "the relationship with Christ," not "Christian values," that would endure.[14]

At the end of his letter, Olivera returns to this central challenge of following Jesus. He reminds his fellow Cistercians that "their vow of *conversatio morum* [conversion of life] can be understood as a promise to follow Jesus in the monastic life" and that this monastic way of following Jesus is set out in the Rule of Benedict, specifically as a "way of obedience-silence-humility (RB 5–7), of good zeal and good works (RB 72 and 4)."[15] So receiving the Tibhirine monks' legacy means considering how they lived as followers of Jesus and how they understood and practiced the monastic way of following Christ, in particular the Cistercian monastic way with its foundations in the Rule of Saint Benedict.

A Cistercian Charism in Algeria

What did it mean to be a Cistercian monastic community in Algeria at this time? In November 1995, two years after the GIA ultimatum and the Christmas Eve visit of Sayah Attiya and his men, the monks reflected on the nature of their Cistercian monastic charism in preparation for a gathering of the leaders of religious communities in Algeria.[16] The resulting

[14] Christophe Lebreton, *Born from the Gaze of God: The Tibhirine Journal of a Martyr Monk (1993–1996)*, trans. Mette Louise Nygård and Edith Scholl, MW 37 (Collegeville, MN: Cistercian Publications, 2014), May 1, 1994, 78.

[15] Olivera, *How Far to Follow*, 122.

[16] Union des Supérieurs Majeurs d'Algeria (USMDA).

report, compiled by the prior of the Atlas community, Christian de Chergé, offers a snapshot of their self-understanding just a few months before they were abducted from their monastery.

The monks were asked to consider how the charism of their order was being embodied in the current situation. Did "the last turbulent two years mark a drift?" Did the circumstances "oblige us to adapt, to compromise beyond the limits of our charism?"[17] As the brothers speak and listen to each other, one thing becomes clear to them: "this charism is an irrevocable gift of God" (*un don de Dieu sans repentance* [cf. Rom 11:29]), and it is this charism, "a living obligation, not set in stone," that allows them to remain faithful to the Gospel in a country "oppressed by terrorism, repression, a crisis of identity, and a marked impoverishment of [their] immediate environment."[18]

How is this charism expressed? The report draws together the community's reflections in three sections: it offers first some different perspectives on the essence of their charism; second, thoughts on the challenges they face within the broader mission of the church in Algeria; finally, and perhaps most important, how they live out their charism in the daily, in the quotidian.

In articulating the essence of their Cistercian charism, Christian gathers the monks' thoughts into key themes: presence, sign, contemplation, and, perhaps surprisingly, *bonheur* (happiness or joy). The report is replete with direct quotations, allowing us to hear a variety of voices from the community.[19] The monks express their understanding of their charism with clarity and confidence.

[17] "Comment, dans la situation présente, rejoignons-nous le charisme de notre Order? (21 novembre 1995)," in *Sept vies pour Dieu et l'Algérie*, ed. Bruno Chenu (Paris: Bayard, 1996), 175.

[18] "Comment, dans la situation présente," 176.

[19] I have followed Christian's text in using quotation marks for the other monks' contributions.

> "To ensure a presence, not missionary-apostolic, but contemplative and prayerful in a Muslim milieu, by means of a community that is stable, united and fraternal, hard-working (with the associates)."[20]
>
> "A discrete, mysterious presence, separate from the world and in communion with people, humbly attentive to the material and spiritual needs of those around us."
>
> "*Ora et labora* [prayer and work] . . . to be together a sign of the Church, invisible to the world, but visible to our neighbors. Witnesses of peace, of the possibility of fraternity, by the grace of God, across our diversities."
>
> . . . on the way: a communal way toward the contemplative experience of union with God.[21]

It is Christian's voice that can be heard in relation to *bonheur*, and it is worth noting that in this same context he speaks of the continuing process of discernment of vocation, and of the departure of two brothers, one returning to secular life and a novice to another monastery. Each monk's well-being (*bonheur*) was central to these decisions.[22] Their joy is predicated on the sense of freedom that arises from confidence in their call:

> A great, unalterable joy [*joi*], with the certitude that God called us not only to live monastic life, but to live it here, at Tibhirine, and that this is just as true today. [. . .] Happiness [*bonheur*] here is risky, but real. It is tasted in perseverance.[23]

[20] The monks worked the monastery vegetable plots and orchards in a cooperative with village neighbors.

[21] "Comment, dans la situation présente," 176–77.

[22] During this period the community had wisely decided not to accept any new novices.

[23] "Comment, dans la situation présente," 177.

The Benedictine vow of stability stood: their commitment was to this place, Tibhirine, living with each other as brother monks and with their Muslim neighbors, seeking a fraternity that embraced difference.

The report also names the prayerful support that the monks received from other Cistercian communities and from the local church. Indeed, they understood their charism in solidarity with the mission of the church in Algeria, a church that had been battered to a point of extreme fragility. Together they had been thrust into a situation where they had experienced the Gospel-inscribed "self-emptying [*dépouillement*] and free gift" that is the shared vocation of all followers of Jesus. Paradoxically, this had allowed the church to live out its Gospel mission—"to love to the very end [*aimer jusqu'à l'extrême*]"—with freedom and authenticity.[24]

Amid these difficult circumstances one might expect the community's monastic way of life to have come unstuck or been impossibly compromised. This is not the case. There were clear pressures, and the report names these: the heavy workload carried by such a small community threatened to impinge on the priorities of prayer and *lectio divina* (sacred reading); the often serious and urgent needs of those around them left them feeling "helpless and powerless," requiring "additional silence and recollection."[25] But the community reflects that over these two years "the monastic charism has seemed to us neither easier nor more difficult." In fact, the realities of their situation provoked the growth of "truth and humility," while awareness of the difficulties faced by all people motivated "prayer and poverty."[26]

In this situation of extreme insecurity, what Christian calls their "daily way of expressing hope" provided an anchor.[27] Foundational to this way was their commitment to living in

[24] "Comment, dans la situation présente," 178.

[25] "Comment, dans la situation présente," 179.

[26] "Comment, dans la situation présente," 178.

[27] "une façon quotidienne d'exprimer l'espérance" ("Comment, dans la situation présente," 179).

community, as cenobitic monks. The presence of others offered "support for each" and "a remedy for the inevitable fantasies."[28] In fact, the pressures of the previous two years had strengthened the bonds among the brothers. A greater level of "consultation and dialogue" underpinned their decision making, deepening their understanding of monastic obedience. Christian characterizes their communal relationships as "mutual dependence."[29] After Christmas 1993 the monks had "re-chosen (re-chosen) to live here together" (*vivre ici ensemble*).[30] In repeating the word "re-chosen" Christian stresses that this hope-oriented way of life is not oppressive: it is chosen in freedom.

Ultimately, the living out of their charism, their following Christ in the monastic way, was to be found in the daily, the quotidian. Christian emphasizes the necessity of accepting life as it is. This is not fatalism. He has an active sense of acceptance in mind here: seeking to choose rather than submit to the constraints imposed upon them.[31] And it was the shape and rhythm of monastic life that powered this possibility. The community's "daily way of expressing hope" was shaped by the core monastic priorities of prayer, work, and hospitality, by the monks' "separation from the world" (their monastic enclosure, by no means typically expressed), and by their particular vocation as a place of Christian-Muslim dialogue (again, by no means typically expressed). This late community reflection offers a candid report card on these core monastic priorities. Again, the monks' voices illuminate the report with their honesty.

[28] "Comment, dans la situation présente," 179.

[29] "Comment, dans la situation présente," 179.

[30] "Tous nous avons rechoisi (rechoisi) de vivre ici ensemble" ("Comment, dans la situation présente," 180).

[31] "Comment, dans la situation présente," 181.

On prayer:

> "To increase the level of faith-hope-charity in oneself is to increase it in the environment in which we live. And this is our way of providing a solution to the country's crisis."

> "My prayer? What can I say? . . . but there is the prayer of Jesus. And his silence as 'they set their mouths against heaven'!" [see Ps 73 (72):9].[32]

On *lectio divina*:

> In the night, take up the Book when others take up arms.

> "In January 1994, I read the Book of Revelation in a different light. I taste Psalms 93, 123, etc. 'God the breaker of war,' here (cf. song of Judith). The reading at Vigils from the Book of Judges, on the conquest of Joshua, made me nauseous!"[33]

On work:

> "Working together with neighbors is the expression of a lived solidarity and a sharing of life, in a climate of friendship that defuses fear. People are not afraid to hang out with us as in the past, and further—we trust each other."

> "The work in the garden and with the associates: practical works of hope!"[34]

[32] "Comment, dans la situation présente," 181.

[33] "Comment, dans la situation présente," 182. Pss 94 (93) and 124 (123).

[34] "Comment, dans la situation présente," 182.

On welcome:

> Redirection [of hospitality] from the guesthouse to the gatehouse. Hospitality in the guesthouse has effectively been almost non-existent for two years now. Hospitality to the neighborhood is offered "in every way imaginable." In various ways: sharing resources, services rendered, listening to people's concerns about the situation—hopes, worries, sorrows, anxieties, family dramas, everything. Concern, understanding, compassion . . . The doctor [Br. Luc] knows a thing or two about that![35]

A Heritage for Us

Taking its cue from their November 1995 report, this book explores the community's "daily way of expressing hope," examining the expression of the monastic way of following Christ at Tibhirine. The monks' legacy, their gift to us, is to be found in their lives: in the way they lived out the vocation that is actually shared with all followers of Christ. So the aim is to offer a taste of their gift, necessarily limited, but illuminating its essential contours by immersing ourselves in their lives and their writings.

The monks left an extensive legacy of writings, much of which is held in France in the archive of the abbey of Notre-Dame d'Aiguebelle, the motherhouse of the monastery at Tibhirine. The publication of their writings has been gathering speed over the last few years. The English-speaking world, however, has had limited access to their gift, as very little of their work has been translated. English translations have been published of Christophe Lebreton's final prayer journal, a growing number of Christian de Chergé's chapter talks and most recently a selection of Christian's writings in the Modern

[35] "Comment, dans la situation présente," 182–83.

Spiritual Masters series—a very welcome addition.[36] Bernardo Olivera's *How Far to Follow: The Martyrs of Atlas*, remains an invaluable source: it includes firsthand accounts of the events leading up to and following the monks' deaths.[37] Research has burgeoned too, but again mostly in French. In English, John Kiser's 2003 book, Th*e Monks of Tibhirine: Faith, Love, and Terror in Algeria*, provides a vivid narrative account of their story and its political context. Christian Salenson's *Christian de Chergé: A Theology of Hope* (translated from French) offers a masterly account of Christian's theological contribution.[38]

[36] Lebreton, *Born from the Gaze of God*; Christian de Chergé, *God for All Days: The Final Monastic Chapters of Christian de Chergé*, trans. Jennifer Rushworth, ed. Matthew Cheung Salisbury, MW 73 (Collegeville, MN: Cistercian Publications, 2025); Christian de Chergé, "Chapter Talks on the Psalms," *Cistercian Studies Quarterly* 51, no. 1 (2016): 93–119; Christian de Chergé, *Christian de Chergé: Spiritual Writings*, ed. and trans. Christian Krokus and Habib Zanzana, Modern Spiritual Masters series (Maryknoll, NY: Orbis Books, 2025). Portions of Christian's chapter talks on humility (RB 7) are translated in Edith Scholl, "Christian de Chergé on Humility," *Cistercian Studies Quarterly* 41, no. 2 (2006): 193–215.

[37] Olivera, *How Far to Follow*.

[38] A handful of more recent books have been translated into English. A more devotionally oriented book was sponsored by the Vatican publishing house and co-authored by journalist Françoise Vayne and Thomas Georgeon, the postulator of the beatification of the nineteen Algeria martyrs (Thomas Georgeon and Françoise Vayne, *Simply Christians: The Life and Message of the Blessed Martyrs of Tibhirine*, trans. Daniel B. Gallagher [Huntington, IN: Our Sunday Visitor, 2020]). Translated from Spanish is Brazilian theologian Maria Clara Bingemer's study of two religious communities, the Cistercians in Algeria and the Jesuits in El Salvador, who suffered violent deaths. Bingemer helpfully draws attention to the influence of Emmanuel Levinas on Christian de Chergé's thought (Maria Clara Bingemer, *Mysticism and Witness in Koinonia: Inspiration from the Martyrdom of Two Twentieth-Century Communities*, trans. Suzana Regina Moreira [Eugene, OR: Cascade Books, 2023]). Published before the death of Fr. Jean-Pierre Schumacher and translated from German is a pilgrimage of discovery by a former postulant to the Atlas community (Freddy Derwahl, *The Last Monk of Tibhirine: A True Story of Martyrdom, Faith, and Survival* [Brewster, MA: Paraclete Press, 2013]).

In telling the Tibhirine story it is impossible to avoid privileging the voice of Christian de Chergé—as both the prior of the Atlas community and its most prolific writer. I have endeavored to give voice to the other members of the community; however, given the wealth of material now available, it is not possible to do justice to all the monks in one slim volume.

The title of this book, *Life Here Together*, intentionally draws on the English title of Dietrich Bonhoeffer's short handbook *Life Together*, written in Nazi Germany on the eve of World War II for the experimental underground Finkenwalde seminary, where young theological students were being formed for ministry in the Confessing Church. The Lutheran-formed Bonhoeffer had rediscovered monasticism—and found a rich source of wisdom for living together in a time of crisis. In a different time and place, a different "here," the Tibhirine monks lived from that same rich source of wisdom until they, like Bonhoeffer, paid the ultimate price for their discipleship.

The book proceeds in four parts:

Part I, "Real Monks of the Present Time," introduces the story of Notre-Dame de l'Atlas and the community at Tibhirine. It outlines the place of the Cistercians (OCSO) in Algeria, from its establishment in the colonial era to the evolution of Tibhirine after independence and the development of the community's particular vocation under Christian de Chergé.

Part II examines the twin foundations of monastic life expressed in the Benedictine phrase *ora et labora* (prayer and work) and how these were understood and lived out at Tibhirine.

Part III, "Living here together" (*Vivre ici ensemble*), explores the intersection of the Cistercian commitment to community and hospitality, and the particular context in which the Tibhirine monks lived. Inherent in the vow of stability is a commitment to place, which encompasses relationships both within and beyond the monastery wall. The result is "encounter," the transformative meeting with God and others.

Part IV, "Loving to the end" (*Aimer jusqu'à l'extrême*) travels to the theological heart of the monks' radical commitment to following Christ—to the very end. Paradoxically, their story is less about martyrdom than about how to choose life.

An Epilogue, "A Heritage for Us," steps into a reflective space, drawing out some key themes and exploring the gift and challenge of the monks' legacy for people of faith.

The text of Christian de Chergé's *Testament*, in translation, is reproduced in full in Appendix I. This might be read as a coda. It is an extraordinary poetic text that speaks with clarity to the choice that Christian and his brother monks made to stay at Tibhirine. While it stands alone, I hope that the depths of its call and challenge might resonate even more strongly after the reader has traveled, through this book, in the company of Christian and the monastic community at Tibhirine.

Appendix II, "The Brothers," offers brief biographies for the seven monks killed in 1996. Each of the monks has a unique story, and Marie-Dominique Minassian's compilation of an astonishing range of biographical material published in *Heureux ceux qui espèrent: Autobiographies spirituelles* (nearly 800 pages) enabled me to immerse myself in their lives—so ordinary, so inspiring. Some of this rich material has made its way into this book; the rest awaits another. Readers may like to explore these biographies alongside the chapters.

"How Far to Follow?"

"How Far to Follow?" is the resonant title of the English publication of four letters sent by Bernardo Olivera to members of the Order in the first year after the monks' deaths. And, of course, the monks' response to this question is "to the end." This book is about the way they did this, how they followed Christ, sustained by their monastic way of life, adapted to their particular context. They followed Christ by simply embracing the quotidian—by simply doing what needed to be done each day. Their gift is not, ultimately, their martyrdom—which can be so easily misunderstood—but the witness of their living, a witness that we can glimpse through the traces that they left, especially in the rich records left by the community.

How did the seven monks live their last days, their fifty-six days of captivity? We will never know, of course. But I believe we can be confident that they lived as they had been living in the years before their abduction: humanly, faithfully, following Christ. The final scene of Xavier Beauvois's 2010 film, *Of Gods and Men* (*Des hommes et des dieux*), so faithful to the Tibhirine story, depicts the monks filing through the late Spring snow between their armed captors, still tenderly caring for each other. The camera pans out, and over the scene we hear the words of Christian de Chergé's *Testament*, completed after that first visit of Sayah Attiya and his men on Christmas Eve of 1993. It begins,

> If it should happen one day—and it could be today—
> that I become a victim of the terrorism
> which now seems ready to engulf
> all the foreigners living in Algeria,
> I would like my community, my Church and my family
> to remember that my life was GIVEN
> to God and to this country.[39]

And this is their gift: not despair at the horror of their end, but their testimony, their witness to living here together.

[39] Christian de Chergé, "Testament spiritual du frère Christian (1 décembre 1993; 1 janvier 1994)," in *Sept vies pour Dieu et l'Algérie*, ed. Bruno Chenu (Paris: Bayard, 1996). Translation Olivera, *How Far to Follow*, 127.

Part I

"Real Monks of the Present Time"

Chapter 1

From Colonial Service to Precariousness

> I had scarcely arrived in that house, their house, so poor and so full of warmth at the same time, when I perceived forming within me . . . the profound conviction that they were the real monks of the present time.
>
> —Phillipe Hémon

In the summer of 1991 Dom Bernardo Olivera, abbot general of the Order of Cistercians of the Strict Observance (OCSO), visited the monastic community at Tibhirine. One night he had a vivid dream: a monk from the community was being held by the throat and lectured harshly by another monk of the Order:

> First, you are wasting your life in this Muslim world that asks nothing of you and mocks you, while there is so much to do elsewhere, so many people who are only waiting for your witness to embrace the contemplative life and come to enlarge your community. . . . Second, you poor fool, our Order really has no use for a foundation like yours; what a dead weight![1]

[1] Christian de Chergé, "Confèrence du frère Christian du chapitre général 1993," in *Sept vies pour Dieu et l'Algérie*, ed. Bruno Chenu (Paris: Bayard, 1996), 84.

At the time the newly elected Olivera was familiarizing himself with the community of Notre-Dame de l'Atlas and its two houses: the foundation at Tibhirine and its small annex at Fez, Morocco, established in 1988. The dream dramatically focused questions that were clearly on his mind: what was this tiny monastic community doing in a Muslim environment? why should the Order continue to support it? These were not new questions—after Algerian independence in 1962 the existence of the monastery had been the subject of almost constant debate within the Order. In the dream it was Olivera himself who took up the defense: as Christian de Chergé observes in his later retelling of Olivera's dream, the monk being throttled was hardly in a position to speak![2] On waking, Olivera immediately recorded his response—and the next day shared his experience with the Tibhirine community.

We will return to Olivera's response in chapter 2, but for now the violent interlocutor of his dream articulates clearly, if dramatically, questions that will concern us in this chapter, and indeed throughout this book. Why would a community of primarily French monks remain in post-colonial Algeria? What is the point of a contemplative, non-missionary, monastic community in a Muslim-majority country? And why stay in an increasingly unstable and violent environment?

This chapter begins to explore these questions and the evolving response lived out by the monks of Notre-Dame de l'Atlas, examining the interweaving of the history of Algerian-French relations with the story of the Atlas community. It outlines the place of the Cistercians in Algeria from its first foundation at Staouëli in the colonial era and the refoundation at Tibhirine in the twentieth century. The chapter traces the Tibhirine community's changing fortunes before and after independence in 1962 and closes with a first look at the

[2] Christian de Chergé recounted the story in an address to the general chapter of the Order in Poyo, Spain, in September 1993. In meetings of the general chapter abbots and abbesses from each house of the Order gather to strengthen unity and to make decisions relating to the Order. The abbot general is elected by the general chapter.

development of its emerging distinctive vocation as a community of prayer among others who pray (*priants parmi d'autre priants*)—a development that was closely linked with the arrival of Christian de Chergé in 1971 and his election as prior in 1984.

Staouëli: A Colonial Foundation

The first Cistercian foundation in Algeria was very much part of the colonial project that began in 1830 with the French occupation of Algiers. Just thirteen years later, in 1843, at the invitation of the French government, Cistercians established a monastery on the Staouëli plain, seventeen kilometers west of Algiers. The French administration granted the Order the concession of a large property (1020 hectares) and supported the monastery with funds, equipment, and labor. The Cistercians were renowned for their agricultural enterprise and were thus ideal partners in the expansion of the colonization that the French government envisaged for Algeria.[3]

Notre-Dame d'Aiguebelle, a thriving Cistercian monastery in southeastern France, sponsored the new foundation, sending an initial cohort of about twenty monks to work with military personnel, engineers, military convicts, and locals in building the monastery and farming complex.[4] Staouëli had

[3] *Concessionaires* were required by contract to clear and develop the land granted as a concession before being given full ownership. Notre-Dame de Staouëli needed to clear 1000 hectares in ten years and plant 2,000 trees each year to achieve ownership (Claude Garda, "Les monastères cisterciens d'Algérie: Notre-Dame de Staouëli—Notre-Dame de l'Atlas," *Collectanea Cisterciensia* 58 [1996]: 203).

[4] Nuno de São José, "Notre-Dame de l'Atlas, mystère d'une secrète fécondité: histoire de la communauté depuis sa fondation jusqu'en 1996," *Collectanea Cisterciensia* 83 (2021): 272. Br. Nuno is a Portuguese-born professed member of the Atlas community. He entered the relocated community at Fez in 2012. Since 2000 the community has been located at Midelt, Morocco. He prepared a comprehensive history of the monastic foundation to mark the beatification of the seven Tibhirine monks in 2018. This chapter draws extensively on his work.

been the site of the French victory over Ottoman troops defending Algiers in 1830. In a ceremony attended by Msgr. Antoine-Adolphe Dupuch, the first bishop of Algeria, and Marshal Thomas-Robert Bugeaud, the first governor general, the foundation stone was laid for the new monastery on a bed of cannonballs collected from the battlefield[5]—cementing the relationship between the colonial occupiers and the nascent monastery. The motto of the Staouëli monastery encapsulates its colonial agenda: *Ense, Cruce et Atato* ("by the sword, by the cross and by the plow").[6]

A hundred and fifty years later, in post-colonial Algeria, in the midst of the civil war engulfing the country, Br. Christophe Lebreton wrote this same Latin motto in his Tibhirine prayer journal, then commented, "War (violence) cross toil: everything is here."[7] The irony is palpable.

The scale of European settlement in Algeria was unique within the French colonial empire.[8] Proponents saw in Algeria an opportunity to implement a new, postrevolutionary (slavery-free) form of colonization focusing on agrarian settlement, characterized as *peuplement et fertilisation* (settlement and fertilization).[9] Further, proponents suggested that Algeria "not be called a colony," but rather be made "one of the most beautiful provinces of France"—an idea that persisted into the twentieth century.[10] Algeria, divided into three *départements* in 1848, was considered an extension of French soil in which European citizens enjoyed benefits similar to those of metropolitan France. The indigenous Muslim population enjoyed no such

[5] Garda, "Les monastères," 204.

[6] São José, "Notre-Dame de l'Atlas," 273.

[7] Christophe Lebreton, *Born from the Gaze of God: The Tibhirine Journal of a Martyr Monk (1993–1996)*, trans. Mette Louise Nygård and Edith Scholl, MW 37 (Collegeville, MN: Cistercian Publications, 2014), 13; October 10, 1993.

[8] Jennifer E. Sessions, *By Sword and Plow: France and the Conquest of Algeria* (Ithaca, NY: Cornell University Press, 2011), 1.

[9] Sessions, *By Sword and Plow*, 183.

[10] Sessions, *By Sword and Plow*, 3.

rights. By 1848 there were almost 100,000 French troops stationed in Algeria and more than 100,000 settlers (*colons*).[11]

French policy makers were influenced by models of settler colonialism forged by the British in Canada, Australia, and New Zealand.[12] For those of us now living in such settler-colonized lands the pattern is only too familiar: wholesale appropriation (theft) of land, incentivized systems of land redistribution directed at wealthy settlers, the provision of cheap labor in the form of immigrant workers, and the "civilizing mission" of a self-proclaimed superior culture.[13] The subjugated indigenous population is viewed as an inconvenience, at best an additional source of cheap labor. By 1871 a combination of warfare and economic dislocation, resulting in disease and famine, had reduced the indigenous population, estimated as around three million at colonization, by a third.[14] Not surprisingly this has been called genocide.[15]

The monks could not have been unaware of the part they were playing in the colonial agenda. Indeed a 1936 account of the history of the foundation comments, "Thus the monastery, its model farm, and its industries served both the spiritual and the material interests of the new country, organized by sword and plough by Marshal Bugeaud and his soldiers, but educated

[11] Sessions, *By Sword and Plow*, 1, 85, 217. The French word *colons* retains its relationship with the language of colony and colonialization in a way that the English *settlers* does not.

[12] Sessions, *By Sword and Plow*, 180.

[13] Session notes that the phrase *mission civilisatrice* came into French usage around 1840 in relation to Algerian colonization (Sessions, *By Sword and Plow*, 6).

[14] Phillip Chiviges Naylor, *Historical Dictionary of Algeria*, 4th ed., Historical Dictionaries of Africa (Lanham, MD: Rowman & Littlefield Publishers, 2015), 15.

[15] Christian Salenson, *Christian de Chergé: A Theology of Hope*, trans. Nada Conic, CS 247 (Collegeville, MN: Cistercian Publications, 2012), 15.

by Cross and plough by Abbot François-Régis and his monks."[16]

Nonetheless, the Cistercian commitment to prayer, to work, including manual labor, and to living simply, unafraid of hardship and deprivation, offered an enduring witness to both settlers and the indigenous population. Notre-Dame de Staouëli may have functioned as a model farm serving the interests of colonization, but it equally offered a visible yet modest spiritual presence that would improve the religious credibility of the French occupiers.[17] The monks' austere and prayerful way of life was noticed and respected by the local population. Muslims recognized the monastery as "the holy house," bowing deeply as they passed.[18] The exiled Algerian resistance leader Abd al-Qadir, a devout Sufi Muslim, on meeting the former abbot Dom François-Régis in Paris, reportedly remarked on the hospitality offered by the monks: "I have known you for a long time because my people speak to me of you: you received them as if they were your own."[19] (The inspiration for the foundation of the monastery is said to have come in response to a remark by Abd al-Qadir to General Bugeaud that "Christians do not pray."[20])

However, the early years at Staouëli were by no means easy. The particularly harsh living conditions and the ravages of disease, especially malaria, took a significant toll: in the monastery's first ten years, around thirty monks died in Algeria, others on their return to France. But the community grew

[16] Sébastien Vandermarliere, "Les abbayes de l'Ordre de Cîteaux (Stricte Observance): Sainte Marie de Maguzzano," *Collectanea Cisterciensia* (1936): 220; "Atlas Martyrs," trans. Donald McGlynn, CSQ 32, no. 2 (1997): 156.

[17] John W. Kiser, *The Monks of Tibhirine: Faith, Love, and Terror in Algeria* (New York: St Martin's Griffin, 2002), 36.

[18] Vandermarliere, "Sainte Marie de Maguzzano," 220.

[19] Garda, "Les monastères cisterciens d'Algérie," 205.

[20] Henri Teissier and Jean-Jacques Pérennès, Introduction to *Heureux ceux qui osent la rencontre: des moines en pays d'Islam*, ed. Marie-Dominique Minassian, Les écrits de Tibhirine (Paris: Bayard-Cerf-Bellefontaine, 2022), 18.

steadily, supplied with monks from Aiguebelle and other French monasteries, reaching a peak of one hundred fifteen monks in 1879. At the turn of the century a period of aggressive anti-clericalism in France led to the dispersal of many religious communities. In 1904, anticipating the possible expulsion of the Order or the confiscation of its property, the abbot sold the monastery, both buildings and land, and relocated the monastic community to northern Italy.[21] The Staouëli chapter had ended.

Notre-Dame de l'Atlas: A New Beginning

It was not until 1934 that another Cistercian foundation was made in Algeria; it had "a very different style and spirit" from the colonially driven Staouëli.[22] Five monks were sent by a Slovenian abbey, Notre-Dame de la Délivrance, Rajhenburg, to establish a haven from the threat of expulsion from Yugoslavia (this abbey had itself been founded as a refuge from persecution in France). The small community was initially based at Ouled-Triff and later at Ben-Chicao, both in the Atlas Mountains, before finally settling in 1938 at Tib-Hirine, "the gardens," a nineteenth-century colonial farm seven kilometers from Médéa.[23] By this time the refoundation had been returned to the jurisdiction of Aiguebelle; in November 1938, the monastic community was formally established as Notre-Dame de l'Atlas. It comprised nineteen professed monks (thirteen choir monks and six lay brothers[24]), drawn from two abbeys and

[21] São José, "Notre-Dame de l'Atlas," 273.

[22] Armand Veilleux, "The Witness of the Tibhirine Martyrs," *Spiritus* 1, no. 2 (2001): 208.

[23] São José, "Notre-Dame de l'Atlas," 273–75; McGlynn, "Atlas Martyrs," 156.

[24] In the second half of the twelfth century the Order introduced lay brothers (*conversi*) to assist the monks with the considerable labor needed to sustain the monastic economy. While lay brothers were similarly vowed, the creation of a separate brotherhood inevitably embedded inequality, and tensions between choir monks, who were focused

three nationalities—nine Slovenians, eight French, and two Czechs.[25] When Br. Luc Dochier arrived in 1946 he found a community divided according to their monastic origins, Rajhenburg or Aiguebelle, "two rivers whose waters do not mix."[26]

The Tibhirine estate was more modest than Staouëli in size, about 375 hectares. There was a reliable spring to water the farm, which included 36 hectares of vines and 80 hectares of arable land as well as a forest. The remainder of the land was wild—steep and rocky. While its elevation (1000 meters) offered spectacular views of the Tamesguida mountains, the climate could be harsh: relatively mild summers—except if the sirocco was blowing, when it could reach 40 degrees Celsius (104 degrees Fahrenheit)—and long, cold, wet winters. The local population was entirely Muslim, primarily of ethnic Berber-Kabyle origin. The few families located nearby were poor and depended on employment on the estate.

The property included a set of buildings that were readily adapted as a monastery: a large villa, two pavilions joined by a terrace, a small bell tower, and a range of agricultural facilities including vats for wine making. The monks established the first chapel in a stable. With the assistance of salaried and seasonal laborers, both French and local, they produced good quality wine (some exported to France), vegetables, fruit, honey, butter, and cheese, as well as raising livestock. The monastery was also supported economically by Aiguebelle and by local donors. By 1939 the monks were able to open a small guesthouse, welcoming a steady stream of local clergy and religious, seminarians and students, settlers, and civil and military personnel.[27] In the early 1970s a young Christophe Lebreton was one such guest during his national service, a

primarily on the work of the liturgy, and lay brothers, focused on manual labor. The distinction was abolished by the Order following Vatican II, after the challenge issued to religious communities in *Perfectae Caritatis*.

[25] São José, "Notre-Dame de l'Atlas," 276.

[26] São José, "Notre-Dame de l'Atlas," 278.

[27] São José, "Notre-Dame de l'Atlas," 27–76.

definitive experience in the discernment of his vocation. Prayer, work, and hospitality: the central features of Cistercian monastic life were now in place.

World War II left its mark on the monastery, with some monks returning to Slovenia or France and others being enlisted for military service. As the mountain locale had proved attractive for scout and youth camps, in 1941 the monastery was asked to provide facilities for them—these facilities in the Tibhirine Forest Park were requisitioned in 1942 for refugees fleeing bombing in Algiers. During the war the guesthouse was made available to convalescing soldiers as well as retreatants. The monastery held, as Nuno de São José notes, "a privileged place in Algeria that settlers, civil and military officials, or wealthy families from Médéa like to frequent," often sharing a meal in the guesthouse "transformed into a small 'restaurant,' renowned for its wine." Women were welcomed at such gatherings, at Mass in the guesthouse chapel, and sometimes as guests—all technically forbidden by the Order at the time.[28] Tibhirine was already pushing established monastic boundaries.

After World War II the monastery began an ambitious building program, stretching both its human and financial resources. São José notes the disparity between the rather grand plans for the expansion of the monastic complex and the poverty of the local monastery workers' housing.[29] In recounting the history of the community in the 1988 annual circular letter, Christian speaks of the "dream of grandiose constructions" during this period, "disproportionate from the moment they were conceived," adding wryly, "but who noticed?"[30] The dissonance between the vision for a grand monastery

[28] São José, "Notre-Dame de l'Atlas," 277–78.

[29] São José, "Notre-Dame de l'Atlas," 279.

[30] Moines de Tibhirine, "Lettres circulaires de la communauté Notre-Dame de l'Atlas Tibhirine-Fès (1988)," in *Heureux ceux qui espèrent: Autobiographies spirituelles*, Les écrits de Tibhirine 1 (Paris: Bayard-Cerf-Bellefontaine, 2018), 703.

(Br. Luc remembered this as "the period of Illusions"[31]) and their neighbors' poverty was embodied in the only additional wing to be built, a source of embarrassment for the small monastic community that had found a more equitable way of living with the local village by the 1980s and 1990s. In the last years of the community the only inhabitant of this wing was their neighbor Ali's cow.[32]

The community was elevated to the status of abbey in 1947 and reached its numerical peak by 1950 with thirty-one members (twenty-two choir monks and nine lay brothers).[33] But the optimistic vision of growth was soon eroded as the Algerian Revolution (1954–1962) unfolded.

Independence for Algeria

By the 1930s there was a growing movement of resistance among Algerian Muslims to the structural inequality that determined the lives of the indigenous population. The economic disparity between settlers (the majority now locally born and increasingly known as *pieds-noirs*[34]) and Algerian Muslims was stark: settlers controlled the most productive land, leaving indigenous Algerians to subsist on often marginal remnant holdings. Starvation was a regular threat, and too often a reality (particularly devastating famines occurred in 1867 and

[31] Moines de Tibhirine, *Heureux ceux qui espèrent: Autobiographies spirituelles*, ed. Marie-Dominique Minassian, Les écrits de Tibhirine 1 (Paris: Bayard-Cerf-Bellefontaine, 2018), 90.

[32] Philippe Hémon, "An En-Visaged Good-By-E," CSQ 34, no. 2 (1999): 207.

[33] São José, "Notre-Dame de l'Atlas," 278–79.

[34] The term *pied-noir*, "black foot," originally referred to urban Europeans in Algeria, while *colons* was reserved for rural settlers but was increasingly used to refer to all European settlers in French Algeria and North Africa. *Pieds-noirs* had diverse origins; some were political and economic refugees from various European countries. By 1954 around half of the *pieds-noirs* population had non-French origins (including Spain, Italy, and Malta). See Naylor, *Historical Dictionary of Algeria*, 425.

1937). Poverty deepened as the Algerian Muslim population increased significantly relative to the settler population, partly because of decreased infant mortality rates.

By the centenary of colonization in 1943, half of the indigenous population was living at or below subsistence level. This impoverishment contributed to the movement of peasants from the interior plains to coastal cities (and to metropolitan France).[35] While there was no formal system of apartheid, Algerian cities were clearly divided, with settlers living in elegant European-style districts and the majority of indigenous Algerians crushed into overcrowded slums. Promises made following World War II regarding greater Algerian participation in political processes were not fulfilled, and hopes for the pursuit of equal political rights gave way to militant nationalism.[36]

On All Saints' Day, November 1, 1954, the Front de Libération Nationale (FLN) issued a proclamation inviting Algerians to join the struggle for national independence, while its military wing, the Armée de Libération Nationale (ALN), began operations across the country. This date is now recognized as the beginning of the Algerian War of Independence, one of the most brutal decolonizing wars of the twentieth century.[37] Estimates of Algerian casualties vary from 250,000 to 1.5 million, with French military casualties at 27,500 and civilian deaths at 2,800.[38] The conflict also resulted in the mass destruction of villages and further deforestation.

[35] "By 1930 only 1 per cent of Algerians had a farm of more than 100 hectares" (Martin Evans and John Phillips, *Algeria: Anger of the Dispossessed* [New Haven, CT: Yale University Press, 2007], 38). See also Sessions, *By Sword and Plow*, 9.

[36] Evans and Phillips, *Algeria: Anger of the Dispossessed*, 39, 48.

[37] Sessions suggests that the protracted length and trauma of the decolonialization process in Algeria can be partly explained by the features of the colonial process itself: its "peculiar ties to France and the drastic inequities they entailed between settlers and the precolonial inhabitants" (Sessions, *By Sword and Plow*, 2).

[38] Naylor, *Historical Dictionary of Algeria*, 518.

The FLN used guerrilla tactics to disrupt the colonial political order, but atrocities were carried out by all parties. Revelations of the use of torture by the French military, as well as mounting casualties, contributed to the collapse of the French government in 1958. With the subsequent appointment of General Charles de Gaulle as president, a political settlement was eventually negotiated. National referendums overwhelmingly approved the Evian Accords (the ceasefire agreement of March 18, 1962) and the granting of independence, and on July 3, 1962, France formally recognized Algeria as an independent nation.

While settler estates in the Médéa region experienced significant violence during the war, the monastery remained largely sheltered, because of the warm relationships the monks had built with the local Muslim inhabitants. In May 1957 Fr. Amédée, sub-prior at the time, wrote to the abbot general, "In spite of the troubles that are shaking our region, the Muslim population retains its attachment and confidence in us, and comes to ask for our moral protection against the abuses of our soldiers, which are far from always being to the credit of our army."[39]

It was not always easy for the community to maintain its position of neutrality. Only the intervention of the archbishop of Algiers, Msgr. (later Cardinal) Léon-Étienne Duval, prevented the prosecution of Br. Luc for treating injured *fellaghas* (armed militants) in the mountains. During this period families from the surrounding mountains sought refuge from the violence and settled close to the monastery, some in abandoned or disused monastery buildings. So the village of Tibhirine was born. Among the exceptions to this relative shelter from the war was the 1959 kidnapping of Fr. Matthew and Br. Luc by the ALN: the two were freed after eight days. Luc's standing as the local *toubib*, the doctor, probably secured their lives.[40]

[39] Quoted in São José, "Notre-Dame de l'Atlas," 282.

[40] McGlynn, "Atlas Martyrs," 157; Jean-Paul Schumacher, "Les frères de Notre-Dame de l'Atlas dans la societé algérienne, à Tibhirine,"

Most of the seven monks who were later killed in 1996 had connections with Algeria that predated their monastic lives. In 1959, while completing his national service, Christian had been posted to Algeria, working as an officer with the Sections Administratives Spécialisées (SAS) in Tiaret. Created in 1955, the SAS had been designed to bring rural communities more tightly under French control. While the SAS helped to deliver improvements in social conditions, it also had an intelligence-gathering function that made officers particular targets of the FLN. The SAS officers worked alongside Algerian recruits, who were trained and paid to protect harvests and civilian infrastructure.

In the course of his work, Christian had become friends with Mohammed, a rural guard in the village of Ain Saïd, a devout Muslim and the father of ten children.[41] Their friendship of just four months transcended their differences in age—Christian was twenty-two, Mohammed over forty—as well as their different faiths. One day, as the two men walked and talked together, their group was met by gunfire. Mohammed's immediate response was to place himself in front of Christian. Mohammed began to receive letters threatening his life if he failed to prove his support of "national liberation." On November 8, 1959, Mohammed was killed while drawing water from his well.[42]

---

in Moines de Tibhirine, *Heureux ceux qui espèrent*, 17; São José, "Notre-Dame de l'Atlas," 281–82.

[41] "Mohammed" has been identified as Cheikh Benmechay. The name "Mohammed" was often used by French colonists and military personnel as a generic way of referring to Algerian Muslim men. It is unclear why Christian used this designation, though it may have been to preserve his identity for the sake of his family's safety. Christian Krokus, "Introduction," in *Christian de Chergé: Spiritual Writings*, ed. and trans. Christian Krokus and Habib Zanzana, Modern Spiritual Masters series (Maryknoll, NY: Orbis Books, 2025), xviii n4. Minassian includes a photograph of Benmechay in Moines de Tibhirine, *Heureux ceux qui espèrent*.

[42] Christian did not write an account of this story until 1974, and he had not shared it until shortly before joining the Atlas community. The 1974 account is found in his Chronique de l'espèrance 3 (Noël 1974),

This event, Mohammed's offering of his own life for his friend, had a profound influence on the rest of Christian's life. The date of Mohammed's death, eight days after All Saints' Day, was inscribed in Christian's own "perpetual calendar."[43] On All Saints' Day 1985 he again reflected on its significance:

> In the blood shed by this friend, assassinated for not wanting to make a pact with hatred, I knew that my call to follow Christ would be lived, sooner or later, in the same country where I have been given this sign of the greatest love possible: "*qui pro vobis et pro multis effundetur* . . . ." I knew, at the same time, that this consecration had to flow through *common prayer* [*une prière en commun*] in order to be a true witness of the church and a sign of the communion of saints.[44]

The situation after independence in 1962 was radically different; the monastery entered a long period of uncertainty and instability. In the newly independent Algeria, Islam was now the state religion and Arabic the official national language. The church had to negotiate the continued presence of the monastery, and the government placed limits on the size of its membership.[45] Further, the new socialist government embarked on a program of nationalization and redistribution of land held by resident foreigners. While religious orders were permitted to retain their property, Archbishop

---

written for family and friends (Moines de Tibhirine, *Heureux ceux qui espèrent*, 366–68). In her biography of Christian, Marie-Christine Ray suggests that Mohammed was killed the day after the encounter with the armed fellaghas (Marie-Christine Ray, *Christian de Chergé, prieur de Tibhirine*, 2nd ed. [Paris: Bayard, 1998], 48). Christian's 1974 account implies a later date.

[43] Moines de Tibhirine, *Heureux ceux qui espèrent*, 366.

[44] Moines de Tibhirine, *Heureux ceux qui espèrent*, 369. The Latin quotation is from the words of consecration of the Mass, "which will be shed for you and for many."

[45] McGlynn suggests that it was limited to twelve members. McGlynn, "Atlas Martyrs," 157.

Duval wisely counseled against their doing so, as at the time Arab landowners were limited to twenty hectares, and he feared that the resulting inequity could result in the monks' simply being seen as successors to the French *colons*. The monks relinquished the operation of the farm and most of the estate at Tibhirine, including sixty hectares of established vines, retaining just twelve hectares, of which only eight were arable.[46]

Finding a Place in Post-Colonial Algeria

In the face of the uncertainties of post-independence Algeria and the community's own fragility, the future of the monastery was never assured. The community itself was divided about its prospects, with some believing that there was still a place for them amid the Muslim population and others unconvinced or fearful.[47] A number of factors contributed to the monastery's continued presence: its relationship to the Algerian church, the support of other Cistercian communities, the growth of the village of Tibhirine and the interdependence between the monastery and its Muslim neighbors, and, at a broader level, the impact of Vatican II on monastic life and on relations with other religious traditions, particularly Islam. Finally, underpinning these factors was the more intangible sense of call, perhaps most clearly embodied in the vocation of Christian, who arrived in 1971.

A Monastery for the Algerian Church

Central to the survival of the monastery was its close relationship to the Algerian church. The situation of the church in Algeria changed dramatically in 1962. As independence became inevitable and then a reality, most of the settler population

[46] São José, "Notre-Dame de l'Atlas," 284 n29.

[47] Schumacher, "Les frères de Notre-Dame de l'Atlas," 18.

fled—more than a million people by August 1962.[48] Archbishop Duval described this exodus as "an apocalypse."[49] Consequently the Christian population of Algeria shrank significantly: by 1964 only 100,000 foreign Christians remained, and by 1970 this number was halved.[50] Duval's vision and leadership were critical in re-orienting the church. Faced with an almost total loss of power, he saw an opportunity to build an Algerian church to serve all Algerians: he declared that the church "did not choose to be foreign [*étrangère*] but Algerian."[51] A longstanding supporter of independence, he had denounced the French use of torture and hoped for a reconciled multi-faith, multi-cultural Algerian society, bringing together its disparate peoples: Arabs, Berbers, and *pieds-noirs*, Muslims, Jews, and Christians. The *pied-noir* press derided him as "Mohammed Duval."[52]

Duval intervened twice to save the Tibhirine community. In 1963, after the regular visitation of the father immediate in May,[53] the Order began to take steps towards closing the community. When negotiations to secure a transfer of the monastery to the Benedictines in Morocco were unsuccessful, in September the monks voted overwhelmingly to leave Algeria. But the process was halted by the sudden death of the abbot general, Dom Gabriel Sortais, on November 13—the evening

[48] Evans and Phillips, *Algeria: Anger of the Dispossessed*, 70.

[49] São José, "Notre-Dame de l'Atlas," 286.

[50] Schumacher, "Les frères de Notre-Dame de l'Atlas," 17. Quoted from Ray, *Christian de Chergé*, 89. After independence, alongside the remaining religious an influx of aid workers, from France, Eastern Europe, and the Middle East helped to reshape the Christian community (Teissier and Pérennès, "Introduction," 25).

[51] Schumacher, "Les frères de Notre-Dame de l'Atlas," 17. The original source is an interview with Duval published in *Le Monde*, January 11, 1964, and quoted in Ray, *Christian de Chergé*, 100.

[52] Evans and Phillips, *Algeria: Anger of the Dispossessed*, 70, 226; São José, "Notre-Dame de l'Atlas," 283.

[53] A formal visit made every two years by the abbot of a monastery's motherhouse (the father immediate) or by another representative of the Order.

of the day that he had signed the decree formalizing the closure. This unexpected event proved a turning point for the community: as Christian wrote, "we were going to be reborn from this death."[54]

Duval, determined to maintain this monastic presence in Algeria, pressed for a deferral: "the immediate departure of the monks, highly esteemed by the population, would be detrimental to the Christians who remained behind."[55] (Thirty years later, after the 1993 Christmas Eve visit of armed insurgents to the monastery, Msgr. Henri Teissier, then-archbishop of Algiers, made a similar plea: the immediate departure of the monks would have a devasting impact on the remaining Christians in Algeria.[56]) When Duval's efforts to find another religious order to take on the monastery failed, in January 1964 he wrote to the OCSO general chapter, meeting in Rome, of the hardships overwhelming the Algerian church, passionately pleading for a continued monastic presence at Tibhirine to support local clergy and to be a prayerful Christian witness in a Muslim environment.[57] The Tibhirine monastery was given a reprieve, and the challenge of rebuilding the community in this new situation was taken up energetically by Dom Jean de la Croix Pryzluski, the newly elected abbot of Aiguebelle, who was responsible for the oversight of the Atlas community.

[54] Moines de Tibhirine, "Lettres circulaires de la communauté Notre-Dame de l'Atlas Tibhirine-Fès (Noël 1987–Noël 1995)," 1988; 704.

[55] São José, "Notre-Dame de l'Atlas," 285. São José is quoting from a document held in the archive of Notre-Dame de l'Atlas, "À propos de la dissolution de l'Atlas."

[56] Bernardo Olivera, *How Far to Follow: The Martyrs of Atlas*, CS 197 (Kalamazoo, MI: Cistercian Publications, 2002), 56.

[57] São José, "Notre-Dame de l'Atlas," 285. In addition to the Cistercians, two other monastic communities were in Algeria in 1962, as well as some smaller fraternities: the Benedictine missionaries in Médéa, who left in 1973–1974, and the Poor Clares in Algiers, who stayed until January 1995 (Henri Teissier, "Le monastère de Tibhirine et l'Église d'Algérie," in Moines de Tibhirine, *Heureux ceux qui espèrent: Autobiographies spirituelles*, ed. Moines de Tibhirine, Les Écrits de Tibhirine 1 [Paris: Bayard-Cerf-Bellefontaine, 2018], 27).

Later, in 1978, Dom Jean de la Croix became prior of Notre-Dame de l'Atlas, a position he held for six years.

Duval intervened again in 1976 when closure was ordered by the Algerian authorities. After he petitioned the head of the national gendarmerie, the order was revoked.[58] He assured the monks that "the monastery was there until the Last Judgment."[59] As Dom Armand Veilleux, procurator of the Order (1990–1998), has observed, Duval saw in the Tibhirine community "a realization of his dream of an Algeria where Algerians and French, Muslims and Christians, could live together as brothers."[60] With a certain sad symmetry Duval died, at the age of ninety-two, on the same day that remains of the seven Tibhirine monks were found. The deaths of the monks, he said, had crucified him.[61] Their shared funeral Mass was held in the Basilique de Notre-Dame d'Afrique, Algiers on June 2, 1996.

For over thirty years the Tibhirine monastery played a significant role in the Algerian church. For the Christian community in Algeria, the monastery provided a much-needed place of retreat, the brothers' presence, prayer, and teaching were a source of spiritual *animation* for the church, and the monastery's harmonious relationship with the villagers of Tibhirine offered hope that Muslims and Christians could live side by side. As Henri Teissier said at a Mass to honor the seven martyred monks held in Rome on October 10, 1996, "Tibhirine was for us an icon of our vocation as Christians seeking God

[58] São José, "Notre-Dame de l'Atlas," 293.

[59] Teissier, "Le monastère de Tibhirine et l'Église d'Algérie," 29.

[60] Armand Veilleux, "Le contexte communautaire de Notre-Dame de l'Atlas," in Moines de Tibhirine, *Heureux ceux qui espèrent*, 42. A similar assessment was made by the historian Martin Evans and journalist John Phillips: Tibhirine represented both a vision of a Christianity that was "neither colonial or crusading" and was a "symbol of a multi-faith post-colonial Algeria where Christians and Muslims, along with Jews, could live together in mutual respect and dialogue" (Evans and Phillips, *Algeria: Anger of the Dispossessed*, 226).

[61] McGlynn, "Atlas Martyrs," 184.

in the land of Algeria, that is to say in a Muslim land. . . . I think there is no other monastery in the world which has such a general relationship with the members of the local church. Most of the priests, religious men and women, as well as the laity living permanently in the diocese, had a personal bond with the community."[62]

Reimagining a Cistercian Monastery

Under the guidance of Jean de la Croix the place and purpose of the monastery were reimagined: "to create a small discreet community, in a country that has become independent and socialist; a Cistercian community that has to fit in as such and harmoniously into an entirely Muslim environment; to realize a community that is poor among the poor."[63] The impact of Vatican II is clear here: beginning with Pope Paul VI's encyclical *Ecclesiam suam* (1964), the path was opened to respect and dialogue with Islam.[64] Similarly, *Populorum Progressio* (1967) recognized the damaging impact of colonialism and the obligation to work toward a shared, just future.

However, rebuilding the monastery in post-independence Algeria was by no means straightforward. Jean de la Croix sought to secure a small number of professed monks from other European monastic houses to bolster the community. Indeed, the ongoing support of the motherhouse, Notre-Dame d'Aiguebelle, and other Cistercian monasteries is a recurrent

[62] Quoted in McGlynn, "Atlas Martyrs," 149–50. See also Teissier, "Le monastère de Tibhirine et l'Église d'Algérie."

[63] "réaliser une communauté petite et discrète, dans un pays devenu indépendant et socialiste; une communauté cistercienne ayant à s'insérer comme telle et harmonieusement dans un milieu entièrement musulman; réaliser une communauté pauvre parmi les pauvres." Quoted in Schumacher, "Les frères de Notre-Dame de l'Atlas," 18.

[64] São José, "Notre-Dame de l'Atlas," 286. Vatican II's Dogmatic Constitution on the Church (*Lumen Gentium*, 1964) and Declaration on the Relation of the Church to Non-Christian Religions (*Nostra Aetate*, 1965) are of critical importance. See chapter 6.

theme in the story of Notre-Dame d'Atlas. Personal relationships built across the Cistercian world continued to nourish all parties. By the end of 1964 four monks from Aiguebelle, two from Cîteaux, and three from Timadeuc had joined the small remnant at Tibhirine. Duval welcomed them with joy: "The desert has bloomed again." But he also cautioned them: "It is necessary to be careful, to avoid anything that would look like proselytism. You are no doubt called upon to be a center of influence, but not yet, you must let things come."[65] Orientation to the changed environment was taken seriously, with the newcomers being provided with Arabic language lessons and instruction on the history of Islam and on local customs.

Even so, in the years that followed, there was considerable internal instability, with ongoing changes in both the leadership and the membership of the community. Between 1962 and 1984 there were nine superiors (all appointed externally), each bringing his own vision of monastic life and of relations with the outside world—which might swing from "excessive openness" to traditional Cistercian "strict enclosure."[66] With recruitment from a range of European monasteries (no local recruitment was possible) came significant differences in monastic formation, experience, and culture. When Christian arrived in 1971, the community consisted of thirteen monks from seven different monasteries.[67] It was no small challenge to form fraternal community amidst this diversity.

[65] Quoted in São José, "Notre-Dame de l'Atlas," 287.

[66] Schumacher, "Les frères de Notre-Dame de l'Atlas," 19.

[67] Peter Gilmore, "Atlas: Reawakened Memories and Present-day Reflections," CSQ 35, no. 2 (2000): 232.

Tibhirine Neighbors

The relationship between the monks and their neighbors was also subject to change and challenge. Before independence the monks were in many ways in a similar position to other wealthy *colons*, employing local laborers to work on their estate. The monastery was consequently the center of the local economy.[68] All this changed after 1962, and relations needed to be constantly renegotiated as political, social, and economic conditions altered.

As the village of Tibhirine grew around the monastery, the monks' ties to the villagers increased, along with an accompanying sense of responsibility for their welfare. In 1962 a school was established in a monastery building, initially in cooperation with the diocese of Algiers, so that local children did not have to travel long distances to receive a basic education. Fr. Amédeé was appointed as a teacher. Responsibility for the school was taken up by local authorities in 1965–1966.[69] The dispensary, opened in 1946 by Br. Luc, continued to serve the region (after a period of hesitancy when Jean de la Croix first assessed the situation in 1964[70]). From 1966 until 1979 a welfare service for mothers and children was provided under the direction of a Belgian lay woman, Madame de Smet. However, as São José observes, "These initiatives were highly appreciated by the population and the local administration, but did not always promote the autonomy of the beneficiaries with regard to the monastery, which thus continued to play a role tinged with 'paternalism.'"[71] Over time, however, the relationship of the monks to their neighbors became one of greater mutuality and cooperation. The poorer they became the closer they were to their neighbors: they were indeed poor among the poor.

[68] Schumacher, "Les frères de Notre-Dame de l'Atlas," 18.

[69] São José, "Notre-Dame de l'Atlas," 283, 288.

[70] São José, "Notre-Dame de l'Atlas," 286.

[71] São José, "Notre-Dame de l'Atlas," 290.

Christian de Chergé: A Shared Vocation

The arrival of Christian in 1971, with his specific vocation to Algeria, to Muslims, and to prayer proved to be decisive for the Atlas community. While Tibhirine was the place where Christian lived out his vocation, his vocation also confirmed and shaped the vocation of the Atlas community as a whole. Not long after his arrival, he was granted leave for two years to study at the Pontifical Institute for Arabic and Islamic Studies under Fr. Maurice Borrmans. Here Christian learned Arabic, studied the Qur'an, and deepened his understanding of how religion in Algeria functioned.[72]

The year 1976 saw further political change for the Algerian church: private education and health services were nationalized, so that the religious working in them either became public servants or left Algeria. The year was also a turning point for the Tibhirine community.[73] On September 29, during the regular visitation by Jean de la Croix (at the time still abbot at Aiguebelle), the community voted unanimously to accept Christian's request to make his solemn profession, the final set of vows committing him permanently to Notre-Dame de l'Atlas. The ceremony was held just thirty-six hours after the vote, on October 1, the feast day of Saint Thérèse of Lisieux, in the presence of a hastily gathered group of local Christian and Muslim friends and colleagues. It was the first solemn profession to have taken place at Tibhirine since 1952, and it marked, in the community's own assessment, a moment of clarity and unity regarding its vocation. It had taken twenty-five years for the community to come to a point of common understanding, and now, in response to Christian's own sense of call, they were able to articulate a vision of their shared

[72] Kiser, *The Monks of Tibhirine*, 40–42. The then-superior Dom Dominique Imbert was opposed to "internships outside the monastery," but the majority of the community agreed to Christian's two-year sojourn in Rome (São José, "Notre-Dame de l'Atlas," 292).

[73] São José, "Notre-Dame de l'Atlas," 293.

vocation: to be "a presence of the Church praying with the prayer of Islam and a monastic presence in the Church of Algeria."[74]

Christian himself was deeply appreciative of this articulation of the mission of the community, which aligned so well with his own sense of call "to live in PRAYER in the service of the Church of Algeria, listening to the Muslim soul."[75] It was no accident then that Christian's solemn profession was timed to correlate with the Friday prayers of the Muslim community. Further, during this same time of consultation and discernment three other monks of the community had requested that their stability be moved to Atlas. As the entry in the community diary notes, "Christian's yes was also, visibly, the yes of the community to become one."[76]

In his visitation report to the abbot general (November 2, 1976) Jean de la Croix expressed a quiet excitement at what had unfolded in the community, as well as his hopes for its future leadership:

> Brother Christian expresses his desire to respond to the uncertainty of current political conditions with an excess of trust and abandonment to Divine Providence. Present at Atlas since January 15, 1971, he feels perfectly in accord with the idea of Cîteaux. . . . Amazed at the continuity of God's plan for Atlas despite all the difficulties, he therefore asks his brothers to accept his definitive commitment. . . . Brother Christian was unanimously accepted to solemn

[74] "présence d'Église priante à la prière de l'Islam et présence monastique à l'Église d'Algérie" ("Profession solennelle du frère Christian 1 octobre 1976," in *Sept vies pour Dieu et l'Algérie*, ed. Bruno Chenu [Paris: Bayard, 1996], 26). This text was prepared for publication in the diocesan bulletin; see Moines de Tibhirine, *Heureux ceux qui espèrent*, 402 n1.

[75] Christian expresses this appreciation in a letter to Maurice Borrmans following his solemn profession (Christian de Chergé, *Lettres à un ami fraternel. Correspondance avec Maurice Borrmans* [Paris: Bayard, 2015], 92–93; October 22, 1976). Quotation from Christian's petition to the community dated September 14, 1976, in Bernardo Olivera, "Monk, Martyr, and Mystic: Christian de Chergé (1937–1996)," CSQ 34, no. 3 (1999): 324.

[76] "Profession solennelle du frère Christian 1 octobre 1976," 26.

> profession. The vote was like a spark setting fire to the whole. . . . Without presuming about the future and looking back on all that happened during the regular visitation, there is no denying that Brother Christian's solemn profession . . . has had a preponderant influence. This religious, by his personality, by his authority, which extends beyond the confines of the monastery since he is in charge of the guesthouse, his great moral character, his knowledge of Islam . . . seems to be the most qualified at the present time to direct the future of Our Lady of Atlas. . . . The continuity of Atlas through all obstacles . . . seems to me the visible sign of the infinite power of God who in spite of everything maintains this Cistercian presence . . . in Islamic territory. The community is aware of this, and I see in this solemn profession . . . and in the choice of the non-stabilized for stability in Algeria, a conscious response to this action of God on the part of the entire community.[77]

Outrageous trust in God is, perhaps, the quality that increasingly became the *basso ostinato*, the ground bass, of the community. Over time the community learned to live peacefully with permanent provisionality. In a letter to his old teacher Maurice Borrmans following his solemn profession, Christian wrote, "Afraid of the future? Why no, because only love has a future."[78]

Real Monks of the Present Time

In 1984 Christian was elected prior of the monastery.[79] As sub-prior he had already taken on leadership over the previous

[77] Quoted in Olivera, "Monk, Martyr, and Mystic," 324–25.

[78] "Peur de l'avenir? Mais non, puisque seul l'amour a de l'avenir" (Chergé, *Lettres à un ami fraternel*, 94; 22 octobre 1976).

[79] For more than twenty years instead of being able to elect their own superior, the community had had an *ad nutum* superior appointed by the motherhouse of Aiguebelle. In 1993–1994 this situation was resolved: the community renounced the status of abbey, becoming a priory and

year, when Jean de la Croix's health had deteriorated. The monastery was still struggling numerically, but a call to French monasteries for reinforcements proved fruitful. Over the next five years a steady stream of recruits, professed monks and novices, came to Tibhirine, including Michel Fleury, Bruno Lemarchand, and Célestin Ringeard from Bellefontaine, and Christophe Lebreton and Paul Favre-Miville from Tamié.

When Philippe Hémon, a monk of the Cistercian abbey of Tamié, first visited the monastic community at Tibhirine in 1990 he was struck by its poverty, its precariousness, and, paradoxically, its sense of freedom—of living with openness to the Divine:

> I had scarcely arrived in that house, their house, so poor and so full of warmth at the same time, when I perceived forming within me, coming from I know not where, the profound conviction that they were the real monks of the present time. Everything in their existence was stamped with the seal of precariousness. The precariousness of their situation as foreigners several times expelled and brought back, the precariousness of the country's political and economic situation, the precariousness of their status as a religious minority. And I thought of what Jean-Baptist Metz had written once, so fittingly: religious life can never be understood apart from that precariousness which demonstrates its eschatological openness. Without that condition as its foundation it installs itself in the transitory . . . and dies as a result. What freedom I felt with those men, stripped of all, able to offer only that in themselves which made them day by day more human. Was I not told recently by a monk who had seen other communities that to his mind they were the poorest community in the Order?[80]

---

clearing the way for a prior (rather than abbot) to be elected by the community (São José, "Notre-Dame de l'Atlas," 296).

[80] Philippe Hémon, "An En-Visaged Good-by-E," CSQ 34, no. 2 (1999): 208.

One is reminded here of Arnold of Bonnevaux's description of the monks of Clairvaux as "poor men . . . bearing a rugged cross" and of the astonishment expressed by the visiting papal party at the Cistercian way of life.[81] No wonder Hèmon calls them "the real monks of the present time."

The Black Decade

By 1990, however, Algeria was experiencing increased political and social instability. The Algerian War of Independence left the country materially devastated and economically vulnerable. From independence until 1989, the FLN, which had led the war against French rule, was the only legal political party, but widespread frustration with the lack of economic progress saw the rapid growth of Islamic fundamentalist groups. In the elections of 1991, the Front Islamique du Salut (FIS) won huge gains, but was subsequently banned. Algeria plunged into a civil war that extended to the early 2000s. Initially, insurgent groups operated from primarily rural and mountain bases, but by 1993, gathered in a loose structure known as the Groupe Islamique Armé (GIA), terrorist cells extended into towns and cities. The violence unleashed on the Algerian population was savage and was perpetrated by both insurgent groups and security forces. Foreign nationals were increasingly targeted after a GIA ultimatum in October 1993 ordered their departure from Algeria.[82]

Precariousness became the mode of existence at Tibhirine for both the monks and their neighbors, and for Algeria as a whole.

[81] William of Saint-Thierry, Arnold of Bonneval, and Geoffrey of Auxerre, *The First Life of Bernard of Clairvaux* 2.6, trans. Hilary Costello, CF 76 (Collegeville, MI: Cistercian Publications, 2015), 85.

[82] Jan Palmowski and Christopher Riches, "Algeria," in *A Dictionary of Contemporary World History*, 6th ed. (Oxford: Oxford University Press, 2021); Evans and Phillips, *Algeria: Anger of the Dispossessed*.

Chapter 2

A Cistercian Monastery in Algeria

Les murs de Notre-Dame de l'Atlas sont à l'image de tout ce qui les entoure: brûles de soleil et couverts de sable. Ainsi la végétation, ainsi le visage de tous ceux qui habitent ici.

The walls of Notre-Dame de l'Atlas are like everything around them: sunburned and covered with sand. Thus the vegetation; so also the faces of all those who live here.
—Bruno Lemarchand

On the feast day of Saint Monica, August 27, 1984, Br. Michel Fleury and Fr. Bruno Lemarchand set out from the monastery of Bellefontaine, in western France, to join the community at Tibhirine. Their departure was timed so that they would arrive for the feast of Saint Augustine the following day: "it is already Africa" Bruno remarks as he recalls his final celebration of the Eucharist at Bellefontaine.[1] The two saints, Monica and her son Augustine of Hippo (now Annaba, Algeria), attest not only to the ancient presence of Christianity in North Africa but also to its significance in the development of Christian thought.

Shortly after their arrival, Bruno wrote an account of the journey and their reception for a circular letter to friends and family. It offers a particularly vivid description of the setting

[1] Moines de Tibhirine, *Heureux ceux qui espèrent: Autobiographies spirituelles*, ed. Marie-Dominique Minassian, Les écrits de Tibhirine 1 (Paris: Bayard-Cerf-Bellefontaine, 2018), 217.

of the monastery and its tiny community, and a helpful snapshot of its way of life: with Bruno's assistance we can begin to imagine life at Tibhirine.

On their Air France flight Bruno is impressed by the provision of a "guaranteed pork-free" meal (adhering to Islamic dietary laws) and strikes up a warm conversation with his Algerian neighbors, who appear surprised by his identity and destination. As the plane descends into Algiers he sees "the Mediterranean and a boat." The pair disembark, move through customs, declaring that they "are coming to Algeria as 'residents'" (unusual for Europeans since 1962), and are met by two monks from the Atlas community, Fr. Jean-Pierre and Fr. Amédée.[2] Bruno describes their hot, dusty trip to Tibhirine:

> In a [Renault] 4L car, we set off in the direction of Notre-Dame de l'Atlas: about a hundred kilometers. The whole scenery has changed. As brother Michel says, it is no longer France.
>
> The temperature is 30 degrees, but a fresh wind is blowing from the sea, succeeding, the fathers tell us, the sirocco that has been blowing in recent days: everything appears to be covered with sand, and thirsty. We drive towards Blida, the city of roses, then Médéa. We cross the gorges of the Chiffa. [. . .] A few kilometers from Médéa, the village of Draa Esmar, "the place where there are rushes"; at the top of the main street, you can still see the small church, closed today . . . . We still have a little way to go to reach the monastery, but the road is now in its most natural state, that is to say unpaved: each passing of a car raises a cloud of dust and sand that combines with that raised by the wind.
>
> [. . .] Here we are bypassing the mountain of Djebel Nador (1108 m), and from the road we sight our new monastery: its appearance is between oasis and desert,

[2] Moines de Tibhirine, *Heureux ceux qui espèrent*, 218.

> but quite the opposite of that of Bellefontaine, as we suspected. The walls of Notre-Dame de l'Atlas are like everything around them: sunburned and covered with sand. Thus the vegetation; so also the faces of all those who live here.[3]

Oasis or desert? Bruno is not simply pondering the physical appearance of the monastery here, its dust-colored walls and the promising green tinge of its gardens set amid the drought-stricken mountains. He is also invoking the theological symbol that underpins Judeo-Christian spirituality: the desert as the place of stripping back and of new birth. Moses leads the Hebrew slaves out of Egypt into a long, hard desert where they will be tested and remade before they are able to enter the Promised Land. The prophets speak from the desert: it is at the edge of the wilderness that John the Baptist calls his fellow Judeans to return to God. Jesus' public ministry begins with his own forty-day time of testing in the solitude of the desert, clarifying and purifying his own vocation. In the fourth century the early Christian monks fled from the cities of the Mediterranean world to the deserts of Egypt and Syria, finding a place where a stripped-back life supported the internal work of re-orienting and re-making the self. And while we now think of Cistercian monasteries, in their rural settings, as idyllic oases in a hyper-urbanized world, the first Cistercians thought of themselves as heading for the desert, even if in the hope of establishing an earthy paradise.

Desert and oasis are found side by side. Moreover, as Cistercian monk and theologian André Louf suggests, "the call of the desert" is foundational to the church: "the desert is the place where the church is born and grows."[4] But if the desert is our common call as Christians, Louf argues, there is also a sense in which religious and monastic orders have a special

[3] Moines de Tibhirine, *Heureux ceux qui espèrent*, 218.

[4] André Louf, *In the School of Contemplation*, trans. Paul Rowe, MW 48 (Collegeville, MN: Cistercian Publications, 2015), 71–72.

responsibility to embody "the spirit of the desert."[5] The nature of the desert is crucial here: it is neither "a refuge where one can take shelter from certain dangers" nor "a greenhouse whose special conditions permit the growth and maturation of spiritual flowers and fruits"—rather it is "a crucible" where one is painfully but beautifully remade. Louf describes this unwelcome but necessary process: "thanks to a certain fire—simultaneously that of the passions and that of the Holy Spirit—a noble metal will emerge, purified of its dross, or a new alloy will see the light of day—daring, novel, and unknown to the present."[6] This stripping and remaking comes as a shock to novice monks.[7] The desert both provokes crisis and brings new birth—reconciliation with God, with oneself, with others. As Bruno and Michel approached the monastery at Tibhirine their monastic vocation could be seen, written into the landscape: desert and oasis, the crucible and the hope of rebirth.

A Tour of the Monastery

The two brothers are greeted by Christian de Chergé and introduced to the monastery and its small community of monks:

> Father Christian, the prior, receives us with great kindness at the guesthouse reserved for women (because it is located right at the entrance of the monastery, although here the enclosure is a little elastic). Introductions. Refreshments. And we start the tour of the monastery. First the chapel (it will be good to pray there) . . . the refectory (the table is already set); the "scriptorium" (or common study room with a small desk for each monk), . . . the

[5] Louf, *In the School of Contemplation*, 72.

[6] Louf, *In the School of Contemplation*, 73.

[7] Louf gently outlines this reality in his classic introduction to Cistercian life (André Louf, *The Cistercian Way*, trans. Nivard Kinsella, CS 76 [Kalamazoo, MI: Cistercian Publications, 1983], 50–52).

large terrace overlooking the mountain all colored by sunshine, the dormitory (our belongings are left there: small cell with a bed, a table, a chair, and even a bed-spread) . . . a few other rooms (kitchen, washroom); and we take a little walk in the "park": a few large and beautiful trees, gigantic aloes, rose bushes, but all of it is affected by the drought (it hasn't rained since May) and the weight of the dust deposited by the wind.

A visit also to the cemetery where the first monk to die at Atlas is buried, and Father Aubin (a monk from Timadeuc in Brittany), who died last spring. We greet the brothers of the monastery: Father Jean de la Croix (resting in his room), Father Jean-Baptiste (wearing a plaster cast following a recent fall from the top of a ladder), Father Roland, who stands at the gatehouse, Brother Luc the doctor (and the cook). In the garden we find Brother Marie and his helper, Ali, who has been working at the monastery for thirty years.[8]

The geography of the monastery is important: each space has a function that contributes to the overall purpose of the monastery. "First the chapel": the life of prayer is central, and the space set aside specifically and solely for prayer is the heart of the monastery. In the early 1970s the chapel had been relocated to the old winery, adjacent to the cloister. More suited in scale for the small community, in style it drew inspiration from the mosques of the region and was considered an "architectural success."[9] The brothers gather here for prayer six or seven times a day. As the Rule of Benedict insists, "nothing is to be preferred to the Work of God" (RB 43.3). Often this work is continued in the "scriptorium" in *lectio divina,* the prayerful reading of Scripture and other sacred texts. The refectory, the

[8] Moines de Tibhirine, *Heureux ceux qui espèrent*, 219.

[9] Nuno de São José, "Notre-Dame de l'Atlas, mystère d'une secrète fécondité: histoire de la communauté depuis sa fondation jusqu'en 1996," *Collectanea Cisterciensia* 83 (2021): 292.

dining room, is the place of physical nourishment: another engine house, requiring considerable labor to ensure that the "table is set," that there is food to share. Bruno gives us a picture of the sparse simplicity of a monk's cell—bed, table, chair. The bedspread is an unexpected luxury. Simplicity, to the point of austerity, is a hallmark of Cistercian monasticism.

Bruno also sketches the interface with "the world": the guesthouse, as the focus of monastic hospitality, and the gatehouse, where contact with neighbors and visitors is mediated. This interface assumes "enclosure," a fundamental element of monasticism in the Benedictine tradition: "the workshop where we are to toil faithfully . . . is the enclosure of the monastery [*claustra monasterii*] and stability in the community" (RB 4.78). Traditionally a monastery is physically separated from the outside world by a wall, with entry controlled at the gatehouse, enabling the work of the monks to be carried out undisturbed in the monastic enclosure or cloister. The desert is separated from the city. The monk has "left the world," and enclosure places limits on both the access of outsiders to the monastery and the movement of the monks outside. In practice the strictness of this enclosure varies, but "the contemplative life" of the monastery remains the priority.[10]

Already Bruno notices that enclosure at Tibhirine is somewhat "elastic." The monastery at Tibhirine was not purpose built; it had been a farm, and efforts to secure physical enclosure had only ever been partially achieved. The growth of the village of Tibhirine complicated this effort. In the mid-1960s the monks' efforts to build low walls and erect fences risked offending their neighbors, who were used to being able to move freely through the monastery grounds. (At this time the solution to problems with animal incursions into the gardens and petty theft was to hire a local as caretaker.)[11] The gatehouse

[10] Constitutions of the Cistercian Order of the Strict Observance (CST) 29.2.

[11] Jean-Paul Schumacher, "Les frères de Notre-Dame de l'Atlas dans la societé algérienne, à Tibhirine," in Moines de Tibhirine, *Heureux ceux qui espèrent*, 19; São José, "Notre-Dame de l'Atlas," 287–88.

was a busy and sometimes noisy place—even more so in the last years of the community—where locals sought advice and assistance. Br Luc's dispensary brought with it a steady stream of patients. Finding a healthy balance in relation to "the monastery wall," one that would ensure its contemplative purpose, was an ongoing challenge. Enclosure was indeed "elastic."

The visit to the cemetery, the burial place of the monks who had lived and died at Tibhirine, is a reminder of the other component of the Benedictine workshop: "stability in the community." Monks do not join a monastic order per se; they join a particular community of that order—a particular community in a particular place—ideally until they die. This dual commitment to a place and to a community feels astonishing in the modern world, where commitments of any sort are rare. But such commitment is no easier for monks than for anyone else. When Bruno and Michel arrived in 1984 it was for a twelve-month trial of monastic life at Tibhirine. Both had made their first profession, or temporary vows, at Bellefontaine in the previous year. Michel found himself very much at home in the small, poor community and quickly settled. Bruno did not and returned to Bellefontaine until 1989. When Bruno made his solemn (final) profession at Tibhirine in 1990, Fr. Jean Scotto, former bishop of Constantine and friend of the community, interpreted the vow of stability in starkly simple terms: "This means: you stay with us."[12]

After their tour of the monastery, Bruno and Michel met their brother monks. The workshop of the monastery is a communal enterprise: "Cistercian monks seek God and follow Christ under a rule and an abbot in a stable community that is a school of brotherly love" (CST 3.1). The life of prayer and work is set in a community—a community, it turns out, that is comprised of ordinary, flawed human beings—held together, sometimes strongly, at other times more tenuously, by their

[12] Moines de Tibhirine, "Lettres circulaires de la communauté Notre-Dame de l'Atlas Tibhirine-Fès (1990)," in *Heureux ceux qui espèrent: Autobiographies spirituelles*, Les écrits de Tibhirine 1 (Paris: Bayard-Cerf-Bellefontaine, 2018), 716.

common purpose. In Bruno's account we meet real people: Jean de la Croix resting in his room, Jean-Baptist in a plaster cast because he'd fallen off a ladder, Roland at the gatehouse, Luc juggling his work as a doctor for the district and as cook for the community, Marie working in the garden with their neighbor Ali. A small, human community at work, in a harsh environment.

Dust weaves its way through Bruno's narrative. The natural world is not simply a backdrop, as Cistercians have long understood. In a letter written to persuade a young protégé to join the monastery, Bernard of Clairvaux says, "Woods and stones will teach you what you can never hear from any master."[13] Writing to the community at Bellefontaine just a few days after his arrival, and later to his cousin, Br. Michel remarks on the spectacular sunrises and sunsets over the mountains and the changes of color as the light shifts: "It leads to contemplation and thanksgiving." And he reminds his brothers that "there is nothing as beautiful as God alone."[14]

The view of the sun setting over the mountains had long nourished the brothers at Tibhirine. In his address to the general chapter meeting in Poyo, Spain, in 1993, Christian recalled a particular sunset, a moment shared with a brother—clearly Luc:

> When I was a novice at Atlas, I saw one of our brothers, a lay brother by conviction, frozen at the window in the evening of an exhausting day. He was watching the sunset. Yet I felt he was exhausted, even exasperated. The show was magnificent, it is true. And I, behind him, just as much admired that after twenty-five years of presence one still knows how to admire a sunset, in the same place as on so many other days. At the end, he turned around and said simply, "We'll wait until tomorrow evening be-

[13] Bernard of Clairvaux, *The Letters of St. Bernard of Clairvaux*, trans. Bruno Scott James (Stroud, UK: Sutton Publishing, 1953; repr. Kalamazoo, MI: Cistercian Publications, 1998), 156; letter 107.

[14] Moines de Tibhirine, *Heureux ceux qui espèrent*, 155–56.

> fore we piss off!" In a flash, I understood what stability was, and many other things about monastic life.[15]

Luc saw many more sunsets, as well as many more exhausting days, before he was taken from the monastery in 1996. He never did piss off!

The tour for the two new recruits gives way to the routine of monastic life: the two chapel bells ring, and "the sound reverberates throughout the mountain" as the community gathers to celebrate the feast of Augustine, bishop of Hippo and doctor of the church:

> The celebration begins with the singing of Vespers, then readings of the day's Mass and the Eucharist follow: the celebration takes place calmly, with long moments of silence, and Father Prior renews his welcome of the two brothers who have come from Bellefontaine: he tells us what Saint Augustine still represents for the Church today, and more particularly for the Church in North Africa. After the Eucharist, a long moment of thanksgiving [*action de grace*]. Then the meal (readings of the Sayings of the Desert Fathers and "Music for Our Time" by Miguel Angel Estrella). And the chapter: Father Prior asks Brother Michel and me to introduce ourselves, to say simply and in broad outline what our past was, and also the reason that made us ask for a year's trial of monastic life at Notre-Dame de l'Atlas.
>
> After this meeting, we went to the chapel for the office of Compline, which ended, as in Bellefontaine, as in all our Cistercian monasteries, with the singing of the "Salve Regina" (in Gregorian [chant] of course) in front of the icon

[15] Christian de Chergé, "Confèrence du frère Christian du chapitre général 1993," in *Sept vies pour Dieu et l'Algérie*, ed. Bruno Chenu (Paris: Bayard, 1996), 82.

of the Virgin Mary, the only one lit by the flame of a candle (in Bellefontaine, there are two and they are bigger . . .).

First night in the Atlas Mountains.[16]

Here we meet some of the key features of monastic life: the rhythm of liturgical prayer (here Vespers, Eucharist, Compline); the shared meal in the refectory (as per tradition in "silence," without chatter, except for the additional nourishment of reading and music); the chapter, the regular meeting of the community, where the monks receive regular teaching from the prior and discuss practical matters. And Mary, who holds a special place in Cistercian monasticism, as "Mother and Symbol of the Church": every community and every monk is dedicated to her (CST 3.5). So the day ends with the chanting of the Salve Regina, the medieval Latin hymn in her honor.

Bruno notes, though, the difference in the way the icon is lit. Here just one candle; at Bellefontaine two, bigger, candles. Everything is smaller here—the monastery buildings, the land they cultivate, and especially the community—and hence the number of monks to share the work. Bruno writes later of the chapel and sacristy that it is "Bellefontaine in miniature."[17]

Bernardo Olivera's Dream

The scale of the monastery was indeed tiny, but it was not Bellefontaine in miniature. It was not France. If the landscape, monastery, and people were "sunburned and covered with sand," so too was monastic life at Tibhirine. In the years since Algerian Independence, and under the influence of Vatican II, the monastic community had been steadily and intentionally engaging with the local culture and continuing to build strong

[16] Moines de Tibhirine, *Heureux ceux qui espèrent*, 219–20.

[17] Moines de Tibhirine, *Heureux ceux qui espèrent*, 220. His remark is recorded in the Bellefontaine chronicle.

relationships with their Muslim neighbors. As early as 1965 Arabic language lessons had been provided for monks (initially by Fr. Amédée), as well as orientation in Islamic history and culture.[18]

In 1979 the Ribât es-Salâm (Link of Peace), a group of Christian men and women seeking to understand Islam better as a lived faith, began meeting at the monastery. They were soon joined by a local group of Sufis, the 'Alawiyines de Médéa, who had asked to meet the monks for prayer. In the years ahead further "modulations" were embraced: after 1989 the monks' agricultural work was carried out in a cooperative arrangement with their neighbors; ongoing adjustments to enclosure were made in light of their relationships with their neighbors; care was taken to recognize Muslim holy days, including Ramadan; on Fridays the Eucharist was timed to correlate with the Muslim community's gathering for midday prayer.

The work of enculturation afforded no certainties, however. When Christian was invited by the abbot general, Bernardo Olivera, to address the general chapter meeting in Poyo, Spain, in September 1993 on the subject "Cistercian contemplative identity," he sensed a trap.[19] Olivera's dream during his visit to the Atlas community in 1991 came to mind, with the sharp rebuke delivered by the monk in the dream throttling and rebuking a brother from the Atlas community: "You're wasting your life in this Muslim country . . . our Order really has no use for a foundation like yours."[20] What was this small contemplative community doing in a Muslim majority country? In the dream, it is Olivera who responds to the monk's aggressive questioning. On waking he recorded his response and later shared the dream with the Tibhirine community. Christian astutely uses Olivera's own response to give weight

[18] São José, "Notre-Dame de l'Atlas," 287.

[19] Chergé, "Confèrence du frère Christian du chapitre général 1993," 79.

[20] Chergé, "Confèrence du frère Christian du chapitre général 1993," 84.

and clear affirmation to the call that the community had embraced:

> Their mission is a presence, silent, living, and vital, that of Jesus, that of the Gospel. It is also a welcome from the heart for the Muslim brother, in order to be a better Christian oneself. For it is in this openness to Islam that their way of being Christians, here and now, will be learned. No need to seek reciprocity. Don't wait for it to continue to open up; this would be contrary to the gift [*la gratuité*] of love. If it presents itself, they will give thanks to the one who allows it and gives it . . . . Of course they have to learn something of the Muslim world, because it has cultural and religious values intended for them. And then, they can contribute to awakening and motivating the contemplative dimension that lies at the heart of every Muslim.[21]

Olivera was fully aware of the risks involved, the tension between enculturation and monastic identity, and when he shared his dream with the community, he drew attention to this challenge:

> You have a mission to enculturate the Cistercian charism so that the expression of this monasticism may be enriched by what you will have gleaned from the local culture [. . .] . This inculturation may provoke a reaction of fear, fear that you will lose your monastic identity. In order not to experience this fear, or to liberate yourself from it, the first thing you need to do is to deepen your monastic culture.[22]

[21] Chergé, "Conférence du frère Christian du chapitre général 1993," 90.

[22] Chergé, "Conférence du frère Christian du chapitre général 1993," 88.

This is the mission that Notre-Dame de l'Atlas had intentionally embraced since 1976, but there was no template for this work of enculturation. As Christian observes, "it is no longer possible to set up a monastery built up in advance, because, more than any other, the contemplative life is discovered to be dependent on the 'human' conditions of life of a country, its culture, its history, its habits, its religious tradition."[23] So there was no template for Tibhirine. In fact, there is no template for any Christian community. But there are traditions of wisdom, wells of experience, and in this case immense resources within the Cistercian tradition that enabled the Atlas community to live deeply and creatively into its monastic identity, with increasing confidence and, indeed, freedom. Their Cistercian heritage was deeply important to them, and they dug deeply into its well.

The following chapters explore the ways in which the monks baptized their Cistercian vocation with the dust of Algeria to become a "silent, living, and vital" presence—a prophetic presence—in a Muslim country increasingly torn apart by violence. A presence that still offers us its fruits.

[23] Chergé, "Conférence du frère Christian du chapitre général 1993," 96.

Part II

Ora et labora

Chapter 3

Prayer

Nous sommes un corps à l'écoute.
We are a body that listens.
—Christophe Lebreton

When Brother Michel Fleury wrote to his cousin shortly after his arrival at Tibhirine in 1984, prayer was central to his thoughts:

> Thank you, Joseph, for reminding me of your "Presence." I beg the Lord Jesus that he might complete my poor prayer. He is the only one who truly prays, the only true missionary, the only "Good Samaritan who bends over the human family in distress," today's Gospel reading. It is not certain that one can say that there is more free time than in Bellefontaine, but the way of working is calmer, favoring union with God, more precisely the "return to God" [*retour à Dieu*]. Rise: 4 a.m. Vigils: 4:15 a.m. Lauds: 7:30 a.m. Terce: around 8:15 a.m. Eucharist: 12 noon. None: 3:30 p.m. Vespers: 6:30 p.m. Retire: 9. Magnificent sunrises and sunsets, beautiful over the mountains, with the differences at dusk. G-d's canticle is "gob smacking," excuse the expression; but Scripture, it is even more beautiful.[1]

[1] Moines de Tibhirine, *Heureux ceux qui espèrent: Autobiographies spirituelles*, ed. Marie-Dominique Minassian, Les écrits de Tibhirine 1 (Paris:

In a note to the Bellefontaine community written just after his arrival, Michel had already remarked on the spacious silence afforded by the monastery's morning routine: "Brother Bruno and I appreciate the two and a half hours of silence in the morning between Vigils and Lauds (wash and dress, breakfast, prayer in the chapel, and reading)."[2] Notice too that as he lays out the pattern of community and personal prayer Michel emphasizes its purpose: returning to God (*retour à Dieu*). He understands the difficulty of prayer and its priority, and how the structure of the day supports its pursuit. Further, the rhythm of prayer mirrors the rhythm of the natural world, the sunrise and the sunset, so that prayer is rooted to this place that offers its own gift in the changing light over the mountains.

We glimpse too the significance of Scripture and *lectio divina* in feeding the life of prayer. The reading of the day's Gospel (Luke 10:25-37) offers an image of Jesus' saving Michel's "poor prayer": Jesus is the "Good Samaritan who bends over the human family in distress." The wounded traveler is not simply a stranger in need but represents our common human condition. Even our prayer needs the support of "the only one who truly prays," Jesus. Mercifully he bends to serve us. (Saint Paul's experience resonates here: "Likewise the Spirit helps us in our weakness; for we do not know how to pray as we ought, but that very Spirit intercedes with sighs too deep for words" [Rom 8:26]).

This chapter explores the Atlas community's understanding and practice of prayer. The surviving traces of the monks' lives—letters, prayers, homilies, talks, journals—offer a window into monastic life, and through that window the reader finds ordinary Christians facing the same challenges in relation to prayer that are faced by all people of faith. The monks display a consistent modesty about prayer as well as an absolute

Bayard-Cerf-Bellefontaine, 2018), 156. Michel's cousin Joseph Crand was a diocesan priest. Michel and Joseph shared a significant correspondence.

[2] Moines de Tibhirine, *Heureux ceux qui espèrent*, 156.

commitment to its practice. Personal prayer is no easier for a monk than it is for the average Christian. Communal prayer is no easier for a monastic community than it is for the average parish community. Even though one might imagine the monks as somehow expert in its craft, prayer remains hard work. In the monks' experience of prayer the personal and the communal, the individual and the community, are delicately interwoven. Above all, as they lived through a deeply troubled time, the call to prayer remained.[3]

Ora et labora, Prayer and Work

The motto *ora et labora*, prayer and work, expresses the balance sought in a monastery founded in the Benedictine tradition. Indeed it was the hallmark of early Cistercian reform. Christian de Chergé speaks of prayer and work as the *mamelles* (breasts), the twin sources of nourishment for monastic life.[4] He reflects on these twin foundations in the context of a long series of chapter talks delivered between February 1991 and August 1993 on the newly revised *Constitutions and Statutes* of the Cistercian Order.[5]

[3] In his lecture for the *Journeés Romaines* in 1989, Christian quoted Pope Paul VI's October 1965 speech to the United Nations: "'The hour has come when a pause, a moment of recollection, reflection, you might say of prayer, is absolutely needed so that we may think back over our common origin, our history, our common destiny' [https://www.vatican.va/content/paul-vi/fr/speeches/1965/documents/hf_p-vi_spe_19651004_united-nations.html]. This necessity is no less urgent today" (Christian de Chergé, "L'échelle mystique du dialogue," *Islamochristiana* 23 [1997]: 4).

[4] Christian de Chergé, *Dieu pour tout jour: chapitres de Père Christian de Chergé à la communauté de Tibhirine (1985–1996)*, 2nd ed. (Montjoyer: Abbaye Notre-Dame d'Aiguebelle, 2006), 403; July 2, 1992. Elsewhere he calls *ora et labora* the two crutches (*béquilles*) (Chergé, *Dieu pour tout jour*, 363; March 12, 1991).

[5] The series covers significant portions of the revised *Constitutions and Statutes of the Monks of the Cistercian Order of the Strict Observance* (approved at Pentecost 1990). The constitutions were the culmination of work carried out in the light of Vatican II, particularly in response to the

While I draw on a range of sources, material from this series of chapter talks provides the backbone for consideration of prayer in this chapter and of work in the next. As prior, Christian delivered carefully prepared short talks (eight to ten minutes) to the community three times a week during the morning Office of Terce, held in their meeting room or chapter.[6] The chapter talk texts—sometimes bullet-point notes, at other times fuller text—display Christian's sharp intellect, his depth of knowledge of their shared Cistercian tradition, and, as is the case across his writing, his capacity to offer fresh insights often expressed in vivid metaphors.

While only Christian's written scripts for his talks survive, they offer the reader enough to imagine how it might have been to listen with the Tibhirine monks. Further, Christian often notes or responds to conversations that have taken place in the community: the chapter talks are never delivered "from on high."[7] While a walk through a constitution might sound like a dry subject, Christian uses this series of chapter talks as an opportunity to examine and deepen the community's understanding of their Cistercian monastic commitments. Bernardo Olivera had no reason to fear that the monastic identity

---

1965 papal encyclical *Perfectae Caritatis* (The Adaption and Renewal of Religious Life). The Order had worked long and hard on the revision of its constitutions, as is reflected in Christian's chapter talks as he discusses earlier drafts and the debates at general chapter, as well as the relationship among the constitutions, the papal encyclical, and the Order's roots in the Rule of Benedict. Christian works from the French version of the revised *Constitutions*.

[6] Chergé, *Dieu pour tout jour*, xiv.

[7] In early 1985 the community diary notes a desire for great community participation in chapter: "we go as far as to say that there is no dialogue in the community." It may well have been that Christian had overloaded his curriculum. Practices derived from larger French monasteries needed to be adjusted. After discussion the community decided to experiment with "mini-chapters" (just five minutes) before Lauds and a pattern of more participatory chapters in the evenings. The later talks, delivered at Terce and somewhat longer, bear the imprint of this early learning for Christian as prior (Moines de Tibhirine, *Heureux ceux qui espèrent*, 448–49).

of the community was at risk: the talks and the discussion around them were an exercise in deepening its monastic culture.[8]

The Goal of Prayer: A Shared Contemplative Vocation

What is the goal or purpose of prayer? Immediately this question invites a broader frame. When Michel speaks in his letter to his cousin of returning to God (*retour à Dieu*) he is referring not only to the goal of prayer but to the goal of monastic life itself, to the monks' contemplative vocation. In fact, it is this all-encompassing purpose that is definitive of Cistercian monasticism. In the words of the Constitutions, "This Order is a monastic institute wholly ordered to contemplation" (CST 2). In his chapter talk on this article Christian elucidates: "everything must be organized to help signify the ultimate vocation of man, which is to SEE God."[9] So while contemplation—*seeing, remembering, returning to* God—is their particular monastic vocation, it is actually a shared human vocation. Cistercian monastic life is simply ordered in a way that signals and supports this call constantly to "return to God." However, as Michel indicates in his letter, no schedule, no way of life, however carefully structured, can guarantee this return to God, though certain conditions (a calmer way of working for example) might favor it.

Nonetheless, Christian is cautious around the word *contemplative*. He begins his 1993 address to the general chapter of the Order gathered at Poyo, Spain, by raising his discomfort with the wording of its theme—"Cistercian contemplative identity"—"because it can imply that contemplation can be possessed as an identity, as a stable state." Instead, he argues, contemplation implies "a process, a tension, a permanent

[8] See chapters 1 and 2 for Dom Bernardo Olivera's visit to Tibhirine and the dream that enabled him both to affirm the monastery's mission and to acknowledge the tension between inculturation and identity.

[9] Chergé, *Dieu pour tout jour*, 355; February 21, 1991.

exodus." Like Abraham setting out from Haran, he says, we are invited by God: "Walk in my presence" (Gen 17:1; see Gen 12). And such a walk, he confesses, "deepens my hunger to 'see' the Presence more than it satisfies it." There is no arrival in this life. Christian quotes the wisdom of the Muslim mystical tradition: "He who declares himself a Sufi is not really a Sufi." Similarly, it would be foolish to declare oneself "a contemplative." Could one really claim to have "always recognized him on the road" (an allusion to the appearance of the resurrected Christ on the road to Emmaus, Luke 24) or in the "naked, sick, hungry" (drawing on the parable of the Final Judgment in Matthew 25)? Instead, Christian suggests, if we recognize ourselves as being perpetually "on the way," we are liberated from the sort of unhealthy preoccupation with identity that prevents the self-forgetfulness needed to see God.[10] So being a member of "a monastic institute wholly ordered to contemplation" does not confer on one a ready-made (or even a slowly acquired) contemplative identity. Rather, the ordering of monastic life is, in Christian's view, intended to "keep awake my desire to see God, [which is] always threatened by blinking."[11]

In his chapter talks Christian similarly stresses that the goal of monastic life is seeing God, remembering God's presence. This is heart work: it is the state of the heart that opens this possibility. The beatitude "Blessed are the pure in heart, for they shall see God" (Matt 5:8) has underpinned the monastic call from its earliest days in the deserts of the Mediterranean world. Seeing God requires purity of heart, and monastic life is dedicated to heart work. As the Rule of Benedict teaches, the monastery is "the school of the Lord's service" (RB Prologue), a place of ongoing formation, a place where hearts are

[10] Christian de Chergé, "Conférence du frère Christian du chapitre général 1993," in *Sept vies pour Dieu et l'Algérie*, ed. Bruno Chenu (Paris: Bayard, 1996), 79–80. Elsewhere Christian speaks of moving from "being for oneself" to "being for him [Christ]" (*d'un "quant à soi" à un "quant à lui"*) (Chergé, *Dieu pour tout jour*, 358; February 27, 1991).

[11] Chergé, "Conférence du frère Christian du chapitre général 1993," 81.

re-formed in the likeness of Christ. This work of re-formation is both personal and communal. Playing on the language of formation, Christian says, "we are striving to acquire a FORM [*une FORME*] that is that of Christ," not just as individuals but as "the whole Body of Christ, each member being informed [*informé*] by all the others."[12]

How does this re-formation take place? Listening, Christian reminds the community, is foundational. Building on the first word of the Rule of Benedict, *listen* (*obsculta*), he images the monastic school as offering a series of *tables d'écoute* (wiretaps or listening devices)—the French here offers a vivid image, literally "listening tables." These *tables d'écoute* deliver "the one and same Word of God," a word that calls us to renewed discipleship—"to begin again" our "discipline of heart and action."[13] All the elements of monastic life—prayer and work, solitude and community—offer places of such listening, invitation, and conversion.

The Rhythm of Prayer: *Opus Dei*

Communal prayer is a privileged and formative *table d'écoute* in monastic life: "nothing is to be preferred to the Work of God [*Opus Dei*]" (RB 43.3). The rhythm of communal prayer not only structures daily life but provides the scaffold for its contemplative purpose: it orients life to the remembrance of God.[14] If the monastery is a school of the Lord's service, the Liturgy of the Hours is its school of prayer—a school, as Christian observes, that one never quite leaves. The typical Cistercian schedule, drawing on the psalmist's "seven times a day I praise you" (Ps 119 [118]:164), begins with Vigils before dawn, then Lauds followed by the daily Eucharist, and the shorter Offices of Terce, Sext, and None punctuating the day, with Vespers

[12] Chergé, *Dieu pour tout jour*, 357; February 26, 1991.

[13] Chergé, *Dieu pour tout jour*, 357; February 26, 1991. Christian also alludes here to Mary and Martha, representing prayer and work, or contemplation and action, as necessarily "inseparably joined."

[14] Chergé, *Dieu pour tout jour*, 380–81; August 22, 1991.

and Compline completing the rhythm. Each of the Offices is comprised of psalms and antiphons, canticles and hymns, Scripture readings and responsories, prayers and intercessions. In the Cistercian tradition much of the Office is sung or chanted. The schedule of community prayer at Tibhirine followed these established patterns, although the Eucharist was generally celebrated in the middle of the day, with Sext as its prelude rather than as a separate Office.

The regular pattern of prayer is of such importance that the constitutions designate it as a statute: "Because the Work of God is a means of sanctifying the day, [each Hour] is to be celebrated at the time assigned to it, determined according to Cistercian tradition and local custom" (CST 19.1A). This "sanctification of the day at regular intervals" is beautifully expressed, as Christian points out, in the term "Liturgy of the Hours." Drawing on Benedict, he reminds the community, "it is at all times that we must keep ourselves under the gaze of God" (see RB 7.12–13).[15]

The heading for Christian's chapter talk on this statute is worth noting. The words of the psalmist, "seven times a day, I have sung your praise," are followed by a list of these seven times in both Arabic and French: "*Al-fajr* (aurore), *as-shurûq* (lever du soleil), *ad-duha* (9h), *ad-dhur* (midi), *al-'asr* (16h), *al-maghreb* (coucher du soleil), *al-'ichâ* (nuit)."[16] Dawn, sunrise, 9 o'clock, midday, 4 o'clock, sunset, night. Seven times a day, in this place, Tibhirine. The monks' rhythm of prayer is not only conducted under the gaze of God but is witnessed by their Arabic-speaking Muslim neighbors.

In naming the seven times of prayer in Arabic, Christian intentionally correlates their monastic rhythm of prayer with the Islamic pattern of prayer (*salat*), five times a day: *fajr* (dawn), *dhuhr* (noon/sun at the zenith), *asr* (afternoon), *maghrib* (sunset), and *isha* (evening/night). As for the Cistercian monks,

[15] Chergé, *Dieu pour tout jour*, 377; July 27, 1991.

[16] Chergé, *Dieu pour tout jour*, 377; July 27, 1991. Retaining Christian's transliteration of the Arabic.

there are two bookends, *fajr* (dawn) and *maghrib* (sunset). The Liturgy of the Hours and the *salat* (daily prayers) share the same intentions: the sanctification of time and the remembrance of God. Indeed the commitment to prayer through the day, to the Liturgy of the Hours, was one of the features of monastic life that, as John W. Kiser observes, had given the Cistercians in Algeria an "affinity" with Muslims that was "natural."[17] In his 1993 address at Poyo, Christian observes that their Muslim neighbors could understand the monks' identity only in terms of their own religious practice: "He prays, he believes in God, he observes Lent and gives to the poor . . . It's almost like us!"[18] (When their young neighbor Mohammed was taken to visit some French Cistercian monasteries he remarked, "You know, there, I met real Muslims."[19])

Daily prayer in Islam is carefully correlated to the sun—and that undoubtedly inspires Christian, in his chapter talk, to explore early Benedictine practice. He notes how much variation there would have been in the "prescribed hours" for the Work of God in Benedict's day (sixth century), when time was calculated using the movement of the sun and dividing day and night separately into twelve parts or "hours." Thus hours during the day were longer in summer and shorter in winter. This meant, for example (and Christian is surprised by this discovery) that Lauds was celebrated at 4 a.m. at mid-summer (June 21) but at 7:40 a.m. in mid-winter (December 21), and Vespers at 8 p.m. at mid-summer and 4 p.m. in mid-winter. He notes that these times closely correlate with the times specified for *salat al-fajr* (prayer at dawn) and *salat al-maghrib* (prayer

[17] John W. Kiser, *The Monks of Tibhirine: Faith, Love, and Terror in Algeria* (New York: St Martin's Griffin, 2002), 37.

[18] Chergé, "Confèrence du frère Christian du chapitre général 1993," 82.

[19] Chergé, "Confèrence du frère Christian du chapitre général 1993," 82. This story is quoted by Louf in a conference on contemplative life given in Rome in November 1993. Christian's Poyo talk had clearly made an impression (André Louf, *In the School of Contemplation*, trans. Paul Rowe, MW 48 [Collegeville, MN: Cistercian Publications, 2015], 14).

at sunset).[20] One can imagine a playful discussion of these discoveries among the monks. Christian leaves the community with an open question: how might the pattern of prayer that they have inherited better reflect "local customs"[21] (reading this phrase from the constitutions more broadly perhaps than the statute intended!).

In fact, in summer the monastery bell signaling Vigils often coincided with the voice of the muezzin signaling dawn and calling the monks' Muslim neighbors to *salat al-fajr*.[22] And for some years the prayers of both, monks and Muslims, came from the same enclosure: in 1988 the monks had invited their neighbors to use the waiting room of the former welfare service for mothers and children as a prayer room while they waited for a planned mosque to be built.[23] The monastic enclosure became a shared *table d'écoute.* In fact listening for, attending to, points of contact had been a long-term priority for the monastic community. In the community's circular letter for 1993, amidst the growing tensions in Algeria, Christian noted that they had become even more aware of the vocation to prayer they shared with their neighbors. After All Saints' Day, while the monks prayed the opening words of their Office, "God, come to my aid! Lord, make haste to help us!" (*Dieu, viens à mon aide! seigneur, vite, à notre secours!*), the same plea for help is echoed in the *Surah el-Fatiha*, "The Opener" (Qur'an 1), recited during Muslim prayers. The repetition of these words five times a day connected the monks' prayer with that of their neighbors.[24]

[20] Chergé, *Dieu pour tout jour*, 377; July 27, 1991.

[21] CST 19.1A.

[22] Chergé, *Dieu pour tout jour*, 405; August 4, 1992.

[23] Moines de Tibhirine, "Lettres circulaires de la communauté Notre-Dame de l'Atlas Tibhirine-Fès (1988)," in Moines de Tibhirine, *Heureux ceux qui espèrent: Autobiographies spirituelles*, Les écrits de Tibhirine 1 (Paris: Bayard-Cerf-Bellefontaine, 2018), 707–8.

[24] Moines de Tibhirine, "Lettres circulaires de la communauté Notre-Dame de l'Atlas Tibhirine-Fès (1993)," 736.

However, regardless of its centrality to monastic life, the Work of God is not an end in itself. It is a scaffold designed to support the remembrance of God, and the intention is that this remembrance, or mindfulness, be extended throughout the day, not just during times allocated for prayer (CST 20).[25] Consequently shared prayer was not the only means of communion, Christian suggests: "With some neighbors, the bond of contemplation can take place without there being an explicit sharing of prayer (this will probably even be the most frequent case)." He illustrates this point by sharing a conversation he had had with two of their neighbors, Mohammed, son of Ali, and an older Mohammed:[26]

> [Mohammed, son of Ali] said that it is through prayer (*salât*) that God GATHERS us together. He calls us to prayer, and there we are together for him. I pointed out to him that at the moment the places [of prayer] and the words used separated us, and very often too the INTENTION (this is more serious) . . . he [son of Ali] tried to defend himself. Mohammed had been silent . . . he then breaks his silence: "There is greater than *salât* . . . what? . . . *al-mahabba*, LOVE . . . and love gathers together, or it doesn't exist!"[27]

The elder Mohammed also understood prayer (*salât*) as a scaffold, as an aid to remembering God—who is love and who draws all into a communion of love. Christian continues: "There is a place for us where the Office and Love come together to speak as one in a total openness of heart to the Father

[25] CST 20: "By constantly cultivating mindfulness of God, the brothers extend the Work of God throughout the whole day."

[26] Chergé, *Dieu pour tout jour*, 381; August 22, 1991. Ali was the long-serving gardener at the monastery. The older Mohammed is probably Mohammed M., the caretaker of the monastery. Christian renders the Arabic name variously as Mohamed and Mohammed. For clarity I have standardized these to Mohammed.

[27] Chergé, *Dieu pour tout jour*, 381; August 22, 1991.

and to the multitude of brothers: it is the Eucharist, which is precisely MEMORIAL."[28] Love, communion, remembering, all come together in the Eucharist, which becomes not only a place of remembering the presence of God, but of being nourished by the presence of God.

The Work of God (*Opus Dei*), the structured life of communal prayer, is then for the Atlas community the scaffold or framework that assists the monk to listen for the presence of God and to orient the whole day towards walking in God's presence. At the heart of this Work of God the Eucharist focuses this remembering, this returning to God, in its invitation to communion with or participation in the paschal mystery of the death and resurrection of Jesus.

The Community of Prayer: Weaving the Carpet

In the monastery prayer can never be a solely individual pursuit. The prayer of the individual monk and the prayer of the community are interrelated. The state of the heart of each individual matters to the whole. Christian uses the vivid image of a woven carpet to describe this interdependence:

> The monastery provides a frame, a weft, but it is up to each person to fill this frame, to weave the carpet. Cistercian labor has its trademark, its specific "graces," but it requires the loving attachment of each to the Lord Jesus. This is to say that the balance and the success of the community is dependent on the intimate relationship of each member with his Lord.[29]

Communal and personal prayer are necessarily interdependent. The nourishment that prayer provides and the difficulties

[28] Chergé, *Dieu pour tout jour*, 381; August 22, 1991. "Il y a pour nous un lieu où l'Office et l'Amour se rejoignent pour se dire ensemble dans une totale ouverture du cœur au Père et à la multitude des frères: c'est l'Eucharistie qui est précisément MÉMORIAL."

[29] Chergé, *Dieu pour tout jour*, 359; March 5, 1991.

that prayer presents are both woven into the carpet, into the Body of Christ.

Weaving the carpet is by no means straightforward. The liturgical life of the community (the Work of God) promises much—and demands much. The constitutions hold out the promise of both personal and communal growth: "The liturgy strengthens and increases both the inner sense of the monastic vocation and communion among the brothers" (CST 17.1). But Christian rightly names the costly nature of this commitment to communal prayer:

> The place where this communion is received is also a place where it is PRACTICED . . . no wonder that there too [the monk] encounters obstacles, knots, the temptation to feel rejected. It is a place of SANCTIFICATION where we learn the cost of communion, which is first of all to totally offer oneself with one's own tastes and one's own will, in order to receive oneself differently, in the symphony of the Holy Spirit.[30]

So practice is needed—a process again, not a one-off deal—and "we learn the cost." For the liturgy to become a place of sanctification requires sacrifice, the offering of oneself. This practice necessarily includes the relinquishing of personal liturgical preferences, undoubtedly the site of many "knots." Christian continues: "No communion is possible if each does not offer oneself personally."[31] So he remarks on the need "to accompany, to precede" the community liturgy with personal prayer, preferably when gathered together. In the liturgical life of the community the offering of self is first and foremost to God, he says, but then also to the community, and indeed to all humanity. He continues: "We offer all the means at our disposal (voice,

[30] Chergé, *Dieu pour tout jour*, 373; July 2, 1991.

[31] Chergé, *Dieu pour tout jour*, 373; July 2, 1991.

intelligence, heart, body too)" to be transformed in "the symphony of the Holy Spirit."[32]

While the symphony is ultimately the creation of the Holy Spirit, it is not played without effort. The community's liturgical enterprise was an ongoing and evolving work, undertaken in a real, human community with limited resources: a handful of monks with different gifts, with different formation and life experiences, with different personalities, and with many other responsibilities calling for attention. We glimpse the tensions (the "knots") in Christophe's prayer journal: "big squall in choir at Vespers." Then, on the following Sunday, "Stormy chapter. As cantor still on duty, I am (painfully) at the epicenter of a mini-earthquake. I'm shaken up."[33] A few days later Christophe records his prior's pastoral wisdom: "'We must have humor,' Christian said to me in connection with the singing on Sunday: 'A joyful disappointment.'"[34]

And lest we imagine that the ongoing commitment to the Liturgy of Hours is easy, in his journal Christophe writes that he is "fed up with the Office" and longs for "pure PRAYER, stripped of all liturgical vestments (antiphons, responses, hymns, etc.)."[35]

Difficulties in the community were not always recorded in writing, but an entry in the community diary following Holy Week 1985 offers a small window into the sorts of discussions that would have taken place regularly, and into the tensions that could arise, particularly in the face of change:

> In chapter, we go round the table so everyone can express their observations—criticism or praise—of the various Holy Week services. Memorably a long speech by brother

[32] Chergé, *Dieu pour tout jour*, 373; July 2, 1991.

[33] Christophe Lebreton, *Born from the Gaze of God: The Tibhirine Journal of a Martyr Monk (1993–1996)*, trans. Mette Louise Nygård and Edith Scholl, MW 37 (Collegeville, MN: Cistercian Publications, 2014), 186; August 25 and 27, 1995.

[34] Lebreton, *Born from the Gaze of God*, 187; August 30, 1995.

[35] Lebreton, *Born from the Gaze of God*, 147, 151; April 9 and May 7, 1995.

> Bruno in which he expressed his astonishment at the liberties taken with the structure of the Good Friday and Vigil services . . . with regard to the latter, he expresses real "dismay," with great sadness that it has come to this . . . Regrets also the removal of the cross on Holy Saturday and finds the one on the altar ("stone of sacrifice") after the Mass of Thursday evening astonishing.[36]

Bruno returned to Bellefontaine a few months later; the time was not yet right for him to join the small community of Notre-Dame de l'Atlas. However, it is likely that we are also encountering here the sorts of challenges being faced by many monastic communities (and indeed other religious and ecclesial communities) endeavoring to implement the liturgical reforms and new freedoms envisaged by Vatican II. Tensions around change—between tradition and innovation, the familiar and the new—are inevitable, but in the monastery the priority of this Work of God and its capacity to build (or destroy) communion make meeting such challenges non-negotiable.

Chant is foundational to the Liturgy of the Hours in the Cistercian tradition—indeed the Office is often referred to as *choir*. One temptation, as Christian notes, is to make the performance of the liturgy, especially its chant, a specialist affair: historically there are many examples, even in monastic life, of "liturgies reserved for a vocal or clerical elite" with participation restricted to "listening and silence."[37] Before the abolition of the distinction between choir and lay brothers, postulants were sometimes directed toward the lay brothers simply because they were unable to sing in tune (as had apparently been the case with their then abbot general, Bernardo Olivera).[38]

Against the temptation to specialize, the revised constitution offers a statute that prioritizes full participation as well as careful attention to context: "The celebration is to be such that

[36] Moines de Tibhirine, *Heureux ceux qui espèrent*, 227.

[37] Chergé, *Dieu pour tout jour*, 378; August 6, 1991.

[38] Chergé, *Dieu pour tout jour*, 378; August 6, 1991.

it expresses the spirit of the community and leads the brothers to full participation" (CST 19.2A).[39] The liturgy at Tibhirine did not need to imitate that of Tamié or Bellefontaine or Aiguebelle or any other Cistercian monastery. The liturgy needed to reflect its own particular spirit, embodied at Tibhirine, and enable the full participation of its small community. "This spirit exists HERE," says Christian.[40]

However, the small size of the community and the variable vocal capacity of the monks at Tibhirine was a continuing challenge (as Christophe's late journal entry indicates). Christian reminds the brothers that God's hearing is different from ours: "when the heart rings true, God hears the wrong notes [as if they were] true."[41] If the celebration of the liturgy is to embody "the spirit of the community," then, Christian suggests, "the best singer is the one who knows how to make the harmonics of this 'spirit' vibrate, who will LISTEN to it, then compose with it."[42] Listening is again foundational, this time listening to one's brother monks with ears attuned to the Holy Spirit working in each. Christian then turns directly to the challenging and sometimes divisive role of the cantor, whose responsibility was to lead the chant, especially of the psalms. He draws on the figures of the prophet Elijah and his successor Elisha, who famously asks for a double share of his master's spirit (2 Kgs 2:9). Surprisingly, perhaps, Christian suggests that the community is Elijah, and the cantor is Elisha, the one who asks the community for a double share of its spirit: "the cantor sings only if he sings the spirit of the community."[43]

In practice, of course, the challenges remained. Philippe Hémon, a monk of Tamié and a friend of Christophe, worked with the community over a number of years revising the Liturgy of the Hours. The monks had been increasingly struggling

[39] Such a principle might be profitably applied to the liturgical celebrations of the whole church.

[40] Chergé, *Dieu pour tout jour*, 379; August 6, 1991.

[41] Chergé, *Dieu pour tout jour*, 378; August 6, 1991.

[42] Chergé, *Dieu pour tout jour*, 379; August 6, 1991.

[43] Chergé, *Dieu pour tout jour*, 379; August 6, 1991.

with Offices that were comparable to those sung at Aiguebelle and Tamié, Offices that had been developed by Fr. Aelred Larbiou (1926–1993) during his extended stay at Tibhirine between 1969 and 1973. A monk of Tamié, Aelred had been a key player in the revision and re-composition of liturgical prayer at Tamié following Vatican II, and his expertise as "the troubadour" of the liturgy was sought by other French-speaking Cistercian communities.[44] He had assisted the Tibhirine community to make the transition from Latin to French for the psalms, as well as introducing new hymns and antiphons. It was at this time that the first Arabic elements were introduced into the liturgy (in particular the Lord's Prayer).[45] It is notable that Christian joined and made his first temporary profession in 1971, during this time of significant liturgical change for the community.

However, by the time that Hémon first came to Tibhirine, for Christophe's ordination as a priest in 1990, the community was struggling with the Offices: "their voices were not so strong, they were less ambitious also, and that sort of repertory, in the long run, was a strain on their throats—and their patience."[46] At Christian's invitation and with "definite instructions," Hémon began working with the community on a complete revision of the Offices. While he initially set about to simplify both the quantity of material and the demand on their vocal capacities, he soon realized that given the centrality of liturgical prayer to their vocation in Algeria (*priants parmi*

[44] Victor Bourdeau, *Vingt ans après le Concile Vatican II ou vingt années de vie liturgique à Tamié (1965–1985)*, 1985, Revised 2003. https://www.abbaye-tamie.com/communaute-tamie/la_liturgie/etudes_liturgie/la-reforme-liturgique-a-tamie.

[45] Nuno de São José, "Notre-Dame de l'Atlas, mystère d'une secrète fécondité: histoire de la communauté depuis sa fondation jusqu'en 1996," *Collectanea Cisterciensia* 83 (2021): 291. Understandably, the principle that the liturgy be conducted in the local language could only be partially fulfilled in a French-speaking community.

[46] Philippe Hémon, "An En-Visaged Good-By-E," CSQ 34, no. 2 (1999): 210.

d'autre priants), they needed an enriched repertory "lest the penury so trying in all domains of their daily life should weigh upon them in church also."[47] Surely a wise and pastoral insight—small need not mean impoverished; all communities of faith, regardless of size, deserve to be enriched through their shared prayer.

Hémon visited the community regularly to continue this project, steadily working through the liturgical year and producing new Office booklets for each season—indeed he had planned to be at Tibhirine, working on the Sundays of Easter, at the time of the monks' kidnapping but had been delayed by responsibilities at Tamié. He later reflected that he "might well be regarded as the third survivor of that tragic event."[48]

Weaving the carpet of prayer is an ongoing process requiring both commitment to personal prayer and the commitment of prayer together. And those commitments are costly. Extending another of Christian's metaphors, we might say that while the symphony is created by the Holy Spirit, the orchestra is always in rehearsal.

Praying Twice: Célestin's Personal Prayer

A brief pause for a vignette. While chant was foundational to the Offices prayed in community, it also formed the basis of Brother Célestin Ringeard's personal prayer. The adage attributed to Saint Augustine, "He who sings prays twice," is apposite here. In Célestin's letters describing his early days at Tibhirine we find him walking for an hour each morning, between the Offices, chanting the Jesus Prayer to a rhythm inspired by the beat of a darbouka that he had heard in the neighborhood.[49] His relationship with God was highly expressive: "God continues to fill me: singing, dancing, rhythm inhabit my heart almost from morning to night, to the point that

[47] Hémon, "An En-Visaged Good-By-E," 210.
[48] Hémon, "An En-Visaged Good-By-E," 204.
[49] Moines de Tibhirine, *Heureux ceux qui espèrent*, 288.

I have recovered the same form that I had in those years before my monastic life, and, I believe, a form beyond that!"[50] Célestin had sung his way back into spiritual shape after the difficult ending to his life as a worker priest.

In assessing the progress of his novitiate Christian had remarked on Célestin's "spontaneous and almost constant link to God" as a solid foundation for monastic life and a potential gift to others.[51] Célestin was highly extroverted, unusual amongst those drawn to monastic life, and his prayer reflected his exuberant nature. He had been a passionate singer since his seminary days, and, as Marie-Dominique Minassian observes, "his singing heart is the basic clue to his interior life: en-chanted [*en-chanté*]."[52] He served the community as a cantor, although the role's collaborative requirements were a challenge to his effervescent style.

In February 1996 (a month before the monks' kidnapping) the regular visitation made by Dom Armand Veilleux gave Célestin an opportunity to review his monastic journey. In his brief preparatory notes, found on a single sheet of paper, he noted the key contours of his journey: his life as a monk "very much linked" to his previous work as a priest in Nantes and to his military service in Algeria; his life as a monk in Algeria linked to his meeting with Si Ahmed Hallouz during the Algerian War of Independence in February 1958 (he had saved Ahmed's life); and then his heart surgery in February 1994, which had limited his capacity to "very modest service" in the community.[53] The additional notes on the back of the sheet of paper reveal something of Célestin's life of prayer: he refers to two notebooks, each a hundred pages, containing his antiphons, the refrains that he had composed to sing, either aloud or interiorly, while he worked. In January he had confided in Fr. Joseph Carmona, then at Tibhirine for a retreat,

[50] Moines de Tibhirine, *Heureux ceux qui espèrent*, 289.
[51] Moines de Tibhirine, *Heureux ceux qui espèrent*, 286.
[52] Moines de Tibhirine, *Heureux ceux qui espèrent*, 289.
[53] Moines de Tibhirine, *Heureux ceux qui espèrent*, 302.

> To secure my services for the day (and it helps me every day), I am singing two little phrases this morning: "O God, you are our hope in the face of all the living" and "Wonder of your grace! You entrust to men the secrets of the Father" [. . .] Every day—I confide this to you!—before singing the antiphon that will animate my work, I run quickly to our chapel, and alone with Him (Jesus) I sing this antiphon aloud and go to the corner of the tabernacle to give a "kiss."[54]

The physicality of Célestin's morning prayer is worth noting: he runs (!) to the chapel, he sings out loud, he connects with the presence of Christ in the reserved sacrament. His sung way of prayer continued to sustain him. In a personal note for his monastic brothers at Bellefontaine added to the community's circular letter of Christmas 1995, Célestin reported that while he no longer performed the role of cantor for the community, he was "asked every three to four weeks to open the services, and to sing the Psalms as a soloist." He clearly delighted in being able to contribute in this way to their communal prayer: "It is a joy for me: 'Lord, open my lips' . . . by uniting myself with all creation, with the wild poppies of the fields . . . ."[55]

The Fuel for Prayer: *Lectio divina*

What fuels the life of prayer? Célestin's prayer was fueled by the repetition of Scripture, crafted as antiphons that he could memorize and sing through the day. Participation in the Liturgy of the Hours and the daily Eucharist immerses—indeed almost drowns—the monk in Scripture. But there is a further practice that deepens this experience. The practice of *lectio divina*, the meditative reading of sacred texts, moves this engagement with Scripture more deeply into personal prayer

[54] Moines de Tibhirine, *Heureux ceux qui espèrent*, 301.
[55] Moines de Tibhirine, *Heureux ceux qui espèrent*, 301.

and contemplation. In *lectio* the reader is drawn, through the work of the Holy Spirit, into conversation and communion with God, who speaks through the words of Scripture. While this practice of prayerful reading of Scripture has its roots in the Jewish tradition, *lectio divina* became a particular feature of Christian monastic life. The Rule of Benedict provides for up to three hours of *lectio divina* each day, with an hour extra during Lent.[56] For the Atlas community, a commitment to *lectio divina* was a given. What is more unusual, however, is that we are in the privileged position of being able to observe in the writings of the monks the way in which the practice of *lectio* both shapes and fruits in their lives.

In his chapter talks Christian reviews the basic features of *lectio*, as articulated in the Cistercian constitutions, before drawing out its challenges—undoubtedly from long experience. The basics: *lectio divina*, practiced with "assiduity," has the capacity to deepen faith in God; it means listening and ruminating on the words of the Scriptures (and the Fathers); it is the "source of prayer" and a "school of contemplation"; it belongs to the "quotidian," the everyday, because we need "daily Bread" (*le Pain quotidien*); and "suitable time" must be found each day.[57] Using the classic schema of the Cistercian tradition, Christian briefly touches on the way in which

[56] RB 48.1: "the brothers should have specified periods for manual labor as well as for prayerful reading [*lectione divina*]." Terrence Kardong suggests that *lectio divina* literally means "reading from God" and that given its centrality to monastic life the term may refer to the Bible. However, in his translation of the *Rule* Kardong leaves the term *lectio divina* untranslated as an indication that "we have yet to discover the full implications of what it meant to the ancient monks." It is generally held that traditionally such reading included the writings of the church fathers as well as the Bible, but in either case, as Michael Casey indicates, reading in Benedict's monastery is a serious, even solemn commitment oriented to listening for God (Terrence G. Kardong, *Benedict's Rule: A Translation and Commentary* [Collegeville, MN: Liturgical Press, 1996], 384; Michael Casey, *The Art of Sacred Reading* [North Blackburn, Victoria, Australia: Dove, HarperCollins, 1995], 2–4).

[57] Chergé, *Dieu pour tout jour*, 382–83; November 7, 1991.

listening to the word moves into prayer—*lectio* (reading), *meditatio* (reflection), *oratio* (prayer)—before adding the Carthusian fourth step, *contemplatio* (contemplation), where words fall away and one "speaks heart to heart" with God. He offers a vivid image here: the words "received in the *lectio* are a bit like the carrier rocket that puts the satellite into orbit."[58] Once in orbit the carrier rocket falls away, no longer required. In this experience of union with God, words are no longer needed. Thus *lectio* becomes a school of contemplation.

However, none of this happens automatically. Christian unpacks two particular phrases from the French text of the constitutions (CST 21) that signal the challenge: *une lectio divina assidue* (assiduous *lectio divina*) and *un temps convenable* (appropriate time).[59] *Lectio* needs to be "assiduous" and given "appropriate time." First, he explores the use of the adjective *assidue,* which derives, he points out, from the Latin *ad-sedere,* meaning "to be seated near (towards)," hence with connotations of "continuity, regularity, or permanence." Sitting, he observes, "expresses an attitude of stability, listening, sharing, dialogue," "the body is at rest, the spirit is awake"—we see this "in the example of Mary of Bethany seated at the feet of Jesus" (Luke 10:39).[60] Our bodily posture reflects our interior preparedness for listening.

Christian also stresses the need for a stable place for the practice of *lectio*. In Benedictine and Cistercian monasticism the scriptorium is traditionally the shared place for the

[58] Chergé, *Dieu pour tout jour*, 382; November 7, 1991.

[59] CST 21: *Une lectio divina assidue favorise grandement chez les frères la foi en Dieu. Cet exercice excellent de la vie monastique, où la Parole de Dieu est écoutée et ruminée, est source de prière; elle est également école de contemplation où le moine s'entretient cœur à cœur avec Dieu. Aussi les frères pratiquent-ils chaque jour une telle lectio pendant un temps convenable.*

The English translation of CST 21—"Careful lectio divina greatly strengthens the brothers' faith in God . . . "—misses the fuller sense of assiduity. Michael Casey similarly retains *assiduity* in his exposition of the monastic practice of *lectio divina* (Casey, *The Art of Sacred Reading*, 19).

[60] Chergé, *Dieu pour tout jour*, 383; November 9, 1991.

community to practice *lectio divina* ("a 'common place' in a place of community"[61]), and the value of *lectio* "done in common" is restated in the revised constitutions (ST 21.A). The practice at Tibhirine is clearly variable. Christian holds up their Benedictine friend Robert, a hermit living in the nearby mountains, as an exemplar of assiduity: he is "regularly present there [in his hermitage] where he needs to be." Assiduity, Christian proposes, is "regular presence in a place where one acquits one's obligations."[62] He concedes that the stable place might be one's cell or the cloister, but "one must stay the distance" (*on doit y durer*).

So while the monks have chosen a life in community ("with the brothers"), the priority is to be "with the Lord"—and it is here that the "freely given" grace (*gratuité*) of *lectio* is clear: we are there because "it is good for us to be here" (drawing on Peter's words at the Transfiguration, Mark 9:5) and "not because we have an office to fulfill, or an office to prepare." Christian continues: "When the *lectio* is regular, there is no problem with something being used if necessary to prepare a service, a homily, etc. The serious thing would be to be interested in Scripture only on these occasions."[63]

Second, *lectio* takes time. Christian draws on the Rule of Benedict, noting that *lectio divina* occurs only in chapter 48, a chapter that ostensibly concerns work.[64] In fact the chapter is concerned with the balance between manual work and reading, and it talks much more about reading than work. Christian observes that the Latin phrase *vacare lectioni* is used six times

[61] Chergé, *Dieu pour tout jour*, 383; November 9, 1991.

[62] Chergé, *Dieu pour tout jour*, 383; November 9, 1991. Fr. Robert Fouquez had lived as a hermit in the Tamesguida mountains since 1963. Célestin was a regular visitor to his hermitage. Fouquez moved to Tibhirine for safety in 1994, living in a dwelling separate from the monks. See São José, "Notre-Dame de l'Atlas, mystère d'une secrète fécondité," 302.

[63] Chergé, *Dieu pour tout jour*, 383; November 9, 1991.

[64] Chergé, *Dieu pour tout jour*, 384; November 12, 1991.

in the chapter and that *vacare* means "to be EMPTY."[65] Reading is to be given space, freedom from work, from other occupations. Christian opens this up further, again playing with the word *form*:

> –It takes time to "inform" all the rest of time, to give it "form," consistency, inspiration.
>
> –It also takes time to ruminate, to savor, to record, to memorize (to ponder in one's heart like Mary: a child) [Luke 2:19]
>
> –It takes time to WAIT for the grace that will illuminate the *lectio* and give it new meaning: begging for our meager portion (it is not a given). "Go into the room with Mary . . . read the texts that speak of the coming of the Messiah . . . and then, wait for the arrival of the angel" (Saint Bernard?).[66]

Lectio requires intentional space, unhurried time, an openness to receiving its gift—and the patience to wait. Christian closes this particular chapter talk with a question: "Tonight, what about the time of our *lectio*?"[67] A suggestion that they might have a conversation later that day about the timing of the community's provisions for *lectio*.

Why is *lectio* so important? Christian returns to its purpose. *Lectio* offers a "privileged way in the school of contemplation and for awakening 'faith in the reality of the PRESENCE of God in oneself and around oneself.'" So he echoes the well-known words of Gregory the Great: "Discover the heart of God in the Word of God."[68] We have returned here to the contemplative vocation: seeing, remembering, walking with God. *Lectio* is "the source of continual prayer," allowing "the

[65] Chergé, *Dieu pour tout jour*, 384; November 16, 1991.
[66] Chergé, *Dieu pour tout jour*, 384; November 16, 1991.
[67] Chergé, *Dieu pour tout jour*, 384; November 16, 1991.
[68] Chergé, *Dieu pour tout jour*, 384; November 23, 1991.

union of the heart with God who SPEAKS to the heart."[69] Union is not, however, a static state, a point of arrival. Rather Christian insists that *lectio* is "a veritable ASCESIS of intellect and behavior" (*de l'intelligence et du comportement*), that is, it is a place of training and transformation: "the one who reads will receive the grace to incarnate this Word in his life and will be completely transformed."[70]

Christian illustrates this point by drawing attention to the story of the scribe who comes to Jesus asking, "what must I do to inherit eternal life?" Jesus first asks him about the law: "What do you read there?" And when the scribe responds correctly with a summary of the law, Jesus responds, "Do this and you will live" (Luke 10:26-28). Reading invites action. If *lectio* opens a path to "union with God," it is not to be understood as a destination but rather as an invitation to participation in a transformative process. So Christian finally proposes his own definition of *lectio divina*: "a reading without haste, appreciative, freely given [*gratuite*], engaging the whole person by allowing him to enter into communion with God."[71] *Lectio* is an ascesis, a form of training in a new way of seeing and being, which brings transformation—setting us on the path toward the reconciliation and communion of all things in God.

Christophe's Prayer Journal

In Christophe Lebreton's last prayer journal (1993–1996) we are given a privileged window into the way in which the practice of *lectio divina* nourishes his prayer and continues to form and transform him—we can observe the process of monastic ascesis in practice. In his journal Christophe regularly engages with the readings of the day, particularly with the Gospels. We can here observe the rhythm of the liturgical year—Advent,

[69] Chergé, *Dieu pour tout jour*, 384; November 23, 1991.

[70] Chergé, *Dieu pour tout jour*, 384; November 23, 1991.

[71] Chergé, *Dieu pour tout jour*, 385; November 23, 1991: "une lecture sans hâte, admirative, gratuite, engageant la totalité de la personne en lui permettant d'entrer en communion avec Dieu."

Christmas, Lent, Easter, feast days, and ordinary time—and the cycle of readings that mark its seasons.[72] And it is possible to see how Scripture anchors Christophe in both exterior and interior storms.

On the feast day of John the Evangelist, immediately after the 1993 Christmas visitation to the monastery by armed insurgents, Christophe copied into his journal parts of the first letter of John, reminding himself that love is the sign of God's presence: "If we love one another [*les uns les autres*], God dwells in us, and his love is FULFILLED in us" (1 John 4:12). He comments, "So, to sustain my spirit, I write Scripture: monk-copyist. I lean on the WORD: In the beginning . . . ." Christophe alludes here to the Prologue of the Gospel of John and its dynamic *logos* theology: "In the beginning was the Word, and the Word was with God, and the Word was God" (John 1.1).[73] Historically, many monks were indeed copyists, major producers of books, an industry that must have also exposed them to a meditative reading of Scriptures. Writing out Scripture is all that Christophe can manage on that particular day, in the wake of the events of Christmas Eve. But it is more than enough to "lean on the WORD." The words of Scripture become Word, the dynamic, incarnate presence of God, of love, in the world.

The following day was the Feast of the Holy Innocents, when the church recognizes its first martyrs in the slaughter of children by Herod (Matt 2:13-18), and Christophe found himself addressed directly by the psalm set for the Common of Martyrs:

[72] The discipline of the lectionary also makes it possible to readily track the Scripture readings behind Christophe's reflections.

[73] Lebreton, *Born from the Gaze of God*, 22; December 27, 1993.

Tonight we chanted psalm 32 [33]. Verse 11 woke me up.
"The plan of the Lord remains forever,
the designs of his heart hold good from age to age."
And I read what follows with delight: "Happy (onwards!) the people whose Lord You are,"
Beloved Son of the Father, people in the LOVE that is over us.
Onwards! You humiliated in spirit. [*En marche, les humiliés du souffle.*]
Yes, you make us run on the way of your commands . . . Not so easy to understand this well.
We are a body that listens [*un corps à l'écoute*].[74]

The imperative "Onwards!" (*en marche)* has come from Christophe's reading of André Chouraqui's daring French translation of the Beatitudes (Matt 5:3-12). Chouraqui's use of the active *en marche* rather than *heureux* (happy) avoids the risk of passivity in the face of suffering, and Christophe has embraced this translation—*en marche,* "onwards," becomes part of his vocabulary.[75] For example, in marking All Saints' Day as the anniversary both of independence for Algeria and of his solemn profession, he quotes the Beatitudes using Chouraqui's translation: "Onward, you humiliated ones who belong to the Spirit; the kingdom of heaven is yours. Onwards, you peacemakers; you shall be shouted 'sons of Elohim.'" The chanting of the psalms, the liturgical reading of Scripture, and the practice of *lectio divina* all cultivate deep listening for the Word ("We are a body that listens").

Scripture also reads the community and their situation. On January 17, 1994, Christophe reflects on the Gospel of the day (Mark 2:18-22):

[74] Lebreton, *Born from the Gaze of God*, 23; December 28, 1993 (translation modified). For the French text, Christophe Lebreton, *Le souffle du don: Journal de Frère Christophe, moine de Tibhirine, 8 août 1993–19 mars 1996* (Paris: Bayard-Centurion, 1999), 49.

[75] Lebreton, *Born from the Gaze of God*, 114; November 1, 1994.

> "The wedding guests," the Gospel says today. Yes, that's what we are here. You are here. You are not here. [*Tu es là. Tu n'es pas là.*] You ask us to be here as witnesses to your indissoluble marriage as God and man. No question of fasting when you are in our midst, saying, "Take, eat, drink. My Body. My Blood. For you and for all."[76]

The monks are guests in Algeria, but being called to witness to the presence of Christ is always a call to eucharistic celebration.

On other occasions Scripture invites renewed commitment to living in the way of Jesus. So the story of the feeding of four thousand (Mark 8:1-10) becomes a vivid prayer echoing not simply the Gospel, but also again the celebration of the Eucharist and its overflowing into eucharistic living: "the Gospel where your insides tremble at the sight of this crowd that has nothing. Lord, there are seven of us here. Take us and speak your thanksgiving over us who are next to nothing, and distribute it among those all around us."[77] Just as seven loaves of bread are given to Jesus to bless and distribute to the hungry crowd, so, Christophe prays, may their lives, offered in this place, be a blessing to their neighbors. But note that the hunger is shared—"this crowd that has nothing" (their poor neighbors) and we "who are next to nothing" (the seven monks). Our longing, our desire, for God is shared.

[76] Lebreton, *Born from the Gaze of God*, 36; January 17, 1994; Lebreton, *Le souffle du don*, 61.

[77] Lebreton, *Born from the Gaze of God*, 137; February 11, 1995.

The Heart of Prayer: Desire

In his chapter talks for Lent 1992, Christian turns to the theme of desire, a theme that is particularly pertinent to this season of preparation for Holy Week.[78] The antiphon sung through Lent highlights this: "Behold the time of longing . . . where man waits for his deliverance" (*Voici le temps du long désir . . . où l'homme attend sa délivrance*).[79] If the structure of monastic life is intended "to keep alive my desire to see God,"[80] then it is prayer that both focuses and purifies this desire. Desire, Christian says, is "the heart of prayer."[81] However, lest we imagine that our desire offers a simple, clear runway to God, he reminds us that "we are the battlefield of contradictory desires."[82]

In the Rule of Benedict, Christian observes, the language of desire is mostly used to warn of "the desires of the flesh" (*desideria carnis*), so Benedict uses "spiritual desire" (*spiritalis desiderii*) for the longing that reorients us toward God. For example, Easter is awaited "with the joy of spiritual desire" (see RB 49.7). The Rule paints a salutary picture of "the battlefield" of desires. Christian summarizes its teaching: disordered desire "tears us apart," so that flesh is separated from spirit; we are "deserted, reduced to an animal state" rather than becoming the "spouse of the Word" and the "temple of the Spirit" as God intends. Confronted by this situation—by "this disgrace of disordered desire" (*cette dis-grâce du désir dé-vié,* the French here neatly plays on the words for grace and life)—we can do nothing to bring about "a different will" (i.e., one that conforms to God's will) except by "rediscovering the sense of [God's] Presence."[83] We join the prayer of the psalmist: "*Ante te est omne DESIDERIUM meum*" (Ps 38 [37]:10: "All my desire is

[78] This is a detour from his series on the Cistercian constitutions.

[79] Chergé, *Dieu pour tout jour*, 389; March 5, 1992.

[80] Chergé, "Conférence du frère Christian du chapitre général 1993," 81.

[81] Chergé, *Dieu pour tout jour*, 390; March 31, 1992.

[82] Chergé, *Dieu pour tout jour*, 389; March 5, 1992.

[83] Christian refers to RB 4.56-58 here, with its simple prescription: listen, pray, weep in God's presence.

before you."). The only way ahead is to place the tangle of one's desires before God. Prayer, as "DESIRE," is

> the place where all our other "desires" converge to be purified, abandoned, or transfigured in the one desire for which we were created, that of God. *All my desire is before you* . . . to thee, my soul yearns! The man who was hiding from his Creator gets back on the road, sets off again, and goes in search of him.[84]

Christian's reflection on the story of the Pharisee and the publican (Luke 18:9-14) further enriches this exploration of desire:

> Today's Gospel . . . offers us two prayers prayed in the same place, at the same time: that of the PHARISEE, too fulfilled (with everything, and with himself) to leave room for DESIRE. He is now "satisfied." One who loves truly, even when he gives thanks, never says SATIS! [Latin: *sufficient, satiated*]. In the Publican, we recognize the sign of an absence, an emptiness, a gaping hole, a dependence.[85]

We are invited, then, to stand with the publican, in this place of desire for God where "the sight of our shortcomings, the awareness of our failings, make them more haunting." Here, Christian notes, we have the essence of prayer in the Orthodox tradition: "Have mercy on me, a sinner." Used by monks of the East in a way similar to a chaplet or rosary, the repetition of what we know as the Jesus Prayer becomes a means of continual prayer where breath and heart are joined in the "only cry in which he can recognize himself." It is then that "he knows that he is praying in the Spirit, and in truth, for these

[84] Chergé, *Dieu pour tout jour*, 389; March 28, 1992.
[85] Chergé, *Dieu pour tout jour*, 389–90; March 28, 1992.

words are from him, and he has no identity except through them."[86] Before God one can only beg for mercy.

If desire stands at the heart of prayer, it is also central to the psalms. Drawing on the writing of Joseph Gelineau, Christian notes that desire is one of the major impulses that motivates and sustains the psalms—and their performance: "It is the desires of the Psalmist that animate the words of his prayer, make them throb with life and truth."[87] The Tibhirine monks would know this from daily experience; the chanting of the psalms occupied a significant portion of each of the Offices of the Liturgy of the Hours—they, like all monastics, knew the psalms inside out. But Christian thinks that Gelineau summarizes these desires too neatly, too positively[88]—rather, Christian argues, the desires expressed in the psalms are a mixed bag, articulating both the "quest for God" and "human interests." So, Christian asks, can desire expressed in this way really be called *"oraison,"* "pure prayer," when it becomes "a request for oneself or for others?"[89] "Can one desire anything other

[86] Chergé, *Dieu pour tout jour*, 390; March 28, 1992.

[87] Chergé, *Dieu pour tout jour*, 390; March 31, 1992. Joseph Gelineau (1920–2008) was a French Jesuit priest and composer of liturgical music. His work on the psalms, especially his responsorial settings, has continued to influence contemporary liturgy. Christian's exact source for Gelineau's writing is unclear ("a small book on Psalmody"). However, a brief introduction to the psalms by Gelineau can be found in *The Psalms: A New Translation from the Hebrew Arranged for Singing to the Psalmody of Joseph Gelineau* (London: Collins, 1966).

[88] Christian quotes the list from Gelineau: "desire for healing and liberation, desire for life and happiness, desire for God and his Word, his Law and this Temple . . . " (Chergé, *Dieu pour tout jour*, 390; March 31, 1992).

[89] Chergé, *Dieu pour tout jour*, 390; March 31, 1992. In his retreat talks for the Petites Soeurs de Jésus in 1990 Christian offers an image of *oraison* from the sculptures of Chartres Cathedral: "a seated woman, eyes closed, and the book mid-breast." Here, he suggests, the work of reading (*lectio*) and reflection (*meditatio*) are done, and prayer (*oraison*) begins (Christian de Chergé, *Retraite sur le Cantique des cantiques*, ed. Christian Salenson, Spiritualité [Bruyères-le-Châtel: Nouvelle Cité, 2013], 83).

than God himself in prayer?" Christian turns to the Lord's Prayer to explore this question:

> what does it mean to DESIRE God . . . if it is not to want His Name to be sanctified, for His Kingdom to come, for His Will to be done . . . on earth as in heaven. And specifically, there is a way to desire God, to live this DESIRE that responds to our current situation, here on earth, without its being an escape to the beyond. Because the GOD that I desire gives himself today, here, because he is forever and everywhere. My desire for God, whether lived well or not, in prayer, in *oraison* (as freely as possible), will inspire me with the means of its incarnation: *You have hollowed out my ear so that I may hear . . . And I said: Here I am . . . my God, I want to do what pleases you* [Ps 40 (39):7-9]. The psalmist who expresses himself in this way began his song by making it clear: *I waited, I waited for the Lord!* The feeling that after this, after this long wait through the night, everything that happens will correspond to God's DESIRE and can become the object of my desire, since to desire God and to desire what God wants for me is all ONE.[90]

[90] Chergé, *Dieu pour tout jour*, 390; March 31, 1992. "Mais qu'est-ce que DÉSIRER Dieu . . . si ce n'est vouloir que Son Nom soit sanctifié, que Son Règne vienne, que Sa Volonté soit faite . . . sur la terre comme au ciel. Et précisément, il y a une façon de désirer Dieu, de vivre ce DÉSIR qui répond à notre situation du moment, sur la terre, sans être évasion vers un au-delà. Car DIEU que je désire se donne aujourd'hui, et ici, parce qu'il est de toujours et de partout. Mon désir de Dieu vécu tant bien que mal, dans la prière, dans l'oraison (aussi gratuitement que possible) va m'inspirer les moyens de son incarnation: *Tu m'as creusé l'oreille pour que j'entende . . . et j'ai dit: Voici je viens . . . mon Dieu, je veux faire ce qui te plaît.* Le Psalmiste qui s'exprime ainsi a commencé son chant en précisant bien: *j'ai attendu, j'ai attendu le Seigneur*! Le sentiment qu'après cela, après cette longue attente dans la nuit, tout ce qui va arriver correspondra au DÉSIR de Dieu et pourra devenir l'objet propre de mon désir, puisque désirer Dieu et désirer ce que Dieu veut pour moi, c'est tout UN."

Christian is making a crucial point here. Desire for God does not send us away from the world, from earthly existence, but towards it. Desiring God is not about longing for an object external to our earthly existence. This would be a misunderstanding of the very nature of God, who is eternally present, now and in all places. While the monk is oriented toward the heavenly, desiring eternal life (RB 4.46; CST 22), such an orientation is never other-worldly. The eternal is now. Neither is the objective simply deliverance from earthly suffering. God is not an escape clause. Rather, prayer is a matter of realignment—it becomes a space in which our disordered desires are opened up, exposed to the desire of God. We stand like the publican before God, with our feet on the earth and our hearts burdened by our tangled desires, and our cry for mercy is met with love, by Love.

The (painful) reordering of desire reorients our way of being in the world, our "doing" (in Christian's words, it provides the "means of incarnation"). God's desire becomes our desire. And this is not a static realization, but a dynamic movement of the Holy Spirit providing the fuel for action. When prayer is, or becomes, shared desire (God's desire for us, our desire for God), then it has the capacity to lead us "to a clearer vision, moment by moment, of what God invites us to do, by giving us the desire to desire it with him."[91] This, Christian proposes, "is the human way of Jesus." Jesus withdraws alone for prayer, into the "night." But where we might imagine Jesus in "full beatific vision" in his dialogue with the Father, the gospels offer instead a glimpse of the human Jesus in prayer. In the garden of Gethsemane we see Jesus struggling to align his will with that of the Father: "not my will [desire] but as you desire" (see Mark 14:36).[92] This way of prayer, we are reminded, is costly. Christian is also offering here a secure foundation for

[91] Chergé, *Dieu pour tout jour*, 391; April 4, 1992. "Comment pourrait-on désirer Dieu dans l'oraison si cette oraison ne nous conduisait pas à une vision plus claire, instant après instant, de ce que Dieu nous engage à faire en nous donnant de le désirer avec lui."

[92] Chergé, *Dieu pour tout jour*, 391; April 4, 1992.

petitionary prayer, modeled on the Lord's Prayer, as seeking first God's desire.

"Caught up in the Work of God"

In Christian's chapter talks we are given the gift of his careful thinking about prayer in the context of its actual, committed practice. For those of us who live on the run, in a world that moves too fast for its own good, this is a rich gift indeed. Monastic life is no less pressured, no less insecure, and yet we are assured that prayer, understood at depth, is our shared human vocation.

So embedded in the monks' lives is their rhythm of prayer that when the seven brothers were kidnapped by armed insurgents from the monastery on the night of March 26–27, 1996, the remaining monks, Fr. Amédée and Fr. Jean-Pierre, continued faithfully to pray the Offices amidst the critical tasks before them—checking the safety of neighbors, informing police and Archbishop Teissier, securing the monastery as best as they were able.

After the disturbances of the night and the discovery of the seven monks' abduction, Amédée and Jean-Pierre, together with the guests who had come to Tibhirine for a gathering of the Ribât, rose at 5 a.m. and gathered in the chapel for the first Office of the day. They did not ring the bell, fearing that the kidnappers would know that they had left some of the monks behind. At noon, after the morning trip to Médéa to inform the police of the abduction, they gathered again to celebrate Mass and sing Sext. Just three now, as most of the guests had departed for Algiers. L. M., a priest, recalls: "It was an intense celebration. Amédée and Jean-Pierre asked me to preside. A deep peace filled me, as well as joy at sharing this day with the two brother monks. I felt I was in my place at that point.

There was an astonishing presence of our missing brothers in that empty chapel."[93]

Scripture continued to nourish them. The reading for that day (Wednesday in the fifth week of Lent) included the story of the three youths thrown into the furnace by the Babylonian king Nebuchadnezzar for refusing to bow to false gods (Daniel 3:14-20, 91-92, 95). The text "really spoke to us," Jean-Pierre wrote. "Although bound, they found themselves free, unharmed in the midst of the flames, praising God with a single heart. Their courage and fidelity towards God, and the powerful intervention of the Lord, brought about a radical change in the heart of the king."[94] In the weeks ahead they, and many others, interceded for such a change of heart in the monks' captors.

In the afternoon Jean-Pierre, Amédée, and L. M. took phone calls (the line had been restored after being cut in several places by the insurgents); they rested, said the Office of None, and sorted and tidied the missing monks' disordered rooms. They had been advised not to stay at the monastery and were escorted to Médéa in the early evening. L. M.'s description of their departure is poignant: "I block all the entrances to the monastery with thick wooden planks. We sing vespers. We eat the soup and beans prepared by Luc [the night before] with a salad from the garden. We take what we need for the night along with a suitcase full of precious objects and the money."[95]

The rhythm of prayer continued beyond the monastery too, though L. M. asked to be excused from Vigils. After accompanying the two surviving monks during this critical time he commented,

[93] Bernardo Olivera, *How Far to Follow: The Martyrs of Atlas*, CS 197 (Kalamazoo, MI: Cistercian Publications, 1997), 89. When quoting from these translated texts I have altered the monks' names to retain their original (French) form.

[94] Olivera, *How Far to Follow*, 90.

[95] Olivera, *How Far to Follow*, 91.

> I am happy to have lived through those two intense days with Amédée and Jean-Pierre, who remained always serene, peaceful, and humble. I am glad to have experienced the strength given from on high to accomplish what needed to be done at the moment without unnecessary fuss, and to have enjoyed the unfolding of a normal monastic day, astonished at having come so close to death and feeling thereby a new freedom. May I spend the time that is left to me in giving thanks![96]

A normal monastic day! As we read the accounts of the days and weeks following the abduction, the strength of the scaffold of liturgical prayer for the surviving monks is evident. One can only trust that it sustained the seven captives in the same way. Clearly Jean-Pierre believed that it would:

> The sanctuary lamp in our chapel at Tibhirine was blown out on that sad night of March 26–27. The chapel, which had echoed with the chants and prayers at the regular hours of the Divine Office since 1937, became suddenly silent and empty. "How long, O Lord?" Our hearts reply, "It is only an *au revoir*, until we meet again." "Our brothers have gone away." It was the time just before Holy Week, and a great, long trial was in store for them. They completed their course while paschal time was coming to an end, during the week before Pentecost: "Come, O Spirit of the Lord, come, alleluia!" They were calling down the Holy Spirit on the Church and on the world. They were caught up into the Work of God down to the innermost depth of their being, body and soul. Through it, they were heard in their fervent desire to be totally one with him and to follow him wherever he goes.[97]

[96] Olivera, *How Far to Follow*, 94.
[97] Olivera, *How Far to Follow*, 95.

Chapter 4

Work

Notre présence laborieuse et notre prière silencieuse se veulent accompagnement dans l'épreuve qui dure, comme dans l'espérance . . .

Our hardworking presence and our silent prayer are intended to be a support in the ongoing trial, as in hope . . .
—The brothers of Notre-Dame de l'Atlas

Each Christmas, from 1987 to 1995, the community of Notre-Dame de l'Atlas sent a circular letter to family and friends updating them on life at Tibhirine and at Fez.[1] The letters offer precious insights into the comings and goings of the monks and their guests, the joys and sorrows of their local and extended communities—those they loved, their families and their neighbors—as well as the challenges of the ever-changing social and political conditions. The last of these circular letters is dated December 14, 1995, the second anniversary of the assassination of the Croatian workers at Tamesguida and the feast day of Saint John of the Cross, the sixteenth-century

[1] The small annex at Fez in Morocco was established in 1988. The 1987 circular letter is signed by Christian de Chergé only, while the letters from 1988 to 1995 are signed variously "Fr. Christian and the brothers . . . ," "the monastic community . . . ," or "the brothers of Atlas and Fez." It is clear that they were all compiled by Christian. Some are illustrated with drawings by Christophe (Moines de Tibhirine, "Lettres circulaires de la communauté Notre-Dame de l'Atlas Tibhirine-Fès (Noël 1987–Noël 1995)," in *Heureux ceux qui espèrent: Autobiographies spirituelles*, Les écrits de Tibhirine 1 [Paris: Bayard-Cerf-Bellefontaine, 2018]).

Carmelite who had both suffered and written about the "dark night of the soul." It was indeed a dark night for Algeria and for its inhabitants, including the brothers:

> 1995: car bombs, savage explosions, murders, reprisals . . . grief sets in, accompanied by fears, rejections. Mistrust, veiled hatred, eat away at the human fabric of relationships. Despite everything, life goes on, with prices soaring, wages suffering, public transport destroyed, not to mention the borders closed; and, very practically, with the risks of the long journey to the city when it is necessary, each day, to walk to work, or to school, and back, in the night and in the cold. The courage of an entire little people![2]

The tally of the dead among Catholic religious and priests, friends of the community, had also mounted. But while the circular letter does not avoid naming the "hard things" (*dura et aspera*, hardships and difficulties, RB 58.8), there is also an intentional articulation of the things that might be forgotten or overlooked. Christian's starting point is careful attention to the realities:[3]

> First of all, we must be silent, for a long time. To hear the clamor of "things" that are unsaid, hidden, stifled, repressed, distorted . . . To let oneself be pierced. To stand upright. A calvary to be shared. A table too, prepared for all, where hope learns, day after day, to be nourished by these "very things" that are happening to us, to drink as

[2] Moines de Tibhirine, "Lettres circulaires . . . (1995)," 744.

[3] Christian's approach here resonates with Carmelite William McNamara's description of contemplation as "a long, loving look at the real." Quoted in Walter J. Burghardt, "Contemplation: A Long Loving Look at the Real," in *An Ignatian Spirituality Reader*, ed. George W. Traub (Chicago: Loyola Press, 2008), 91.

> brothers from this very cup that would be easier for us to pass on than to choose.[4]

Christian's use of paschal and eucharistic language underlines both the seriousness of the monks' situation and its gift. Attending in this way, Christian sees more than "hard things." He also sees and names "simple things," "beautiful things," "good things," and "the things . . . to follow"—those things that are simply placed in God's hands, in the light of hope. And in the simple, the beautiful, and the good things, we find the fruit of work, the work of the monks and their neighbors, named and celebrated. It is their hardworking presence (*présence laborieuse),* with their prayer, that underpins hope. *Ora et labora.* Prayer and work.

Among the simple things:

> As for the rain, it also falls on "the just and the unjust." Thanks to [the sun and the rains] the seeds placed in the ground in the gardens have become, for the wellbeing and honor of our associates, tomatoes, green and red beans, squash and zucchini, turnips and potatoes . . . And the trees in the orchard bore fruit, each according to its species and season.[5]

Among the beautiful things:

> If your heart speaks to you, come also and take a walk around our park at Tibhirine. Flowers will speak to you. A carefully maintained avenue will welcome your steps. Perhaps you will exclaim, like the Algiers family who came for a wedding: "How peaceful it is!" Robert works here, still in exile among us. Zealous and attentive servant of the beauty of this place.[6]

[4] Moines de Tibhirine, "Lettres circulaires . . . (1995)," 742.

[5] Moines de Tibhirine, "Lettres circulaires . . . (1995)," 742.

[6] Moines de Tibhirine, "Lettres circulaires . . . (1995)," 743. The Benedictine hermit Fr. Robert Fouquez had moved to Tibhirine for safety in 1994.

Among the good things:

> Coming up from the garden, other very good "things" are lovingly prepared for us by our cooks, the doctor and his assistant, Brother Michel. During the night from Thursday to Friday, Brother Luc hatches his fraternal plot: an abundance of fries at the shared table. Gilles comes regularly to compete for them with us. Our baker also knows how to find an opportunity to spoil us with some sweetness . . .[7]
>
> . . . In his shopping in Médéa, an imperturbable rhythm, Brother Jean-Pierre always receives a warm welcome from the shopkeepers.[8]

The eight monks at Tibhirine continued to work: in the kitchen preparing meals to nourish and delight both the brothers and their (now) few visitors; in the dispensary and at the gate caring for neighbors in need of medical attention, material help, or a listening ear; in the gardens and orchards working alongside their associates producing food for the community and for sale at the markets; in the grounds repairing machinery and the homemade irrigation system managing their precious and sometimes scarce water; in the sacristy and chapel preparing the materials needed for their shared rhythm of liturgical prayer.

Ora et labora. Prayer and work. Two constants in a world of violence and uncertainty. At the end of the circular letter Christian sums up: "Our hardworking presence and our silent prayer are intended to be a support in the ongoing trial, as in hope . . . ."[9] He leaves the sentence unfinished.

[7] Moines de Tibhirine, "Lettres circulaires . . . (1995)," 745.
[8] Moines de Tibhirine, "Lettres circulaires . . . (1995)," 745.
[9] Moines de Tibhirine, "Lettres circulaires . . . (1995)," 747.

The Workshop of the Monastery

The monastery is a workshop, or, as it is expressed helpfully in French, an *atelier*—with its rich connotations of craft and skill. Not a workhouse, where laborers are enslaved, but a workshop where laborers are valued and always learning, developing their skills. It is no accident that the Rule of Benedict uses the vocabulary for work (both *opus* and *labor*) in relation to the entire monastic enterprise, not just physical labor.

In the Benedictine tradition the monastic enclosure is the place where the monk both prays and works: "The workshop [Latin: *officina*] where we are to toil [*operari*] faithfully at all these tasks is the enclosure of the monastery and stability in the community" (RB 4.78). There is a connection, not a conflict between the two, as Christian points out in a short chapter talk. The Office, the Liturgy of the Hours, is "celebrated where the community works"; their communal prayer is the "office of workers"—there is a nice play here on the word "office" which connotes not just the form of liturgical prayer, but the place where work is carried out.[10] Work and prayer are not separate. Indeed, the Rule of Benedict specifies that the work of God (*Opus Dei*), the "Office," can be prayed where the monks are working should they find themselves a long way from the oratory or chapel (RB 50).

Christian finds this close relationship between work and prayer in a resurrection story from the Gospel of John. The disciples have returned to work as fishermen when Jesus appears and invites them to breakfast on the beach (John 21:1-13). We are called, Christian says, by the "Risen One" who "joins us in this hardworking [*laborieux*] reality," to "stop the work [of our hands]" to do "something else"—to come together for prayer. But the work comes too: "Hey, children—bring what you've just caught!" (cf. John 21:10). And this is what God chooses to use. "It is existence itself that is the substance of the

[10] Christian de Chergé, *Dieu pour tout jour: chapitres de Père Christian de Chergé à la communauté de Tibhirine (1985–1996)*, 2nd ed. (Montjoyer: Abbaye Notre-Dame d'Aiguebelle, 2006), 427; February 9, 1993.

offering."[11] While the eucharistic overtones are clear here, Christian's point is that prayer does not arise from a different space, or time, but from embodied life, from the here and now of human existence. Work is part of that reality and a gift. And, in fact, it is the (divine) integration of work and prayer glimpsed in this resurrection story that motivates the monastic project. Christian recrafts the familiar words of the Rule: "We will truly be monks where we live by the work of His hands" (cf. RB 48.8).[12] His hands, rather than our hands. Christian here expresses a longing for full participation in the work of God, a form of union or oneness with God—where our work equals God's work—a hope that orders the present but is beyond human reach.

This reflection comes towards the end of a series of chapter talks on work given over a three-month period beginning in late November 1992, part of Christian's series on the Cistercian constitutions. The traditional twin commitment to *ora et labora*, prayer and work, can be said easily enough, but in practice there is a danger that work might simply be thought of as a support player. The radical commitment to work (particularly to manual work) in the monastic tradition is worthy of fuller consideration, and in this series one senses Christian endeavoring to attend to work on its own terms. A number of questions drive his explorations: what is the place of work in human life? Why the emphasis on manual labor in the Cistercian tradition? What can this mean in the face of modern life, and especially in view of technological developments? Does this monastic commitment have anything to say to the wider world?

Over the course of these talks Christian articulates a nuanced (though not systematic!) theology of work. He draws broadly on biblical sources, wisdom from the monastic tradition, particularly the Rule of Benedict, and the teaching of the

[11] Chergé, *Dieu pour tout jour*, 427; February 9, 1993.

[12] Chergé, *Dieu pour tout jour*, 427; February 9, 1993. RB 48.8: "When they live by the labor of their hands. . . . then they are really monks."

church, including the pastoral constitution *Gaudium et Spes* (1965) and the papal encyclical *Laborem Exercens* (1981), as well as grappling with the contemporary conditions of work, especially the social and political realities of Algeria. It is practical theology at its best—honed from tradition, speaking to the present. However, nothing is wrapped up once and for all—Christian often returns to the same puzzles and paradoxes, which remain.

At the end of this series on work Christian invited Michel to share his experience of factory work with the community.[13] Each of the monks had a work story, and it is impossible not to be curious about the discussions that must have occurred in the community around this subject.

Work in Cistercian Monasticism

Work, particularly manual work, has been a central feature of Cistercian life since emergence of the Order during the twelfth century. The roots of this commitment, especially to manual work, lie in the practices of the fourth-century desert monks who often supported themselves by weaving rope or baskets, as well as by tending small vegetable gardens on their marginal land. Cenobitic monasticism complicated matters: a monastery became, unavoidably, a more complex economic unit in which a community needed to be housed, clothed, and fed. The Rule of Benedict assumes the necessity of work and simply seeks to order the economic life of the monastery in a way that not only serves but is consistent with its overall purpose "to establish a school for the Lord's service" (RB Prol.45). The monastic regulations, "nothing harsh, nothing burdensome," support this overall goal (RB Prol.48).

Historically, as Christian notes, liturgical prayer had come to dominate monastic life at the expense of work, so the reform

[13] Moines de Tibhirine, *Heureux ceux qui espèrent: Autobiographies spirituelles*, ed. Marie-Dominique Minassian, Les écrits de Tibhirine 1 (Paris: Bayard-Cerf-Bellefontaine, 2018), 172.

that emerged from Cîteaux in the twelfth century sought to rebalance the monastic day between work and prayer.[14] In the paring back of monastic life that occurred in the context of this reform, particularly in the commitment to poverty and simplicity, work and especially manual work was once again prioritized. The reformers took seriously the words of the Rule of Benedict: "When they live by the labor of their hands, as our fathers and the apostles did, then they are really monks" (RB 48.8). The Cistercian constitutions, in fact, list work first as one of the "means" of monastic asceticism, of training or formation in monastic life.[15] From its earliest foundations the Cistercian commitment to manual work was focused on agricultural enterprise: monks, increasingly with the assistance of lay brothers, farmed the large estates within which the monastic enclosure was set. Other work, the production of wine or cheese for example, was derived from this agrarian base.

This focus on agricultural enterprise persisted well into the twentieth century. (Indeed, this was the model exported to Algeria with the establishment of the Cistercian monastery at Staouëli in 1843, and on a smaller scale to Tibhirine in 1937.) However, as Christian observes, mechanization had completely transformed modern agriculture—and, consequently, the traditional economies of monastic communities. Cistercian communities had adapted in various creative ways, but one can hear a note of regret in Christian's description of a not-uncommon path, especially in aging communities, when "it is finally decided to replace the dairy herd, or even the cheese factory, with a large shop (bookshop or sale of monastic handcrafts)."[16] Christian admits that there is no easy way

[14] Chergé, *Dieu pour tout jour*, 412; November 24, 1992.

[15] The other means are "hidden life, voluntary poverty, vigils and fasting" (CST 25). Christian treads carefully around the term *asceticism*, noting its unhelpful history of pitting mind again body. The intention of the CST, he suggests, is to restore harmony between body and mind, for the health of the whole person (Chergé, *Dieu pour tout jour*, 425–26; February 3, 1993).

[16] Chergé, *Dieu pour tout jour*, 413; November 26, 1992.

forward, but he remarks on the persistent desire among fellow monastics "to balance themselves through truly manual work." He concludes with a remark that speaks presciently to a world that has now begun to consider the human consequences of artificial intelligence: "The vocation of human hands is to remain industrious even in the age of the robot."[17]

Called to Work

Work is not a curse. In line with the teaching of both the church and the Cistercian constitutions, Christian locates work in "the Gospel of creation."[18] God is the first worker. In the second creation story God forms the human being from the dust of the earth (Gen 2:7) and is thus the first to get his hands dirty. The French expression Christian uses is resonant: *"le premier à avoir mis la main à la pâte,"* literally, "the first to have put the hand to the dough."[19] Manual work has its beginning in God and, in the Genesis narrative, is not at first a curse: "The LORD God took the man and put him in the Garden of Eden to till and to keep it" (Gen 2:15). These twin observations—that God was the first worker and that work is God-given—are the foundations of Christian's thinking about work. Christian expands: "Work is thus a constitutive part of man created in the image of God." God did not simply set the human being to work, but rather invited participation. (In a later talk Christian speaks of such participation as "a privileged place of union with God."[20]) Work, Christian stresses, "partakes of the very nature of the Creator" and offers, in the words of the constitutions, "the opportunity to participate in the divine work of creation" (CST 26).

[17] Chergé, *Dieu pour tout jour*, 413; November 26, 1992.

[18] Chergé, *Dieu pour tout jour*, 427; February 16, 1993. The phrase "the Gospel of creation" is the title of chapter 2 of Pope Francis's encyclical *Laudato Si'*.

[19] Chergé, *Dieu pour tout jour*, 413; November 28, 1992.

[20] Chergé, *Dieu pour tout jour*, 423; January 21, 1993.

Further, he argues, work is valued not just as necessary for human equilibrium or well-being, but as a place where one may experience a form of self-transcendence: "where man learns to 'surpass' himself by exploiting both the hidden resources of the universe and his own ([human] intelligence functioning in the service of the hands)." The implications of the absence of work become clear. As Christian says, the unemployed can experience the "feeling of a ruinous mutilation of life and progress." [21] He makes this point even more strongly at the beginning of his next chapter talk: "unemployment is contrary to human nature." Again, this is because work is a blessing, not a curse, located within "the grace of the creation, which is to be subjected and transformed." Paradoxically, he observes, it is human success, human ingenuity that "has the result not only of relieving him in his work but even of replacing him completely."[22] Machines and robots are economically superior, rendering human hands superfluous. It may be that monastic life at Tibhirine, Christian implies, offered a privileged experience in this regard:

> It is also good that we take the measure of grace given to us to be able to find the equilibrium of our creative being in the effective work of our hands. We are even given the opportunity to experience, in the complementarity of our tasks, the diversity of services that man can attain from his hands.[23]

The range and load of work that each carried in this small community was substantial, but Christian saw this work as a gift enabling the complementarity and balance between head and heart that God intends. In fact, Christian quips, the diversity of their manual work makes "our little monastery a microcosm of this work and almost a museum insofar as we continue to do by hand so many things that elsewhere are now

[21] Chergé, *Dieu pour tout jour*, 414; November 28, 1992.
[22] Chergé, *Dieu pour tout jour*, 414; December 1, 1992.
[23] Chergé, *Dieu pour tout jour*, 414; December 1, 1992.

totally mechanized."[24] However, while Cistercians were once "pioneers in progress" in agriculture, Christian no longer sees this legacy as an imperative. As he observes later, in the modern world progress is too often associated with unemployment and alienation from meaningful work.[25]

Microcosm or museum? The question seems to hang in the air as Christian considers the place of the monks' very modest agricultural enterprise at Tibhirine in the context of their Cistercian heritage. He draws attention to the teaching of *Gaudium et Spes* (67) regarding the dignity of work. He also reminds the community of Paul VI's affirmation of the Cistercian commitment to work, particularly the work of the hands; his valuing of a new style of apostolate where priests live "as workers among workers"; and the possibility of bringing Cistercian expertise to agricultural development in new places, a mission that is captured by the motto "by the cross and the plough, *cruce et aratro*—Staouëli's motto minus 'the sword.'"[26]

But perhaps more important at a local level, Christian reminds his brothers of the words of a former mayor of Médéa, in 1973: "You are doing us a great service . . . . Of course, men of prayer, etc. . . . but above all, in a rural *wilaya* where young people abandon the land, you show that intelligent men, who could have done something else, do not believe that they are demeaning themselves by working the land."[27] Rural depopulation had been a long-term challenge in Algeria, as elsewhere.

[24] Chergé, *Dieu pour tout jour*, 415; December 1, 1992.

[25] Chergé, *Dieu pour tout jour*, 418; December 15, 1992. Christian returns to the complex question of progress as well as the structural imbalances in employment evident in developing economies such as that of Algeria.

[26] Chergé, *Dieu pour tout jour*, 415; December 3, 1992. Christian is drawing on the message of Paul VI to abbots meeting in Rome for the general chapter of 1969.

[27] Chergé, *Dieu pour tout jour*, 415; December 3, 1992.

Jesus and the Work of the Hands

Christian understands work as fundamental to the human vocation: we are called by God to work. He returns, again and again, to the Genesis creation narrative, and to this call to work, which he perceives as "the beginning of the Good News, of the Gospel."[28] The incarnate life of Jesus confirms this understanding. While only the Gospel of Mark identifies him as a carpenter, growing up in the household of a manual worker in the midst of a peasant community was deeply formative for Jesus. This is the context that shapes his speech and storytelling. His teaching is steeped in metaphors derived from the everyday working world. His parables, Christian observes, "are obviously aimed at people who can understand what it means to 'put your hand to the plow,' 'sow in a field,' plant a tree without forgetting the manure, prune a vine, harvest fruit, lead a flock knowing how to distinguish between sheep and goats, thwart the tricks of the wolf or the fox, or read the signs of the times in the sky . . . ."

Jesus' words come from acute observation and from the experience of getting "his hands dirty." This drawing on "the realities of work," Christian suggests, "contributes greatly to giving his Word all of its convincing depth."[29] It is in this way that the Word invites one to discover God's call in the midst of concrete realities, in the quotidian, the daily. Christian is pressing into the meaning of incarnation here: in order to perceive God we are drawn more deeply into embodied life, not away from its realities. Further, he says, while it is "the things of the earth" that become sacraments, in almost every instance these things (bread, wine, oil) have been "enriched through the WORK of man." So for the Eucharist, rather than a lamb, or fruit, Jesus chooses bread, a "'worked' element," to "signify his Presence," thereby placing in the sacrament "something that is indissolubly linked to the truth of his own human

[28] Chergé, *Dieu pour tout jour*, 416; December 5, 1992.

[29] Chergé, *Dieu pour tout jour*, 416; December 5, 1992.

nature."[30] Christian is making a subtle point here. Not only is the bread "the work of human hands," but Christ, present in the bread, identifies himself with those who have worked to produce it. Fully human, he too is called to work.

Both *Gaudium et Spes* and the Cistercian constitutions articulate the solidarity of Jesus with workers in terms of Jesus' (hidden) working life in Nazareth: Jesus "conferred an eminent dignity on labor" when he worked with his hands at Nazareth (*Gaudium et Spes* 67), and manual work affords the monk an opportunity "to follow in the footsteps of Jesus" (CST 26). It is no accident, Christian suggests, that Jesus was born into the home of a craftsman. There were other options: "At the time when the Word *(le Verbe)* became flesh, there was no lack in Israel of cultivated or erudite households, wise and literate, scribes or lawyers, priests like Zechariah and Elizabeth . . . it is not in these circles that Jesus is born, still less in a royal court, nor in the shop of a merchant. God chose to entrust himself to a woodworker, and Jesus' first school was that hard-working home in Nazareth."[31]

When Jesus leaves the carpenter's house, however, he continues to work with his hands. Christian notices the prominence of *hands* in the gospels. In the healing miracles, word and gesture work together: Jesus stretches out his hand to touch a leper (Mark 1:41); he takes Peter's sick mother-in-law by the hand, restoring her to her household service (Mark 1:31). Christian continues:

[30] Chergé, *Dieu pour tout jour*, 416; December 5, 1992.

[31] Chergé, *Dieu pour tout jour*, 422; January 16, 1993. Christian uses both *la Parole* and *le Verbe* to designate the Word. He tends to use *le Verbe* when he wishes to echo the *logos* language of the Johannine writings in the Christian Scriptures and its cosmic overtones. With its basic meaning of *verb*, *le Verbe* offers a more active sense of the Word than *parole*, which primarily connotes *words* or speech. Nazareth for Christian also symbolizes the ordinary, repetitive work that is the ground of the monks' shared life (the "cycle of Nazareth"); see January 12, 1993, p. 420.

> The Word [*le Verbe*], who is creator and re-creator, has hands when he becomes incarnate . . . perhaps he incarnates the hands of his Father. One could say that Jesus worked manually for a long time, like his earthly father Joseph in Nazareth. Then he moved to "the business" of his Father in heaven, and his work is changed, but it remains, it is intended to be MANUAL, because this is how God works. And even more it will still truly be a manual "work" to take the bread "in one's hands" . . . then the cup . . . and finally "to stretch out his hands in the hour of his Passion," not that they may taste rest but that they may abandon themselves to their work of eternity: *Into your HANDS, Father, I commend my spirit* (Luke 23:46).[32]

Work and Sin

While Christian lays the foundations for understanding work in the "Gospel of creation," he does not avoid addressing the persistent connections between work and sin. The view that work is a curse, a punishment for sin, stems from a reading of the story of the Fall: when the man and woman eat forbidden fruit they are expelled from the Garden of Eden, cursed with bitterly hard labor in order to produce their bread (Gen 3). Christian ponders the Genesis text, with its "strong images" and "inexhaustible symbols," in the context of his

[32] Chergé, *Dieu pour tout jour*, 421; January 14, 1993. "Le Verbe créateur et recréateur a des mains quand il s'incarne, . . . peut-être incarne-t-il les mains de son Père. On pourrait dire que longuement Jésus s'est exercé à ce travail manuel qui est celui de Joseph à Nazareth, de son père nourricier. Puis il passa 'aux affaires' de son Père des cieux, et son travail est autre mais il reste, il se veut MANUEL parce que c'est ainsi que Dieu travaille. Et ça sera encore un vrai 'travail' manuel que de prendre 'en ses mains' le pain . . . puis la coupe . . . et enfin 'd'étendre les mains à l'heure de sa Passion', non point qu'elles goûtent le repos mais pour qu'elles s'abandonnent à leur travail d'éternité: *En tes MAINS, Père, je remets mon esprit* (Lc 23,46)."

meditations on hands. There is a connection, he observes, between the sin and the curse: "They had thought they could stretch out their hands to the forbidden fruit to live forever in idleness: it would have been 'divine.' An old dream!"[33] The temptation is to avoid work, and, paradoxically, succumbing to this temptation condemns them to harder work. Hands that were made to create instead play a dangerous game. The "supreme ruse" of the serpent, the Tempter, is to "act through the hands of others":

> [The Tempter] rejects creation insofar as it comes out of the hands of an Other. This creation escaped him. He wants it to self-destruct. He wants to ignore everything to do with the work of the hands: a snake has no hands. He does not know that this is his curse: for even if it is arduous, manual work is going to remain the place where man escapes a fate of death. Hands can still take HARD bread, offer it, share it, and make it the sacrament of LIFE.[34]

Hard work, especially manual work, still has the capacity to become redemptive work. Hands are capable of taking, offering, and sharing bread, so that work becomes life-giving. The eucharistic reference here is clear, but the intention is that this pattern be extended into all life: we are invited to take, offer, share the work of our hands so that all may enjoy the gift of life.

In a later talk Christian returns to the question of the human relationship to work. At a personal level sin manifests itself in our "tendencies to laziness," in our neglect of questions of justice (the rights of others) or of morality (harvesting our neighbor's produce), or in pride (exhausting ourselves by

[33] Chergé, *Dieu pour tout jour*, 419; December 19, 1992.
[34] Chergé, *Dieu pour tout jour*, 419; December 19, 1992.

working alone).[35] But it is structural oppression that makes work a curse:

> Sin does not appear to be linked to work in itself, but rather to a wrong relationship with the worker who is subjected to a quasi-absolute servicing of the idea of work. Working with bricks is good. Multiply it heavily, and it's unbearable. Abolish it, you go to the desert of unemployment . . . there you miss the onions of Egypt, which pleasantly seasoned the work of a slave.[36]

The Exodus story paints a damning picture of forced labor, but liberation takes the Hebrew slaves to a desert where food is scarce and where even the rations of a slave seem attractive. It is a wicked problem. Work is enmeshed in systems driven by greed rather than human well-being, but the necessity of work for survival renders participation in these systems unavoidable.

Work is not per se linked to sin; rather, Christian concludes,

> Work, in its nature, its objectives, and its conditions, thus depends on what man does with it. If it contributes to shaping man, it is because it concerns not only the harmony of hands and intelligence, but above all perhaps because it is, together with prayer, one of those places where the deepest unity of the human being is sought, whose spiritual nature demands that love be involved in everything he undertakes. Yes, it is from the heart that all activity worthy of man created in the image of the triune God must ultimately proceed. When the heart is not or cannot be in it, we sense that work can cause harm, and be harmful.[37]

[35] Chergé, *Dieu pour tout jour*, 427; February 16, 1993.

[36] Chergé, *Dieu pour tout jour*, 428; February 16, 1993.

[37] Chergé, *Dieu pour tout jour*, 428; February 18, 1993. "Le travail, dans sa nature, ses objectifs et ses conditions, dépend ainsi de ce que l'homme en fait. S'il contribue à façonner l'homme, c'est parce qu'il intéresse non

Ultimately the source of sin is to be found in the human heart, not in the hands: "the sin of the spirit [. . .] precedes and surpasses that of the hands."[38] Heart and hands need to be aligned. If work plays a role in "shaping man" (as God shaped the first human being), then it is not simply a matter ensuring "the harmony of hands and intelligence" but also a matter of the heart, of love.

A Prophetic Apostolate

Midway through this series of chapter talks on work Christian comments that "monastic life is essentially prophetic." The immediate context of this remark is his observation that Jesus' first disciples were workers, primarily from the same social milieu as himself, who were called out of their various trades in order to work "differently." The prophetic nature of their witness is not simply found in the message that they conveyed, but in their very being—"what they were, what they remained." Among the first disciples, fishermen become fishers of men; Luke, the doctor, tends souls as well as bodies; and Paul, the weaver, becomes a weaver of communities. Their encounter with the Gospel brings about the reorientation of their work: "A new grace will change the point of application of their professional life." Christian notes a similar pattern in the call to monastic life: "The disruptive call of the Gospel in a life marks a radical change, including in human activity. A long personal and community novitiate will make it possible to understand how God uses the abilities of each: I will make

---

seulement l'harmonie des mains et de l'intelligence, mais surtout peut-être parce qu'il est, avec la prière, un de ces lieux où se cherche l'unité la plus profonde de l'être humain dont la nature spirituelle exige que de l'amour soit engagé dans tout ce qu'il entreprend. Oui, c'est du cœur que doit sortir, en définitive, toute activité digne de l'homme créé à l'image du Dieu trinitaire. Quand le cœur n'y est pas ou ne peut pas y être, on pressent que le travail peut faire mal, et aussi mal faire."

[38] Chergé, *Dieu pour tout jour*, 429; February 18, 1993.

you a doctor, a lawyer, an educator DIFFERENTLY."[39] It is a life that becomes, or seeks to become, "a prophetic apostolate"—that is, a life of discipleship that in itself proclaims the Gospel.

Monastic life offers a context in which work is valued and workers are supported in the long journey towards integrating hands, minds, and hearts "in the Lord's service." The Rule of Benedict, Christian observes, never speaks about work in terms of theory but is, rather, concerned with its practice, establishing "a spirit of work."[40] Christian's bullet-point notes on this spirit are brief but important and so worth expanding a little. First, the monk should work humbly. Artisans are not to become "puffed up," but rather "practice their craft with humility" (RB 56). Humble or even hard manual work is not to be rejected (RB 48.7). Christian also has in view here the sixth step of humility: "that a monk is content with the lowest and most menial treatment, and regards himself as a poor and worthless workman in whatever task he is given" (RB 5.49).[41]

Second, in the Rule work is always viewed in the context of community life and is to be carried out "in a spirit of charity and service." Work is to be useful. Elsewhere Christian admits that in the past rigid obedience around work had often violated its dignity: "The monk also needs to understand the why of what he is ordered to do and not only the how. He is legitimately worried if the next day he is made to uproot the tree he had difficulty planting the day before."[42] A third and persistent concern, found throughout the Rule, is the priority of peace and the avoidance of sadness and murmuring. Christian also highlights RB 64 and presumably the responsibility of the

[39] Chergé, *Dieu pour tout jour*, 423; January 19, 1993.

[40] Chergé, *Dieu pour tout jour*, 424; January 23, 1993.

[41] Christian gave a long series of chapter talks on humility between December 1988 and May 1990. See Edith Scholl, "Christian de Chergé on Humility," CSQ 41, no. 2 (2006); Jane Foulcher, *Reclaiming Humility: Four Studies in the Monastic Tradition*, CS 255 (Collegeville, MN: Cistercian Publications, 2015), 255–61.

[42] Chergé, *Dieu pour tout jour*, 418; December 12, 1992.

abbot in promoting such an atmosphere by being "discerning and moderate" in assigning tasks around the monastery (RB 64.17).

Fourth, work requires a level of responsibility: it is to be conscientious. Both negligence and laziness are to be avoided. Tools and objects are to be respected (RB 32). Finally, the monastery runs what we might call a countercultural economy: "without a spirit of profit, without a spirit of gain"[43] (see RB 57.7–9). Traditionally the monastic economy, founded on the work of the monks, has been styled as a form of self-sufficiency. However, the monastery is not impervious to the needs of the world in which it is located: "the house of God remains open to external needs."[44] So goods may be sold more cheaply (RB 57.8) and alms distributed to ensure the well-being of those who approach the monastery for assistance. The Cistercian constitutions recognize this responsibility: the "hard and redeeming work" of the monks provides "a livelihood for the brothers and for other people, especially the poor" (CST 26).

Christian recognizes that the monastery presents a complex economic equation. The community received donations (financial and in kind) as well as generating income from their small agricultural enterprise. But they also regularly offered their labor and the fruit of their work freely, making calculations impossible, and indeed they cultivated a practice of giving "without counting." Nonetheless Christian suggests some principles, some "flashing lights" to guide their economic relations: justice in their dealings with those who work with or for them, care not to overstretch their financial commitments, taking "account of the buyer's condition" in setting prices, complying with local laws, attending to the "average condition" of those around them and hence avoiding "expensive purchases," and resisting a fear-fueled accumulation of "savings."

[43] Chergé, *Dieu pour tout jour*, 424; January 23, 1993.
[44] Chergé, *Dieu pour tout jour*, 425; January 30, 1993.

Much of this thinking is evident in the way in which the Tibhirine community lived: the cooperative way in which they worked the land, the assistance given at the monastery "gate" and in the dispensary, the modesty of their own living. Philippe Hérmon's first impression of the community springs to mind again: "their house, so poor and so full of warmth" that led him to the conviction that "they were the real monks of the present time."[45] After the seven monks were kidnapped from Tibhirine, the police who came to examine the scene were equally "surprised by the monks' simplicity of life."[46]

Participation and Communion: The Promise of Work

In the context of a talk given during the Week of Prayer for Christian Unity, Christian explores two themes that sum up the gift and promise of work: participation and communion. First, he reiterates that work affords the monk, indeed all human beings, the opportunity to participate in God's work. However, he stresses, this participation requires alignment with God's way of working: "our work cannot be just, praiseworthy, and truly profitable for man if it is not situated in the continuity and logic of what God has undertaken and asks us to continue." Work that is so aligned has the potential, Christian suggests, of being "a privileged place of union with God." Indeed, it becomes in a very real sense *opus Dei*, the work of God. But, he observes, "It is not as easy as it seems to bend to God's conditions . . . which first of all may be to respect the laws of creation and the instructions for use of creatures."[47]

[45] Philippe Hémon, "An En-Visaged Good-By-E," CSQ 34, no. 2 (1999): 208.

[46] Bernardo Olivera, *How Far to Follow: The Martyrs of Atlas*, CS 197 (Kalamazoo, MI: Cistercian Publications, 1997), 91.

[47] Chergé, *Dieu pour tout jour*, 423; January 21, 1993. "Il n'est pas si facile qu'il y paraît de se plier aux conditions de Dieu . . . qui peuvent être d'abord de respecter les lois de la création et le mode d'emploi des créatures."

This idea is neatly expressed. It is human disrespect of these conditions that now threatens human survival on earth.

Second, Christian continues, work that is aligned to the Gospel bears fruit in communion. God's redemptive purpose is "to gather into one the dispersed children of God" (John 11:52). Apostolic work, he suggests, should contribute to this purpose: "The Gospel surely helps us to respect and use the astonishing capacity of work, whatever it may be, to GATHER, to seal the understanding and the complementarity of human strengths and talents."[48] In the context of the monastery, the Cistercian constitutions similarly state that work "contributes greatly to the unity of the whole community" (CST 26). Christian was aware that the small number of monks at Tibhirine meant that it was rarely possible for them to work together as a community. The risk was that rather than work facilitating a consciousness of their "mutual dependence," each monk, in his individual work, would become isolated and "succumb to the temptation of doing as he pleases." On the other hand, work "conceived in the spirit of the Gospel," carried out "in the humility and availability that the Holy Spirit gives," draws one into communion with Jesus.[49]

Importantly, this sense of unity or communion is not for the monastic community alone. Rather, it is on this basis that "monastic work can claim to serve a unity without borders," enabling both a "solidarity with the POOR [. . .] and with the CROWD of WORKERS." Christian insists that the social and political consequences of this redemptive gathering of all into unity cannot be ignored—the poor, the workers "also have the right to discover their dignity and freedom in a world of work so strongly marked by discrimination and oppression." This hope, of dignity and freedom, is founded in a different sort of economy, "the economy of the Kingdom," where "there is no longer 'slave or free', there is only God who accomplishes

[48] Chergé, *Dieu pour tout jour*, 423; January 21, 1993.

[49] Chergé, *Dieu pour tout jour*, 424; January 21, 1993.

everything in all, harmonizing charisms for the wellbeing of the whole Body."[50]

Monastic life is oriented towards this hope—the hope that the ordinary, daily work of the community, and of each monk, will indeed become *Opus Dei*, the work of God, revealing the coming kingdom and gathering all into one. Participation and communion. This can never be fully realized in this life—the kingdom is both now and not yet—but it is this hope that orients and orders the present. And in the writings of the Tibhirine community we glimpse what they sometimes glimpsed of the economy of this kingdom. When Michel speaks about his factory work to the community, he is able, looking back, to see it as the work of God. One senses too that he has been absorbing Christian's chapter talks in thinking about his current work in the kitchen and garden. His insights are recorded in the community diary:

> Brother Michel [. . .] evokes his experience of working in a factory as a miller [fitter and turner] with the certainty of participating both in the work of creation and in the Eucharistic offering of which his workshop table would have been the altar. There remains this double dimension of praise and consecration in his office in the garden or in the kitchen, with the suffering of slowness, impatience, etc.[51]

And, Michel confesses, "it is difficult to leave work to join the *lectio* table." For him the work of the hands is his natural habitat, not a desk in the *scriptorium*. His comments (even though they do not survive in full) are grounding. Work is the site of continuing work on the unruly self: it is both "hard and redeeming" (CST 26), a place of both joy and struggle, a place of both thanksgiving and offering, a place for continued transformation. A eucharistic table.

[50] Chergé, *Dieu pour tout jour*, 424; January 21, 1993.
[51] Moines de Tibhirine, *Heureux ceux qui espèrent*, 172.

Christian's recrafting of the words of the Rule of Benedict on the work of the hands expresses the hope of transformation and redemption, rehearsed in every Eucharist, understood as an eschatological hope: "We will truly be monks where we live by the work of His hands" (RB 48.8). And then Christian adds, "It is finished."[52] The monastic project is done, of course, but these words also echo the words of Jesus on the point of death (John 19:30)—Jesus, the Son whose work was perfectly aligned with the will of the Father (John 5:19) and in whose footsteps they follow, as in hope . . . .

[52] Chergé, *Dieu pour tout jour*, 427; February 9, 1993. "Nous serons moines en vérité où nous vivons du travail de Ses mains. C'est fini!"

Part III

Living Here Together
Vivre ici ensemble

Chapter 5

Community

I don't want to live this alone, I feel far too weak.
—Christophe Lebreton

I believe that your community is,
spiritually and monastically,
at one of the best times in its history.
—Armand Veilleux

When the young Christophe Lebreton fled back to the monastery of Notre-Dame de Tamié in the French Alps in November 1977, after his first, failed attempt to join the small community at Tibhirine, he imaged himself as the prodigal son. "I'm at the end of my rope," he had confided in a letter to the abbot of Tamié, Dom François de Sales:

> it remains for me to express to you my request, that of a son who is always prodigal, but on the way to the Father, and who does not want to walk alone, so he cries and cries for a little help so that he does not inevitably fall into the fatal pit, into incurable sadness, into solitary misery . . . Could you take me in at Tamié, with all that I am . . . above all with my desire—not that it belongs to me—to follow Jesus, to truly seek his Will in the monastery until death. I ask nothing more than to allow myself to complete my one-year commitment in Tamié. You and

> the community will then be able to discern the Lord's will.[1]

Christophe knows that he needs companions. He cannot save himself. He cannot discern God's will alone. He needs a community of brothers. Three years later, when he came to make his solemn profession at Tamié, he addressed the community in similar terms: "I don't want to live this alone," he reiterates.[2]

"Whose feet will you wash?"

The Benedictine tradition has always held that we need the support of companions in the journey to God. While the Rule of Benedict recognizes the validity of monastic life for a hermit or anchorite, it warns that healthy solitary life is only possible after "the test of living in a monastery for a long time," after the monk has received "the help and guidance of many" (RB 1. 3–5).

The early emergence of cenobitic, communal forms of monasticism was unsurprising. The risks of solitary life (self-delusion, pride, despair) and the need for training and oversight were clear from the earliest monastic experiments in the deserts of Egypt and Syria. There was also Basil of Caesarea's sharp question, articulated in his late fourth-century Rule, "Whose feet will you wash?" For Basil monastic life was simply Christian life, and Christian life cannot be lived without the neighbor. We cannot see ourselves without the help of an other. Further, we cannot fulfill the commandment to love: "the very character of Christ's love does not permit an individual to seek his own interest, for Love . . . seeks not its own."[3]

[1] Moines de Tibhirine, *Heureux ceux qui espèrent: Autobiographies spirituelles*, ed. Marie-Dominique Minassian, Les écrits de Tibhirine 1 (Paris: Bayard-Cerf-Bellefontaine, 2018), 555.

[2] Moines de Tibhirine, *Heureux ceux qui espèrent*, 575.

[3] Anna Silvas, *The Asketikon of St Basil the Great*, Oxford Early Christian Studies (Oxford: Oxford University Press, 2005), Longer Rule (LR) 7.5.

Jesus, Basil points out, did not simply teach "the law of love"; he enacted it, he "girded himself with a linen cloth," and he "washed the feet of his own disciples."[4]

Christophe's entry into the novitiate at Tamié in December 1974 had been marked by a ritual modeled on this enactment of fraternal love: the mandatum or washing of feet, a ritual that symbolically fulfills Jesus' command (*mandatum*) that just as he had washed his disciples' feet, they should wash one another's feet (John 13:14). The mandatum has a long pedigree in the Western monastic tradition. Found in Cassian's *Institutes* as well as the Rule of Benedict, historically this rite was performed on Saturday evenings to mark the changeover of kitchen servers. Lowly kitchen service was thus affirmed as a sign of fraternal love. The use of the mandatum in welcoming a novice into the monastic community similarly powerfully underscores the communal nature of the monastic journey: love of God and love of neighbor cannot be separated:

> After Vespers, [. . .] the community goes up to the novitiate, emptied of its tables and decorated with flowers by Brother Didier. Everyone sits down in a circle for the rite of the "mandatum," the washing of the feet . . . I am helped by Brother René, a novice, and girded with an apron I circle and wash the feet of each of my brothers with a jug and a wooden basin equipped with a crossbar to support the feet. During this time, zither and songs.
>
> After the washing: Brother Victor reads me a passage from the Rule of Saint Benedict, chosen before with him (Ch. 4 The Tools of Good Works). Then I'm in the middle, and I address my request (*postulare* = to ask).
>
> Father Abbot: What are you asking for?

[4] LR 7.34–35.

> I said: "The Love of God close to Mary and Joseph, close to my brothers, especially my brothers in the novitiate, Brothers Victor, Paul, Didier, Raffaele, Philippe, Yves, Christian, René."[5]

The ceremony concludes with prayers—not just for the new novice but for "the whole community that welcomes him."[6] If this entry into monastic life constitutes a radical change for the novice, the presence of a new member also changes the community, the relationships among all the brothers. They are in this together.

The Problem of Community

Nonetheless the question remains: why did Christophe flee from Tibhirine in November 1977, the place to which he had felt called, after just eighteen months? What had gone so wrong for him in that community of brothers? There are some very specific answers to these questions to which we will return: factors such as his youth, his fragility after difficulties during his novitiate at Tamié, his sudden isolation from peers (his "brothers in the novitiate"), his unfinished novitiate training, the realities of living in an isolated location in a different culture, the complexity and fragility of the Tibhirine community itself, all of which alert us to the complexity of this creature we call *community*.

In English at least, *community* is a tired word, one that has had to bear too much and risks being weighed down by idealism, even fantasy: we long for *community* yet find it elusive; we propose *community* as a solution to social ills yet operate from a paradigm of individualism, of manifest self-interest. Christian groups are not immune to this "quest for community," often deriving motivation from the idea of recovering some supposedly pure form from the past, whether it be the primitive church or an earlier pristine version of religious life.

[5] Moines de Tibhirine, *Heureux ceux qui espèrent*, 523.
[6] Moines de Tibhirine, *Heureux ceux qui espèrent*, 523.

Reforms (including those that have occurred within monastic traditions) often rest on nostalgia for a past that never existed.[7]

And yet community, living together, remains central to monasticism, and indeed to Christian life. Building community requires two things. First, a robust theological foundation for the practice of Christian community. Second, a prudent modesty regarding its possibility. In this regard it is notable that the situation report prepared by the Atlas community for the meeting of the Union des Supérieurs Majeurs d'Algeria (USMDA) in November 1995 speaks in such terms. In the context of *ora et labora* (prayer and work), the brothers sought "to be together a sign of the Church, invisible to the world, but visible to our neighbors. Witnesses of peace, of the possibility of fraternity, by the grace of God, across our diversities."[8] The key words here are *sign* and *possibility*—nothing is assumed, there is no overreach. Further, there is a recognition that community, here expressed as "fraternity," is dependent on "grace." We are powerless to effect this sign, or this possibility, aside from God. What the Tibhirine monks offer us is a glimpse of "the possibility of fraternity"—hard-won, costly, always fragile.

Theological Foundations

In thinking about the theological foundations of Christian community it will be helpful to briefly sketch the cultural shifts that have rendered commitment to community essentially countercultural in the modern world. To do this I draw on the analysis of philosopher Charles Taylor and theologian Scott Cowdell.

[7] Stephen Pickard, *Seeking the Church: An Introduction to Ecclesiology* (London: SCM Press, 2012), 224–31. Pickard maps the impact of the "rush to community" on contemporary ecclesiology.

[8] "Comment, dans la situation présente, rejoignons-nous le charisme de notre Order? (21 novembre 1995)," in *Sept vies pour Dieu et l'Algérie*, ed. Bruno Chenu (Paris: Bayard, 1996), 176.

In his seminal 2007 book, *A Secular Age*, Taylor examines the changing relationship of religion and society in the post-Enlightenment West. We have moved, he observes, "from a society in which it was virtually impossible not to believe in God, to one in which faith . . . is one human possibility among others."[9] Modernity has dislodged the presence of God from the social order. In the pre-modern period, in the West, a shared Christian cosmology shaped social relations. By contrast the modern world operates without cosmological bearings and, driven by what Taylor calls "instrumental rationality,"[10] prioritizes "the optimization of the individual's goal fulfilment."[11] In the absence of a shared *telos* (goal), as Cowdell suggests, "this is now a world that we make, largely for our own ends, with nothing of compelling significance determining what those ends should be."[12] The social space is constructed to meet individual goals: individualism trumps community, which became "secondary and derivative in the West."[13] Following Taylor, Cowdell helpfully articulates the consequences for the church, particularly in its Protestant expressions: "the Church became less of a body constituted from above and more a fellowship entered into from below—a social contract, a human community derived from godly individuals."[14]

By contrast, Roman Catholic teaching has confidently retained an understanding of the God-givenness of the church and of Christian community. It is possible too that monasticism, with its long, stable tradition of living fraternal community, has been helpfully resistant to the cultural shifts of

[9] Charles Taylor, *A Secular Age* (Cambridge, MA: Belknap Press, 2007), 3.

[10] Taylor, *A Secular Age*, 542.

[11] Scott Cowdell, *Why Church? Christianity as It Was Meant to Be* (New York: Church Publishing, 2024), 31.

[12] Cowdell, *Why Church?*, 31.

[13] Cowdell, *Why Church?*, 32. In this context "believing" precedes "belonging." See also Taylor, *A Secular Age*, 541.

[14] Cowdell, *Why Church?*, 32.

Western modernity.[15] Here I turn to the work of monastic theologian André Louf, where one can sense both the continuous tradition of thinking about Christian community and its refreshment in the context of Vatican II. His work has helped significantly in framing this chapter. Given his place in the French Cistercian world of the late twentieth century, his writing was undoubtedly familiar to the Atlas community.

In his essay "Living in Fraternal Community" (1984), Louf maps out its theological foundations, beginning with this precis: "The Christian community is an ecclesial event, a divine event, a locus of grace."[16] Christian community is "an ecclesial event" because the church encompasses "every group within her." The Cistercian tradition holds monastic community and the church together: its first foundation was known as "the church at Cîteaux"—it understood itself as "a sign of the people of God," the "Church of the desert," which together with the "Church of the world" constitutes the people of God.[17] It is "a divine event" because every Christian community is called into existence by God. This is the bedrock: Christian community is always the result of divine, not human, initiative. (Monks are well aware of this since their presence in the monastery is the result of being called by God into that life.) Further, this divine initiative is located in the unfolding story of redemption. It is "Easter that creates the church." All Christian

[15] Pickard helpfully draws attention to David Bosch's classic work on mission and his observation of the "extraordinary resilience and recuperative power" of monasticism, and its embrace of a "spirituality of the long haul." While Bosch's comments were made in the context of his discussion of medieval mission, they remain apposite (Pickard, *Seeking the Church*, 218; David J. Bosch, *Transforming Mission: Paradigm Shifts in Theology of Mission* [Maryknoll, NY: Orbis, 1991], 232–33).

[16] André Louf, *In the School of Contemplation*, trans. Paul Rowe, MW 48 (Collegeville, MN: Cistercian Publications, 2015), 34.

[17] André Louf, *The Cistercian Way*, trans. Nivard Kinsella, CS 76 (Kalamazoo, MI: Cistercian Publications, 1983), 120. Similarly, the Constitutions and Statutes of the Cistercian Order, CST 5: "Gathered by the call of God the brothers constitute a monastic church or community that is the fundamental unit of the Order."

community, Louf says, is "the fruit of the paschal event": a shattered, scattered group of disciples is reconstituted as a first "fruit of the resurrection."[18] Christian de Chergé similarly understood the paschal foundation of Christian community. In 1973, in the midst of struggles regarding his own fit at Tibhirine, Christian wrote a series of long reflections on his vocation as a monk and its expression in community:

> There is Good News in me, and it is simply Jesus Living among men; they can only call themselves brothers since Jesus has ascended to his Father and his Spirit whispers in us the fraternal call of his universal prayer. All fraternity is a myth outside of this paschal mystery. By resolutely penetrating into the logic of Easter, the monk allows the Father to beget in him brothers of the Christ.[19]

The "fraternal call of his universal prayer" is, in part, an allusion to Jesus' prayer for his disciples in the Gospel of John "that they be one"—as well as to God's eternal desire for us. Communion, fraternity, derives from being drawn into the divine life that Jesus shared with the Father: "as we are one, I in them and you in me" (John 17:22-23). Fraternity is both paschal and Trinitarian. (Notice too that Christian uses the more relational language of fraternity rather than the language of community. If the call is to communion, to oneness, it is via fraternal relationships.)

However, as Louf argues, in this world, there is always a tension between "dispersion and gathering, between *diaspora* and *ekklêsia*"—the community of the church, the first fruit, is

[18] Louf, *In the School of Contemplation*, 35.

[19] Moines de Tibhirine, *Heureux ceux qui espèrent*, 356. "Il y a une Bonne Nouvelle en moi, et c'est simplement Jésus Vivant parmi les hommes; ceux-ci ne peuvent se dire frères que depuis que Jésus est remonté vers son Père et que son Esprit murmure en nous l'appel fraternel de sa prière universelle. Toute fraternité est un mythe hors de ce mystère pascal. En pénétrant résolument dans la logique pascale, le moine laisse le Père engendrer en lui les frères du Christ."

inevitably "timid and fragile."[20] Indeed, our scatteredness makes community humanly impossible, so that it is only the operation of grace that enables its existence:

> Man left to himself is not capable of living in community. His normal condition is *diaspora*, in dispersion in the midst of the world, separated from others, and more profoundly, from himself. This being so, a Christian community, wherever it comes to birth, can only be a gift, a sign of the mercy of God, an anticipation, a prefigurement and foretaste of the kingdom that is to come, of that which only later will be a reality for the whole Church. The Christian community is always something prospective: a window opening out to heaven.[21]

Christian community is, then, "a locus of grace" constituted, amidst human frailty, by divine initiative and oriented toward the future, coming, kingdom. It is this understanding that anchors the Atlas community—not with any sense of presumption or arrival, but as a vision, an eschatological hope, to be renewed again and again in the midst of the quotidian, the daily.

Louf recognizes that Christian community functions as a human group as well "as an event of the Church"—and that there is an inevitable tension between these, as there is always between nature and grace.[22] This makes discernment particularly challenging: what is of God, what is human? We need, Louf stresses, the careful "discernment of spirits . . . for perceiving the life of God in us and in others."[23] Still, the witness of Scripture and the long experience of being the church offer some clues, some signs of divine life, and Louf articulates these as three criteria for a Christian community: it is "built on human weakness," it is "a place of forgiveness," and it is "a

[20] Louf, *In the School of Contemplation*, 35.
[21] Louf, *In the School of Contemplation*, 37–38.
[22] Louf, *In the School of Contemplation*, 40.
[23] Louf, *In the School of Contemplation*, 41.

place of healing."[24] No ascending sequence is implied here. Each of these characteristics remains in play this side of eternity, but their presence, together, are signals that the community is indeed "a locus of grace," open to the transforming love of God.

Open to Grace: The Vowed Life

The structures of monastic life help to open the community to grace. In the Benedictine tradition monks "serve under a rule and an abbot" (RB 1.2). Both the individual and the community are shaped by their shared monastic commitments: the vows of stability, obedience, and *conversatio morum* (fidelity to monastic life). However, while the taking of vows happens at a particular time, living them is a lifelong process.

The entry and incorporation of a new member into the monastic community is a matter for careful, often lengthy, discernment. The movement from postulancy to novitiate, from novitiate to temporary vows, and finally from temporary to permanent vows is a matter for both individual and community discernment. The abbot, in consultation with his council, admits the postulant into the novitiate, but it is the whole fully professed community (the conventual chapter) that must vote on a novice's request to take temporary vows, as well as a monk's request to take permanent vows. The three vows of stability, obedience, and *conversatio morum* constitute serious commitments for the one being admitted—but also for the community welcoming a new member. Both parties are changed. All will be reshaped by the presence of the new monk.

Stability, the dual commitment to a particular fraternity of brothers and to a particular place, is foundational to community life. The Rule of Benedict is sharp in its condemnation of gyrovagues, monks who flit from place to place (RB 1.10–12). In the history of Tibhirine, as in all monastic communities,

[24] Louf, *In the School of Contemplation*, 41.

volatility in membership and in leadership threatened its health, and at times its survival. While much of this volatility was unavoidable, the community understood its impact. Stability (and its lack) impacts the spiritual health of the whole community, not just the individual monk.

Obedience is similarly central to monastic life in the Benedictine tradition, although in contemporary life, the word *obedience* feels weighed down by unhealthy histories of the abusive use of power in religious institutions. In monastic life the reference point is always the example of Jesus Christ, who "became obedient even to the point of death—even death on a cross" (Phil 2:8). Obedience in this context is not primarily a mechanism for imposing and maintaining social order. Yet the need to order a community and make decisions does not disappear—obedience cannot be simply spiritualized. In a chapter talk on obedience Christian draws attention to the careful wording of the revised Cistercian constitution: "By the vow of obedience, a brother desiring to live under a rule and an abbot promises to fulfill all that lawful superiors command in accordance with these Constitutions" (CST 11). Obedience is predicated on alignment with the Cistercian charism to be a "school of brotherly love" (CST 3.1). Christian notes that it is now more common to speak of "mutual obedience" or "responsible obedience," but he does not want to lose track of its foundations.

When Paul recites the hymn of Christ's self-offering (*kenosis*) in his letter to the Philippians, it is to urge the imitation of this way of self-offering ("Let the same mind be in you that was in Christ Jesus," Phil 2:5). What is essential, Christian says, is "to escape from one's own aloof self-possession [*quant à soi*]." And this is where outward (or social) and interior (or spiritual) obedience come together: "A perfect external obedience can very well leave this 'self-possession' intact: one thinks of it no less. Inner obedience sometimes requires a time of dialogue, consultation, mutual illumination, not in order not to obey, but to obey BETTER."[25] Obedience, then, becomes a communal undertaking oriented to the building of a loving community.

It is not surprising that in the biographies of the seven Tibhirine monks questions around the vows of stability and obedience often arise, and often in the context of struggles around vocation and community. Further, in these struggles we often see Louf's three criteria for Christian community woven into the interrelated stories of monk and community: weaknesses are revealed, while the graces of forgiveness and healing allow all to continue their journey to God, sometimes together, sometimes apart. While the complex dynamics of a community can never be fully known, nor indeed the interior life of a monk, in Christophe Lebreton's case we have access to some rich material—correspondence and journals—that offer at least a glimpse into the complex interweaving of the life of a monk and his community. In the remainder of this chapter, then, I offer two windows into Christophe's story: his early, difficult experience of community life, and then his mature understanding of commitment to community. A third window views the Tibhirine community after the Christmas Eve visit of 1993, the monks' discernment processes, and their ongoing commitment to each other and to their place in Algeria.

Window 1: Community as Crucible of Grace

When Christophe entered the novitiate at Notre-Dame de Tamié at the age of twenty-four he had Notre-Dame de l'Atlas firmly in view. He had encountered the small community in Tibhirine whilst completing his national service as a *coopérant* in Algiers during 1972–1974. Deeply influenced by his

[25] Christian de Chergé, *Dieu pour tout jour: chapitres de Père Christian de Chergé à la communauté de Tibhirine (1985–1996)*, 2nd ed. (Montjoyer: Abbaye Notre-Dame d'Aiguebelle, 2006), 366; April 18, 1991: "Une obéissance extérieure parfaite peut très bien laisser intact ce 'quant à soi': on n'en pense pas moins. L'obéissance intérieure exige parfois un temps de dialogue, de concertation, d'éclairage mutuel, non pas pour ne pas obeir, mais pour obéir MIEUX."

involvement with the Emmaus camps founded by Abbé Pierre, Christophe had already begun to explore a call to religious life in service to the poor. The small Tibhirine community appeared a perfect fit.

Just after his entry into Tamié as a postulant in November 1974, Christophe articulated his attraction to Atlas in his journal. He saw in the community the features to which he was himself attracted: poverty (living among their poor neighbors in material and even liturgical simplicity), hospitality (serving the local population via the dispensary and the oil press, and Christians via the simple guesthouse, all in an atmosphere of respect for Muslims), and truthfulness in fraternal relationships ("arguments and then forgiveness"):

> Monks clinging to a work, humanly, on the way to being lost (no recruitment allowed . . .), in an Islamic country where the "politico-social-religious" pressure is very intense, wearing: a manifestly absurd uselessness that witnesses in the same proportion to God.
>
> Few in number, seven and six at the time I was there: much greater demand on common life, no escape possible, a very strong human and spiritual solidarity and . . . human tensions . . . a healthy life, but not idyllic at all.[26]

The superior, Fr. Jean-Baptiste Bruneau, had also spoken frankly about the difficulties of life at Tibhirine: "the monotony, the tensions between brothers."[27] The youthful Christophe was perhaps not ready to hear the cautions. In his imagination Notre-Dame de l'Atlas fit his ideal. But it was not idyllic in any sense: it was simply a small group of monks, with very different life and monastic experiences, committed to living in a difficult environment. Christophe was correct about one thing: in such an environment escape was not possible.

[26] Moines de Tibhirine, *Heureux ceux qui espèrent*, 517.

[27] Moines de Tibhirine, *Heureux ceux qui espèrent*, 517.

But neither was escape possible in the novitiate at Tamié, where Christophe began his monastic journey. For all those entering monastic life the honeymoon, the first flush of love and affirmation, inevitably ends as the novice begins to notice the "faults and limitations" of the other monks.[28] The hard work of learning to live in a community then begins. What one is being offered, of course, is a mirror of the self: what becomes painfully clear is one's own "faults and limitations." This is precisely what Christophe experienced.

By the end of his first year as a novice Christophe was facing significant difficulties. He wrote to his parents,

> The beginning of my life here was a time of peace and joy, knowing that I belonged. And then I was appointed assistant cantor, and this triggered a whole process that quickly overwhelmed me: difficulties in expressing myself, in accepting my brothers and their own expressiveness . . . and more generally I felt within me a struggle to accept my brothers and at the same time a very clear tendency to close myself off, to withdraw. And then there was the announcement of the expulsion of the Atlas abbey [from Algeria], later reversed, which occurred when I was "not strong" and which caused a morbid, haunting sadness, a withdrawal into myself, a very great susceptibility to bursting into anger that made me ashamed and pushed me deeper and deeper into my hole.[29]

How one faces this revelation of weakness is crucial to one's future in the community. If, as Louf suggests, this is "a community built on weakness," then the mutual recognition of frailties is not intended to shame, but rather to encourage mutual dependence—on God and on each other. The monastery is intended to be a place of forgiveness and of healing, of

[28] Louf, *The Cistercian Way*, 126.

[29] Moines de Tibhirine, *Heureux ceux qui espèrent*, 526.

love. Or as Christophe himself wrote much later, it is "a school of peace," a place of learning Jesus' way of peace.[30]

Christophe worked with a psychologist on his difficulties, gaining in self-understanding, but this crisis raised questions regarding his readiness to join the monks at Tibhirine.[31] The community at Atlas was equivocal: first a "yes" from the then-superior Jean-Baptiste, then a "no"—"you need a balanced nervous system," the community is "already going through trials and fragile."[32] The young Christian de Chergé, though, discouraged a delay as adding a further, difficult burden for Christophe. After lengthy correspondence between the monastic communities of Atlas, Aiguebelle, and Tamié, an open-ended trial was finally proposed, and Christophe joined the community at Tibhirine on May 11, 1976.

In many ways, for Christophe going to Tibhirine was like beginning again, but in more challenging circumstances. He was asked to extend his novitiate, which was a source of some pain for him. By the end of summer 1976 he was already tired and struggling. He was unable to participate in Vigils.[33] He confided to Dom François de Sales, the abbot of Tamié, "I feared, because of my situation as the only novice, of falling back into a partially closed personality, solitary and a little blasé (the same one that life in Tamié had shaken up and changed)."[34] He felt lonely and isolated, lacking the fraternal relationships that he had enjoyed at Tamié. His sensitivity and lack of confidence made him vulnerable to grumbling (or

[30] Christophe Lebreton, *Born from the Gaze of God: The Tibhirine Journal of a Martyr Monk (1993–1996)*, trans. Mette Louise Nygård and Edith Scholl, MW 37 (Collegeville, MN: Cistercian Publications, 2014), January 16, 1995.

[31] Christophe again worked with a psychiatrist in 1979 after his return to Tamié (Moines de Tibhirine, *Heureux ceux qui espèrent*, 569). The openness of the monastic community to utilizing mental health professionals is reassuring—the community was not "closed" to external assistance.

[32] Moines de Tibhirine, *Heureux ceux qui espèrent*, 527–28.

[33] Moines de Tibhirine, *Heureux ceux qui espèrent*, 527.

[34] Moines de Tibhirine, *Heureux ceux qui espèrent*, 537.

"murmuring," in Benedictine parlance) in the community, which was itself in a fragile state. For Christophe, only in his mid-twenties, these were still early days in terms of his monastic formation: in a personal note he includes the "problem of chastity for an isolated young person" and the need for "relaxation—human joys."[35] The loss of the companionship of other young novices at Tamié made these burdens acute.

It took more than a year for the parties involved to come to a shared decision that Christophe would leave Atlas and return to Tamié. These were serious decisions, matters for careful discernment—what was best for Christophe? for his well-being and growth? for the community? what was God's will in this situation? And there was additional complexity. Typically, in such decision-making processes, the community is represented by the abbot (supported by a council of senior monks), who carries responsibility for the well-being of the community. However, the small community at Tibhirine was under the jurisdiction of Aiguebelle, so while Jean-Baptiste was the Atlas superior, he was required to consult with the abbot of Aiguebelle.[36] Tamié was also involved as the monastery that had welcomed Christophe as a postulant and had overseen his initial formation in the novitiate. Christophe had retained strong ties with Tamié, entrusting the abbot with his difficulties (indeed it is clear that Christophe regarded Dom François as his spiritual father). So there were three monastic communities concerned with securing the well-being of this young novice while also ensuring the well-being of the communities. This added complexity undoubtedly slowed the discernment process.

While the painful process of stripping and reorienting the self that Christophe had begun during his novitiate at Tamié was normal, it had exposed weaknesses that affected his capacity to engage in fraternal life: his sensitivity, his tendency to

[35] Moines de Tibhirine, *Heureux ceux qui espèrent*, 539.

[36] A *superior ad nutum* is appointed by the motherhouse to serve temporarily, until the community is able to elect its own superior.

withdraw, his emotional outbursts. Christophe was painfully aware of these weaknesses. But these are human weaknesses, not reasons for expulsion from a community. Was it possible for him and the community to work with these challenges at Tibhirine? All parties clearly hoped that this would be so.

In fact, on December 31, 1976, Christophe took his first, temporary, vows at Tibhirine. The way had been cleared during the regular visitation to the community at the end of September that year by the then abbot of Aiguebelle, Dom Jean de la Croix—the same visit that had culminated in the solemn profession of Christian de Chergé on October 1 and the transfer of stability of three other professed brothers.[37] This was a time of renewed hope for the future, celebrated as a Spirit-inspired turning point, as the community clarified its shared call to be a monastic presence in Algeria, a community of prayer alongside others who pray (*priants parmi d'autre priants*).

Christophe had carefully prepared for his own meeting with Jean de la Croix, a meeting that clearly predated this communal turning point. His notes offer an astute assessment of the community in which he had now lived for five months. He saw a community "shaped by its Lord in the crucible of many sufferings," but one for which he held out little hope: "I would like it to live, but I believe it is quite ill, affected in its heart, altered by too much suffering."[38] Nonetheless, there was much that he admired that conformed to his original attraction and to Gospel values: its simplicity (inspired by contact with the challenging socio-economic realities surrounding it), its poverty (living with insecurity as well as the struggle for authenticity when surrounded by material poverty), its commitment to truth, "human relations without artifice," the commitment

[37] Fr. Aubin Le Mouillour and Fr. Jean-Pierre Schumacher had come from Notre-Dame de Timadeuc in 1964. Fr. Roland Lacas came from Notre-Dame des Neiges in 1974 (Nuno de São José, "Notre-Dame de l'Atlas, mystère d'une secrète fécondité: histoire de la communauté depuis sa fondation jusqu'en 1996," *Collectanea Cisterciensia* 83 [2021]: 287 n30; 293 n51).

[38] Moines de Tibhirine, *Heureux ceux qui espèrent*, 538.

to prayer (corporate and individual), its "simple and true" hospitality.[39]

And yet we can feel Christophe's hesitation in the question he articulated for himself. He believed that he was called to "serve under a rule and an abbot" (RB 1.2). Yet he asks, "Will I even be able to continue here to inhabit and to practically live the desire for a relationship of true openness with my Superior, and of a common life expressed through sharing everything that makes up the core—as well as the daily rhythm [*le quotidien*]—of our life?"[40] One senses here the limits of trust in his relationship with his current superior and the absence of deep connection or friendship with the brothers at Tibhirine. Christophe is asking, can I really entrust myself, my deepest self, to this community?

He pushes on, giving further shape to his hesitancy, listing the risks involved in remaining at Tibhirine. He is aware of his own temperament, his tendency to "close down," his ongoing battle to control his sensitivity and his emotions. He is concerned with how these traits impact an already fragile community. He is struggling too with the balance between solitude and community. He experiences monastic life at Tibhirine as primarily solitary: "friendships seem difficult if not excluded (many fears and mutual prejudices)." Solitude and silence, as conducive to "interior quiet" (CST 3.3), are normative features of Cistercian life. Indeed, these are precisely the conditions that enable the monk to grow in "mindfulness of God and fraternal communion" (CST 24).

Nevertheless, these are practices that require practice and are predicated on interior growth. Christophe was still in the early days of formation in this way of life. Healthy solitude is

[39] Moines de Tibhirine, *Heureux ceux qui espèrent*, 538.

[40] Moines de Tibhirine, *Heureux ceux qui espèrent*, 538. "Question qui me concerne . . . c'est à la vie commune sous un abbé qui interprète la Règle que je me sens appelé. Pourrai-je même ici continuer à porter et à vivre concrètement le désir d'une relation d'ouverture vraie à mon Supérieur, d'une vie commune s'exprimant en partage de ce qui fait l'essentiel—comme du quotidien—de notre vie?"

not loneliness. If other brothers appeared to have little need for friendship, this was not true for Christophe. While it is not possible to verify his perception, for someone prone to unhealthy withdrawal, as he was, his lack of friends and the absence of peers were potentially dangerous. Christophe rightly assessed the risk "of personality alteration if my fragile human base is shaken too much."[41]

There was also risk, harder to articulate but of critical importance, in relation to his sense of vocation, of God's call. It is clear that Christophe did not yet feel settled in relation to the shape of his particular vocation (a dual vocation both to monastic life and to the poor) and was experiencing doubts about whether he would be able to explore it fully and freely at Tibhirine. Was this the place where he could fully live into God's call on his life? Would this community support him in this journey?

Christophe understood the interrelationship of vocation and community. Three years later, in preparation for his solemn profession at Tamié, he articulated this interrelationship in his desire "to live this call in a community that defines its realization."[42] Vocation and community are interwoven. While the monk arrives with a sense of call, it is living in community that shapes its expression. Vocation ceases to be an individual project; one's vocation grows (or not) in the context of a community. At Tibhirine Christophe feared that his individual vocation would be constrained by the need to work around certain elements of monastic life that he understood to be core, in particular the centrality of one's relationship with the superior or abbot, and the gift of "fraternal communion." There was a risk, he believed, that he might settle into, and the community consequently support and serve, a compromised "individual vocation" and that, in the absence of "true dialogue at this level," he would miss out on a "glimpsed ideal." Christophe expressed a further fear: the "risk of living one's

[41] Moines de Tibhirine, *Heureux ceux qui espèrent*, 539.

[42] Moines de Tibhirine, *Heureux ceux qui espèrent*, 575.

vocation with a heart (which is at the core of our monastic life) agitated, affected by the bitterness that comes from the reality of the situation."[43] The fear here is, I think, of unhealthy self-denial, a loss of agency, of freedom, of genuine participation in the shaping of one's vocation and life ("of a real dialogue").

Surprisingly perhaps, in their September 1976 meeting Jean de la Croix encouraged Christophe to continue at Tibhirine and, with the agreement of the community, opened the way for him to make a "temporary" commitment at the end of the year. Christophe was buoyed by this prospect and by the changed atmosphere in the community surrounding the solemn profession of Christian. In a letter to a brother monk, Fr. Placide, Christian noted the change in the young novice: "The biggest change is Christophe: a metamorphosis, a big kid who unfolds and risks exercising his talents, which are great. On October 1st, there was a very nice interlude on the guitar."[44]

Nonetheless, Christophe's difficulties continued after his first profession, into 1977, and as the time for the renewal of his twelve-month temporary vows loomed Christophe was convinced that he needed to leave Tibhirine and begged his old abbot to accept his return to Tamié. But the decision was not his alone.

Underlying the whole discernment decision-making process was the monastic commitment to obedience. The risks that Christophe had articulated for his meeting with Jean de la Croix had been prefaced with an important proviso: they were "blessed risks as long as the Lord calls me to stay here through the voice of my Superiors."[45] For Christophe, and for his superiors, the discernment process was difficult and painful. In April 1977 Jean-Baptiste wrote to the abbot of Tamié, "his case is delicate . . . it is a question of finding the place and the environment where God wants [his gifts] to bear fruit. With

[43] Moines de Tibhirine, *Heureux ceux qui espèrent*, 539.

[44] Moines de Tibhirine, *Heureux ceux qui espèrent*, 542.

[45] Moines de Tibhirine, *Heureux ceux qui espèrent*, 538.

the temperament of an artist, a bit of a poet, sensitive (excessively), it can only be very trying for him; we are confronted with many problems on the ground . . ."[46]

It was not a period without joys for Christophe, but the weight and loneliness of his suffering ultimately made staying untenable. He was torn. On August 20 he wrote in his journal, "My Cistercian vocation: a deep conviction, to stay here as long as He wants." Then the following day: "I ask the Lord for forgiveness for not believing in the fruitfulness of crosses, in the uselessness of my life—and also for being so often sad because I do not know how to see the good, the good people, the beautiful around me, in my life."[47] To his mother he confided, "I am discouraged by my faults, by these terrible fits of violence that dominate me and then leave me completely annihilated. I doubt myself, I have so much trouble escaping from myself to turn to God, to present to Him my wretchedness, my suffering, my sin . . . and so many judgments, condemnations, and pride."[48]

In the end it is the cry from Christophe's heart that must be heard: "It is too hard, much too hard for me," he wrote to François de Sales.[49]

Christophe left Tibhirine on November 11, 1977, returning to Tamié, where he continued his monastic journey until 1987. While the community diary simply notes his departure "in the best of spirits," with "humility and gratitude to each member of the community,"[50] Christian reflected on its impact on the

[46] Moines de Tibhirine, *Heureux ceux qui espèrent*, 548.

[47] Moines de Tibhirine, *Heureux ceux qui espèrent*, 551.

[48] Moines de Tibhirine, *Heureux ceux qui espèrent*, 551. "je me dépite de mes défauts, de ces mouvements de violence terribles qui me dominent et ensuite me laissent tout anéanti. Je doute de moi-même, j'ai tant de mal à échapper à mon moi pour me tourner vers Dieu, pour lui présenter ma misère, ma souffrance, mon péché , . . et puis tant de jugements, de condamnations et d'orgueil."

[49] Moines de Tibhirine, *Heureux ceux qui espèrent*, 552.

[50] Moines de Tibhirine, *Heureux ceux qui espèrent*, 557.

community in the chronicle he was writing for friends and family. Here we get another perspective:

> His decision has been made for nearly two months, but today when it is carried out, it still seems to us very quick and brutal. Thus our brother Christophe (twenty-seven years old) leaves us after eighteen months of physical presence among us, day by day. He chose to return to Tamié, where, during his novitiate, he had longed so much for us. Mystery of obedience and of freedom. A brother leaves. For days, it will be necessary to relearn to live differently, and without him, the definition of the Cistercian monk: "AMATOR LOCI ET FRATRUM!" [lover of place and of his brothers]. There is a void in each brother, and in the landscape itself, a void that preserves the sense of a vivacious, jealous affection, an interior void, deep as an unanswered question, as remorse too.[51]

For the community there was immense grief in Christophe's departure—regardless of the difficulties on both sides. When Christian speaks of the "mystery of obedience and of freedom," he reminds us that the monastery is not an autocracy, ruled by an all-powerful abbot, nor an institution in which the shape of one's life is controlled by a rigid set of regulations, but rather a community of brothers who have chosen to listen together to the call, in each, to follow Christ—carefully, respectfully, often falteringly. Obedience and freedom are not opposed, but work together, mysteriously—as we witness in the life and death of Jesus.

For Christophe his early years of living in monastic community, at both Tamié and Tibhirine, were hard. It was a crucible, with all its connotations of being crushed and remade. But it was a crucible of grace where he came to know himself better, to know his limits, and to trust his heart. It was a place of weakness, forgiveness, and healing. A school of love.

[51] Moines de Tibhirine, *Heureux ceux qui espèrent*, 557–58.

Window 2: Stability in Christ

When Christophe returned to Tibhirine in October 1987 much had changed. Ten years down the track Christophe himself had matured into monastic life, and the community, under the leadership of Christian, had settled into its particular vocation: living next to their Muslim neighbors in the village of Tibhirine as a community of prayer alongside others who prayed. This time Christophe's integration into the small community went well. Christian reported on his progress to the abbot of Tamié, Dom Jean-Marc Thévenet, "He is the same: sensitive, attentive, generous, courageous . . . but with a quality of rootedness in the essential and of being present to everything and to everyone that touches our hearts and leads us to give him a large place in the community equilibrium."[52]

It is not long before Christophe begins, once more, to think about his stability,[53] but with a more settled trust in the unfolding of his vocation, and a healthy detachment and freedom. Writing to the abbot of Tamié in April 1988 he says, "I am here with *no conditions or limitations* other than . . . my own limits and the Will of the One who wills. I understand stability as loyalty and availability. As long as this vow makes sense for you (in Tamié) and for me (here) I ask permission to leave it at that."[54]

In his thinking about stability Christophe's focus has shifted from self to self-in-community. He has a broader, ecclesial vision, seeing stability as essentially about commitment—"loyalty and availability"—to a community, and as something received as a call of the Spirit. In August 1988 he wrote jointly to the superiors of Tamié and Atlas:

> The question of the future is posed to the Church here, to the community of Tibhirine-Fez, and to each one here

[52] Moines de Tibhirine, *Heureux ceux qui espèrent*, 606.

[53] Christophe had made his solemn vows at Tamié on All Saints' Day 1980. He was therefore "stabilized" to that community.

[54] Moines de Tibhirine, *Heureux ceux qui espèrent*, 612.

> . . . in my heart it takes the form of a listening [*une écoute*], and my life would like to be able to answer yes to the Spirit who speaks to this Church.
>
> What is said to me, without ecstasy or revelation, but in ordinary time where the Eternal dwells and is revealed: God is with us [*Dieu avec nous*]. I would like to entrust it to both of you so that you can . . . judge for yourselves!
>
> Regarding stability: a call to leave everything, even Tamié, in order to enter more deeply into the Gospel of Jesus Christ, Son of God . . . like Abraham . . . like Mary. The reasons for this bond of stability with the Atlas community: to allow this community to live as such and to be a *sign* for the Church here and for the "other" believers living in this country . . .[55]

While Christophe himself senses the call of the Spirit he also experiences what he names as the "grace of 'detachment.'" This is surprising to him—hence his naming it as a grace, as a "gift of God."[56] There is no urgency. The desire to respond to the call that he senses, to change his stability to Atlas, sits alongside the desire for obedience—to submit this call to the discernment of his superiors.[57]

Christophe's understanding of stability has expanded and deepened. Stability, he now sees, has its ultimate source and place in God. He expresses this poetically in an undated note:

[55] Moines de Tibhirine, *Heureux ceux qui espèrent*, 613. In this letter Christophe also raises a second call, that of his call to priesthood. He is very clear that these two calls, to stability and to the priesthood, must be considered separately: "ordination cannot be monetized as a 'bonus' for my (eventual) change in stability."

[56] Moines de Tibhirine, *Heureux ceux qui espèrent*, 614.

[57] Moines de Tibhirine, *Heureux ceux qui espèrent*, 614. This is Minassian's editorial observation.

No stability for
those who love

as long as the heart has not found its place

in the heart of the Other

as long as he has not received from his gaze

the mission of living here [. . .] .[58]

Stability is received from God and is found in God, not as a permanent achievement or state, but as a life-long process of conversion to the way of Christ. Christophe also reminds himself of the words of his superior when he made his first vows at Tibhirine in 1976: "true solemn profession is expressed on the day of death."[59] It is God who stabilizes. Christophe explains: he is aware "of being stabilized by the Choice of his great love: Christ loved me and gave himself for me," and it is the awareness of this "Gift" (*le Don*) that "orients my life and stabilizes it in the long term."[60] There is an eschatological focus here: of life oriented toward its end or *telos*, the coming kingdom of God. Stability is simply aligning oneself with this goal: "stabilized there so that your Kingdom may come and your Name may be sanctified." Further, Christophe is aware of "a salvation" (*un salut*) that comes "through the brothers." After a "year of fraternal life, of ecclesial life," he had come to believe that what had begun as being sent on a "mission" from

[58] Moines de Tibhirine, *Heureux ceux qui espèrent*, 615.

[59] Moines de Tibhirine, *Heureux ceux qui espèrent*, 616. Christophe had noted these words in his journal on January 9, 1977, and he alludes to them in a testimony prepared for publication in a book on contemporary religious and monastic life. See Moines de Tibhirine, *Heureux ceux qui espèrent*, 547, 687.

[60] Moines de Tibhirine, *Heureux ceux qui espèrent*, 616–17.

Tamié now required his commitment to the Atlas community:

> Stability is linked to a concrete "dwelling." As I believe in the future of this house of the Atlas as well as in that of its annex, Fez, (a future welcomed as a coming of the Kingdom), it seems to me today that I must manifest this faith by committing myself further to this evolution of a community.[61]

Finally, Christophe reframes the understanding of his conversion of stability as a vow "to convert his stability to Christ [. . .] so that He may use it as he wills," for the sake of the Gospel, in this place, in this situation.[62] An image found in Paul's first letter to the Corinthians seems apposite here: Christ as the rock that moves with us (1 Cor 10:4). The stability found in Christ paradoxically offers freedom to respond to the present. And just as the choice to follow Christ is one that must be renewed again and again, stability is an ongoing choice. In the years that lay ahead, the community's choice to stay at Tibhirine, their "concrete 'dwelling,'" was predicated on their commitment to this deeper "stability in Christ."

Window 3: "all together to everlasting life." (RB 72.11)

Living in community, day by day, year by year, requires commitment to the long haul—stability, patience—and an openness to the grace that allows the growth of fraternal love. It is through grace that human weakness, our incapacity to live with each other and even ourselves, is met with forgiveness and healing. Life together is both challenging and joyful. Under external pressure the strength of that life is tested. Crisis can bring communities together, but it can also tear them apart.

[61] Moines de Tibhirine, *Heureux ceux qui espèrent*, 617.

[62] Moines de Tibhirine, *Heureux ceux qui espèrent*, 617.

The Tibhirine community was not protected from the political and social instability of post-independence Algeria. After the failed elections of 1992, opposition groups went underground, and insurgency became more organized and violent. After the Groupe Islamique Armé (GIA) issued an ultimatum in October 1993 giving foreigners a month to leave Algeria, several embassies withdrew staff. In mid-November Christian was called to the office of the *wali* (*préfet*), the head of the local administrative district, and the monastery was offered a police guard. Christian refused any armed presence but agreed that the monastery would no longer be open at night.[63]

Soon after the ultimatum expired on December 1, four foreign nationals were assassinated in Algiers, and on December 14 twelve mainly Croatian workers were massacred by a group of around fifty insurgents at a hydro construction site at Tamesguida, just four kilometers from Tibhirine. The victims were known to the community; they had joined the monks for Christmas and Easter celebrations. Christian was again summoned to the *wilaya* (*préfecture*). During an hour-long interview the *wali* suggested various security measures: that the monks "take a vacation in France" and that they withdraw to a "protected hotel" in Médéa for the nights, and, again, he raised the need for armed protection. The community's chronology of events notes that these measures were considered inappropriate for "the religious state." A temporary departure was unlikely to be temporary—and their "neighbors would not understand."[64]

There was more than monastic community at stake. Their small monastic community was set in a larger community. Their neighbors mattered. For the Tibhirine community the

[63] "Chronologie des événements (5 janvier 1994)," in *Sept vies pour Dieu et l'Algérie*, ed. Bruno Chenu (Paris: Bayard, 1996), 112–13. This chronology was one of a number of documents sent to Abbot General Bernardo Olivera in January 1994 after the Christmas Eve visit of Sayah Attiya and his men. It is reproduced and translated in Bernardo Olivera, *How Far to Follow: The Martyrs of Atlas*, CS 197 (Kalamazoo, MI: Cistercian Publications, 1997), 54–57.

[64] "Chronologie des événements," 114.

call was not simply to life together, but to life *here* together. Christian left his meeting with the *wali* agreeing to an improvement of their telephone line and to remaining vigilant to changing conditions. It was December 19. The chronology soberly records, "We have no illusions, and we decide to lock ourselves in at night more securely and earlier. We are also aware of being in rather exceptional conditions of monastic *conversatio*. We agree to avoid what the *wali* called a 'collective suicide.'"[65]

A few days later, on Christmas Eve 1993, the monks received their first "visit" from the "men from the mountains": three men inside the monastic enclosure, three outside, all armed, though "without being directly threatening."[66] They entered the guesthouse, demanding to see the "pope of the place." Christian duly spoke with their leader, Sayah Attiya, who was armed with a knife and submachine gun, "pointing out that weapons were entering a 'house of peace' for the first time, where they had no place."[67] They continued their conversation outside, and the *Emir* laid out his demand that the monks effectively collaborate with the insurgents by providing medical, economic, and logistical support.[68] Christian maintained their neutral position but was able to de-escalate the situation. In a later account Christian shared a moment of understanding between them. As their meeting came to a close Christian said, "We are preparing to celebrate Christmas; for us it is the birth

[65] "Chronologie des événements," 114. Translation draws on Olivera, *How Far to Follow*, 55.

[66] The monks regularly referred to insurgent militia as the "men from the mountains" and to government-sponsored militia as the "men from the plains."

[67] "Chronologie des événements," 115. Sayah Attiya is not named in the chronology. Christian gave the details of his weapons in a retreat talk given in Algiers in March 1996 (Christian de Chergé, "'L'Église, c'est l'Incarnation continuée': Récollection de carême, 8 mars 1996," in *L'invincible espérance*, ed. Bruno Chenu [Paris: Bayard, 2010], 309).

[68] The details of Sayah Attiya's demands were deliberately omitted from the chronology of events and are simply numbered (1, 2, 3). They are outlined in a report prepared by Fr. Jean-Pierre Schumacher after March 1996 (Olivera, *How Far to Follow*, 71–72).

of the Prince of Peace, and you are coming like this, with arms!" Sayah Attiya replied, "Excuse me, I didn't know . . ."[69] It was, as the community's chronology notes, "a rather exceptional Christmas."[70] It had a profound and lasting impact on the community.

The Christmas Eve visit marked the beginning of an intensive period of discernment for the community. What was their future now? Should they leave? Should they stay? In fact, their eventual choice to stay was not a one-off decision, but one that they revisited many times over the next three years.

When a community meeting was convened on December 26, the majority of monks understandably favored almost immediate departure. They did note, however, that "one of the Christmas visitors made it clear that the GIA made a distinction between 'Christians' and 'foreigners'. . . ."[71] It was the visit of their bishop, Henri Teissier, the following day that helped them situate their decision making in the context of the broader Christian community: "he emphasizes the effect that our abrupt departure would have on all the Christians who face the same trial." They were one community of Christians among other communities of Christians. All were suffering. Tessier suggested a "progressive" or gradual approach "that would allow for a transition period in relation to the surrounding area and would safeguard the future."[72] There was no question of the bishop's imposing a decision. Nor was it the prior who would decide on a course of action. The community would decide together.

The monks saw wisdom in the bishop's advice and began to discuss a staged withdrawal—planning for the immediate departure of three brothers, for medical care or for study, while the others prepared to leave. In his journal Christophe mentions burning papers—serious preparations were being

[69] Chergé, "'L'Église, c'est l'Incarnation continuée,'" 310.

[70] "Chronologie des événements," 115.

[71] "Chronologie des événements," 116.

[72] "Chronologie des événements," 116. Translation draws on Olivera, *How Far to Follow*, 56.

made.[73] However, by December 31 their thinking had evolved further, and a series of formal "conventual votes" clarified their decisions and future. There was strong consensus on three things: First, the refusal of "collaboration" with the insurgents, except for medical attention at the monastery. Second, a staged withdrawal, "even reserving the possibility of staying if nothing stands in the way." Third, a desire "to stay together" with the hope of returning to Algeria, using Fez as a base.[74]

The chronicle of events (probably written by Christian) is followed by a summary of the "situation" as of 6 a.m. on January 5, 1994.[75] By then Paul and Célestin had departed for France to brief the abbot of Aiguebelle and for "long-planned health checks," and Philippe had departed for Algiers to study.[76] Twenty-four foreign nationals had been murdered, but many more Algerians had already been killed—police, soldiers, and civilians. Many foreign nationals had fled, but as yet no religious had been targeted directly. Most religious communities had stayed in situ. The political situation remained volatile. The economy faced severe challenges. And yet, in all of this, Christian writes,

> In community, we have above all lived an experience of deep communion, moment by moment, welcoming the words of prayer and the elements of regular life as a true gift of God dictating to us what needs to be "said and

[73] Lebreton, *Born from the Gaze of God*, 24; December 30, 1993.

[74] Olivera, *How Far to Follow*, 18.

[75] A separate document in the papers sent to Bernardo Olivera in January 1994.

[76] Not to be confused with Philippe Hémon from Tamié. Brother Philippe had joined Atlas in 1987 as a novice and was temporarily professed on May 31, 1989. He spent time away from Atlas for formation and study at La Trappe and Soligny, and in Lebanon. He later continued his Arabic studies in Morocco (Moines de Tibhirine, "Lettres circulaires de la communauté Notre-Dame de l'Atlas Tibhirine-Fès [Noël 1987–Noël 1995]," in *Heureux ceux qui espèrent: Autobiographies spirituelles*, Les écrits de Tibhirine 1 [Paris: Bayard-Cerf-Bellefontaine, 2018]).

done," here and now.[77] A crucial role played by Brother Luc, doctor and elder![78]

Living, here, together. The situation summary offers a snapshot of an even smaller community preparing for the weeks ahead. There were now just six monks. The guest house was temporarily closed. They remained confident in their local associates in jointly managing their small estate with Christophe, while anticipating pressures at a material level (no different from their neighbors) and ensuring the provision of "the most urgent" in case of "an imposed 'absence'" (hoping to avoid looting, or occupation of the estate by the army). And, importantly, they noted the support they were receiving: "In all this, we feel very strongly the support of our Church. The bishop, the [papal] nuncio, and others call frequently." If the monastic community itself experienced a "deep sense of communion," this communion extended well beyond the monastic enclosure. Indeed, what is clear in relation to the story of the Atlas community is how deeply connected it was to the local church, to its Cistercian family, to the families and friends of the monks, and to its Muslim neighbors. In its last three years this sense of communion, within and beyond the enclosure, grew.[79]

At the end of 1994 the monks once more discussed and voted on their future, reaffirming the decisions they had made after the Christmas Eve visit.[80] In fact, as Dom Armand

[77] *Regular life,* i.e., following the Rule of Benedict.

[78] "Chronologie des événements," 119–20. "En communauté, nous avons d'abord vécu une expérience de profonde communion, instant après instant, accueillant les mots de la prière et les choses de la vie régulière comme un véritable don de Dieu nous dictant ce qu'il y a lieu 'de dire et de faire,' ici, maintenant. Rôle capital de frère Luc, médecin et ancien!"

[79] While Xavier Beauvois's 2010 film, *Of Gods and Men* (*Des hommes et des dieux*), is faithful to the monks' story, it does give an impression that the monks were alone and isolated, so that one might overlook their connectedness with people and communities beyond the monastery.

[80] Olivera, *How Far to Follow,* 18.

Veilleux, the then procurator of the order (1990–1998), indicated, the community revisited this discernment at least six or seven times over their last three years: "Every time a new tragedy changed the situation, or every time one or some of their friends were murdered, they made this discernment again, in dialogue and prayer, and always came to the same conclusion." Further, Veilleux noted, their discernment was not made on their own. Twice Christian asked their bishop, Henri Teissier, to meet individually with each one, "to make sure that everyone was truly free in his decisions." [81]

At the end of 1995 Christian invited a representative of the order to review with them the community's decisions. Veilleux's visit to Fez in December 1995 and Tibhirine in January 1996 (a week in each monastery) was for this purpose, under the umbrella of a regular visitation. By then eleven religious had been killed, so the possibility of violent death, as a consequence of their choice to stay, was even sharper.[82] What Veilleux found was "a community exceptionally united in beautiful friendship and unhesitating acceptance of the decisions taken together." Given their diverse backgrounds, formation, and personalities ("each with a strong character"), "this unity was not a given." [83] However, as Veilleux later reflected, "the miracle"—of community, of fraternity, of communion—"happened, especially during the three years when, in the heart of violence, they had to confront ceaselessly, together, the demands of their vocation."[84]

Community—Christian community, fraternity, communion—is always a miracle. Beyond our human capacity, communion is sourced in the God who calls us, in Christ and through the Spirit, "to be one." As Veilleux observes, the communion that the Tibhirine monks shared with the Algerian

[81] Armand Veilleux, "Le contexte communautaire de Notre-Dame de l'Atlas," in Moines d'Atlas, *Heureux ceux qui espèrent*, 39.

[82] Veilleux's report (*Carte de visite*) refers to eleven martyrs (Veilleux, "Le contexte communautaire," 44).

[83] Veilleux, "Le contexte communautaire," 40.

[84] Veilleux, "Le contexte communautaire," 41.

church, with the people whom they served without partiality, with the neighbors they worked alongside, with Muslim friends and fellow seekers of God, was founded in the communion they experienced with each other—which was itself predicated on each of them living "an authentic personal communion with Christ."[85] Living in the crucible of monastic community enabled a larger vision of community, of communion, without boundaries.

Indeed, this is how Christian understood the communion of saints—as communion without boundaries. The very meaning of religious community is, he suggested, "that of anticipating the communion of saints."[86] Anticipating, not achieving, through the long, difficult process of ongoing conversion that was "founded on the FAITH that one day the face of God will be ALL in ALL and that it is imperative for us from this very moment to seek out this ALL, this face of God in every person."[87] Ultimately communion has no boundaries. In one of his very last chapter talks Christian reiterated this same theme: "community is only possible when there is an openness to the contemplation of the wonders of God hidden in each person, signs of the Unique that are written on our faces as so many differences destined for the communion of saints."[88] The Rule of Benedict nudges in the same direction: "all together to everlasting life" (RB 72.11).

[85] Veilleux, "Le contexte communautaire," 42.

[86] Christian de Chergé, *God for All Days: The Final Monastic Chapters of Christian de Chergé*, trans. Jennifer Rushworth, ed. Matthew Cheung Salisbury, MW 73 (Collegeville, MN: Cistercian Publications, 2025), 148; February 18, 1995. Christian is reflecting on the deaths of the four Pères Blancs (White Fathers) at Tizi Ouzou, killed on December 27, 1994. The four were Alain Dieulangard, Charles Decker, Jean Chevillard, and Christian Chessel. Christian Salenson offers a thorough discussion of the significance of the communion of saints in Christian thinking (Christian Salenson, *Christian de Chergé: A Theology of Hope*, trans. Nada Conic, CS 247 [Collegeville, MN: Cistercian Publications, 2012], 95–109).

[87] Chergé, *Dieu pour tout jour*, 143; August 13, 1986. Trans. Salenson, *Christian de Chergé: A Theology of Hope*, 108.

[88] Chergé, *God for All Days*, 230; March 12, 1996.

Veilleux's report, delivered at the end of his visit on January 19, 1996, a little over two months before the brothers were kidnapped, not only affirmed their careful discernment to stay at Tibhirine but offered the monks encouragement and heartfelt thanks for their courage. It is worth quoting at length:

> During this visit, I wanted above all to confirm you in your fidelity to the graces you have received. I do not believe it makes you proud, because you know yourselves that you are not perfect. But I believe that your community is, spiritually and monastically, at one of the best times in its history. You still need conversion, no doubt, but the best conversion for you will consist in your application to live ever better and more intensely what the Lord already gives you to live: a life of community united in the bonds of charity; affection and respect for your Prior, whom God has sustained and guided during the difficult years that have just passed; a life of continual prayer and assiduous celebration of the *Opus Dei*; serious work to make a living; and, finally, openness to dialogue of prayer and material services with your neighbors.
>
> As a visitor, and above all as the first person to be able to visit you since the beginning of the current crisis in the country, I feel that it is in the name of the Order that I address you. It is a word of thanks to God who has protected and guided you, and to you who have responded courageously to his calls. It is also a word of encouragement. In closing, I assure you of my prayers, asking God to continue to protect and enlighten you as he has done so far, and I count on your own prayer.[89]

[89] Veilleux, "Le contexte communautaire," 46.

Chapter 6

Hospitality and Encounter

My house is a house of prayer for all people.
—Isaiah 56:7

the Gospel tells us constantly to run the risk of a face-to-face encounter with others
—Pope Francis

Among Christian de Chergé's papers there is a note dated Sunday September 21, 1975. It begins,

> A quarter of an hour after Compline, return to the chapel. Silence of the evening, this beach at the shore of the Word where all the words and sounds of the day come to break like waves.
>
> Shadow of the night, in the shadow of a Presence entrusted to the vigilance of the flickering lamp at the sanctuary.
>
> Prayer of abandonment, prostrate, between the altar and the tabernacle: "Seek the Lord while He may be found, call Him while He is near," said Isaiah (1st reading of this 25th Ordinary Sunday, Year A).
>
> And then, this other presence that approaches softly, unusual . . .
>
> So you were there too, still watching from the last pew, in your chosen place for the office of Compline that you

> had loved to pray with us during your retreat and your Ramadan fast among us. Tomorrow, Monday, you would leave.
>
> And here you are too, against the same altar, a brother kneeling, prostrate.
>
> The silence continues, for long time.
>
> A murmur rises, coming from the depths, then grows louder, tearing itself from some abyss, such a peaceful spring, yet irresistible:
>
> 'ALLAH! "God." 'ALLAH 'AKBAR "The All-Great." Sigh. "God." Again and again this sigh, like the child who feeds and who only stops for a moment to catch a breath before asking for more; the sighs of one who knows insatiable prayer, and who is not satisfied being there, turns, so small, towards the All-Other.
>
> Silence. Then you turned toward me: "Pray for me." Another silence, you wait.[1]

Two human beings, one Christian, one Muslim, kneeling, prostrate in humility before the One they seek, the One they long to know more deeply. The note continues with an account of three hours of shared prayer with this Muslim guest during

[1] Moines de Tibhirine, *Heureux ceux qui espèrent: Autobiographies spirituelles*, ed. Marie-Dominique Minassian, Les écrits de Tibhirine 1 (Paris: Bayard-Cerf-Bellefontaine, 2018), 376–77; Christian de Chergé, "Nuit de feu (21 septembre 1975)," in *L'invincible espérance*, ed. Bruno Chenu (Paris: Bayard, 2010), 33–34. The Minassian text includes some additions to that reproduced in Chenu's collection. Minassian notes that the text is sourced from an appendix to Christian de Chergé's "Chronique de l'espérance" 10 (September 1976). Following Chenu, I have simplified the lineation of what is clearly a poetic text.

Ramadan 1975,[2] the prayers of each interweaving in French and Arabic, and through deepening silence, as they "both [*l'un et l'autre*] seek to enter together into the Love that speaks of God." Soon they are joined by "their mutual friend," and, as Jesus promised—"where two or three are gathered in my name, I AM there among them" (Matt 18:20)—their prayer continues to flow, building a "symphony" from the "fusion" of "three different expressions of one and the same fidelity" to the Holy Spirit. [3]

When Bruno Chenu included this account in a collection of Christian's writings published in 2010, he gave it the title *Nuit de feu* (Night of fire), recalling Blaise Pascal's visionary experience and its centrality in reorienting Pascal's life.[4] For Christian, though, the experience of shared prayer on this night was less a reorientation than a confirmation of his vocation to prayer in Algeria, received in 1959 from another Muslim, his friend Mohammed, in the offering of his life. Nonetheless this unique experience echoed through the remaining twenty years of his life.

The night of fire, this unexpected gift of shared prayer initiated by a Muslim guest, came at a time when Christian's radical openness to Islam was not necessarily well received by the whole of his community. His careful account of this experience from "notes thrown on paper" was important to him: on the first anniversary of this event, a few days before his solemn profession, he added, "To this anniversary day (September 21, 1976) I have not seen this brother of one night again. He exists. He evokes for me all others [*tous les autres*]."[5] The other here

[2] Ramadan is the month of fasting, prayer, community, and charity observed by Muslims in honor of the revelation of the Qur'an, and of all sacred Scripture. The timing of Ramadan is tied to the lunar calendar, hence its seemingly late date in 1975.

[3] Moines de Tibhirine, *Heureux ceux qui espèrent*, 377–78.

[4] Christian de Chergé, *L'invincible espérance*, ed. Bruno Chenu (Paris: Bayard, 2010), 33.

[5] Chergé, "Nuit de feu (21 septembre 1975)," 38; Moines de Tibhirine, *Heureux ceux qui espèrent*, 378 n1.

is, of course, the Muslim other. Christian knew the work of philosopher Emmanuel Levinas and echoes here the vocabulary central to his thought.

Christian's experience on the night of fire was possible because of the unbounded hospitality offered by the monastery. Hospitality opens the way for encounter with the other, with difference. In fact, hospitality and encounter are two sides of the same coin. But there is risk here: the guest may require something of us; the guest may offer us something of their own; the encounter may change us.

This chapter explores the commitment of Notre-Dame de l'Atlas to hospitality, its shape at Tibhirine, and the experiences of encounter that in turn challenged and re-shaped the monastic community. Of course this experience includes the encounter with Islam. However, interreligious dialogue in a formal sense will not be the primary focus of this chapter. The significant and ongoing contribution of the Atlas community to Christian-Muslim dialogue has been the subject of much scholarly work. Christian Salenson's thorough analysis of Christian's theology of hope (happily translated into English) reveals the theological underpinnings and the originality of Christian's thought and its significance for the theology of religions and interreligious dialogue.[6] But interreligious

[6] Christian Salenson, *Christian de Chergé: A Theology of Hope*, trans. Nada Conic, CS 247 (Collegeville, MN: Cistercian Publications, 2012). As well as examining Christian de Chergé's thought in relation to the theology of religions, Salenson draws out its implications for Christology ("a greater Christ"), ecclesiology ("the communion of saints"), the problem of difference and unity ("the quasi-sacrament of difference"), and the centrality of eschatology. In English, see also Christian Salenson, "Monastic Life, Interreligious Dialogue, and Openness to the Ultimate: A Reflection on the Tibhirine Monks' Experience," *The Way* 45, no. 3 (2006); Pierre-François de Béthune, *Welcoming Other Religions: A New Dimension of the Christian Faith*, trans. William Skudlarek, Monastic Interreligious Dialogue series (Collegeville, MN: Liturgical Press, 2016); Timothy Wright, *No Peace Without Prayer: Encouraging Muslims and Christians to Pray Together. A Benedictine Approach*, Monastic Interreligious Dialogue (Collegeville, MN: Liturgical Press, 2013).

dialogue was never a *project*, for either Christian or the Atlas community as a whole. Rather "dialogue" simply arose from the outworking of their shared contemplative vocation, lived out in a Muslim country—it was, as Christian calls it, "existential dialogue," arising from the quotidian, from the everyday. So the focus of this chapter is on the underpinnings and the living out of hospitality, together with its fruiting in transformative encounter.

The Guesthouse

While monks have intentionally withdrawn from the world to pursue lives of work and prayer in fraternal community, this same world regularly knocks on the monastery door. The stories of the fourth-century desert monks are peppered with tales of visitors asking for the *abbas'* and *ammas'* wisdom about seeking God. The Benedictine and Cistercian monastic traditions recognize and provide for this. Guests are to be expected and indeed are to be welcomed as Christ himself: "I was a stranger and you welcomed me" (RB 53.1; Matt 25:31).

From its inception in 1939 the monastery guesthouse at Tibhirine had been a place of warm hospitality. After his return from studies in Rome in mid-1974, Christian was assigned to assist Fr. Placide in the guesthouse, and in July 1976 he took on the role of guest master, a role for which he was well equipped and which in turn nourished him. A leaflet intended for guests bears Christian's imprint.

The leaflet outlines the story of the Cistercians in Algeria and the nature of the monastic vocation, then continues,

> The GUESTHOUSE—or house reserved for guests—comes from the same vocation of welcome and sharing, listening and praise, silence and unity, in the joyful revelation of what is unique in each person in the sight of the

> One [l'*Unique*] and for the well-being of the whole universe.[7]

The hospitality offered by the guesthouse was simply an extension of the monks' vocation, an opening of the door of the monastery so that other seekers might taste the life to which they had dedicated themselves—a life of seeking, open to the divine presence, a life oriented toward hope and joy. So, the leaflet notes, "this guesthouse is not a boarding house, nor a hotel (with or without stars!), and even less a tourist *gite*." Rather, the monastery was "a place of prayer and restoration open to all who come searching for a climate of silence and recollection." Welcoming all because, the monks believed, such a climate was capable of "illuminating the walk of a man and/or a woman, on the path of life, with or without awareness of the loving presence of God, orienting existence towards its greater good." The guesthouse was open to seekers of all faiths, and none.[8]

In its provisions for the management of guests the Rule of Benedict seeks, in the interests of monastic life, to preserve a distance between monks and visitors—both physical and social (RB 53.16–24). Separation may have been possible in a large monastery, but in a small monastery like Tibhirine, guests were much more visible, and the work of the guesthouse inevitably involved the whole community. The workload was often heavy.[9] In 1977 Christian took stock of its operation. As well as the guest master, who carried the formal role of hospitality on behalf of the whole community, other monks were inevitably drawn into the work: the brother who helped guests find

[7] Bruno Chenu, ed., *Sept vies pour Dieu et l'Algérie*, 2nd ed. (Paris: Bayard, 1996), 24.

[8] Chenu, *Sept vies pour Dieu et l'Algérie*, 24–25.

[9] This fact is abundantly clear from the sources (community chronicle, letters, etc.) gathered for an anthology dedicated to the theme of hospitality (Moines de Tibhirine, *Heureux ceux qui accueillent: vivre l'hospitalité*, ed. Marie-Dominique Minassian, Les écrits de Tibhirine 4 [Paris: Bayard-Cerf-Bellefontaine, 2023]).

their place in the Offices of prayer; the sacristan and the cantor (making provisions for visiting priests, groups, and special occasions); the cook (often requiring "flexibility" and "imagination"—there was no separate kitchen for the guesthouse as had been recommended in RB 53.16); the brothers undertaking laundry, provisioning, accounts; and of course the porter at the gate of the monastery. Beyond this work, Christian noted that the presence of guests put the whole community "in a situation of reception [*accueil*]"—they were all welcomers.

This necessity presented some challenges to community life: while the prayer requests of guests were welcomed into the Offices, their reception at the monastery gate during the Offices could be disruptive; visiting priests and male guests sometimes shared the monks' table in the refectory; and guesthouse matters inevitably arose in chapter.[10] Hospitality was a work of the whole community. Still, it would be a mistake here to imagine the monks as operators of a supporting, tent-making business. Hospitality was part of their vocation, not a troublesome add-on.

A further, important point: the guest leaflet names the monks themselves as guests—guests of the Algerian people, guests in a country where the majority of people are Muslim. Nonetheless the monks are guests who wish to give or, perhaps more accurately, to bear witness. Their hope is expressed in terms that are simultaneously ambitious and humble:

> these brothers would like to contribute to witness that peace between peoples is a gift of God given to men of all places and all times and that it is up to believers, here and now, to manifest this inalienable gift, especially through the quality of their mutual respect and the robust support of a healthy and fruitful spiritual imitation. Alongside the praying people of Islam [*priants de l'islam*], they profess to celebrate, day and night, this evolving communion, and to tirelessly welcome its signs, as

[10] Moines de Tibhirine, *Heureux ceux qui accueillent*, 38–39.

> perpetual beggars of love [*mendicants de l'amour*], throughout their lives, God willing, within the walls of this monastery dedicated to the patronage of Mary, mother of Jesus, under the name of Notre-Dame de l'Atlas.[11]

Ultimately, God is the host—the host who offers peace. All are guests—monks and visitors—beggars at God's table, simply invited to participate in a "evolving communion" (*communion en devenir*) that is pure gift.

A Wide Door

The monastery at Tibhirine was a place of wide and generous hospitality, as was its annex at Fez after 1988. As well as providing a place of retreat and spiritual nourishment for the local church and for Christians living or working in the region, with an open door to Muslim guests, the Atlas community also built significant relationships with other communities.

At the end of 1977 the community agreed to offer the Petites Soeurs de Jésus space in an unused wing of the monastic complex as a safe place of refuge and refreshment during the hot summer months of the Sahara. Inspired by the example of Charles de Foucauld (1858–1916) and modeled on the hidden life of Jesus in Nazareth, the sisters lived in small communities, of just three or four, seeking to live contemplatively amid poor, marginalized people. At Tibhirine the two small communities, sisters and brothers, would from June to September live side by side, celebrating the Eucharist around the same table.[12]

[11] Chenu, *Sept vies pour Dieu et l'Algérie*, 24. According to Henri Teissier, this information leaflet was attached to the wall of each guest room, not only expressing welcome to Muslims but also challenging Christians to reflect on their own spiritual relationship with their Muslim neighbors (Henri Teissier, "Le monastère de Tibhirine et l'Église d'Algérie," in Moines de Tibhirine, *Heureux ceux qui espèrent*, 34).

[12] Moines de Tibhirine, *Heureux ceux qui espèrent*, 411–12; Teissier, "Le monastère de Tibhirine et l'Église d'Algérie," 30. The Petites Soeurs de Jésus were founded in 1939 by Madeleine (Magdeleine) Hutin. Their first

The monks also built a relationship with a community based in southeastern France, the Bergerie de Berdine (Sheepfold of Berdine), founded in 1973 to provide a place for people who were marginalized and often struggling with addictions to rebuild their lives.[13] Through a relationship formed when Jean de la Croix was abbot of Aiguebelle, the Berdine community approached the Atlas community in 1989 to secure a spiritual guide. It was an unusual request and initially considered to be rather at odds with the monastery's primary focus. However, after some months of discernment, including a visit to Tibhirine by a member of the Berdine community, the two communities agreed on a "twinning" arrangement: Jean de la Croix would spend two months with the Berdine community over the summer, and Berdine members would be welcomed to Tibhirine.[14] It was never a matter of the Tibhirine community's giving lessons to Berdine. With each community committed to prayer and work (*ora et labora*), the relationship was intended to be a mutual one.[15] In the following years the annual circular letters of the Atlas community noted the ongoing exchanges between the two communities: Jean de la Croix's periods of residency with the Berdine community and those of their members at Tibhirine. Referring to the charter that held the widespread Cistercian family of monastic communities

---

community was among nomadic Muslims in the Algerian Sahara. During the twentieth century the figure of Saint Charles de Foucauld was of considerable significance to religious communities in North Africa. His life had been closely entwined with the Maghreb: in his youth as a soldier, geographer, and ethnographer and, after his conversion, as a priest and hermit. De Foucauld was killed at his hermitage at Tamanrasset, southern Algeria, in 1916. He was beatified in 2005 and canonized in 2022.

[13] Established by Josiane Saintpierre and Henri Catta, the Bergerie de Berdine acquired an abandoned hamlet in the Vaucluse that residents of the community have slowly reclaimed. The community has welcomed over 7,000 people since its inception: https://berdine.fr/.

[14] Moines de Tibhirine, *Heureux ceux qui accueillent*, 113–19.

[15] Christian de Chergé, "Conférence du frère Christian du chapitre général 1993," in Chenu, *Sept vies*, 89.

together, Christian says this "twinning" is "a charter of charity under another name."[16]

In a development of immense significance, the Ribât es-Salâm (*Lien de la Paix*, Bond of Peace)[17] found a home at Tibhirine, following its establishment in 1979, meeting there twice a year, in spring and fall. The Ribât, the initiative of Fr. Claude Rault, sought to provide a forum for Christian men and women to deepen their understanding of living and praying alongside their Muslim neighbors.[18] In March 1979 the first small gathering was held over four days at the Tibhirine guesthouse. Part of the plan was to reflect and pray while listening for links between the two spiritual traditions—drawing from both biblical and Qur'anic texts. On this first occasion Surah 24, An-Nur, "the Light," was selected for this purpose.[19] At the conclusion of the gathering the participants met with the monastic community to request the monks' support: they were seeking a place where they might find "with Islam, a place of encounter in prayer," and Tibhirine, it seemed to them, was exactly this

[16] Moines de Tibhirine, "Lettres circulaires de la communauté Notre-Dame de l'Atlas Tibhirine-Fès (Noël 1987–Noël 1995)," in Moines de Tibhirine, *Heureux ceux qui espèrent* (1992), 730.

[17] The Arabic term *Ribât* was historically used to describe frontier fortifications during the conquest of the Maghreb and retains connotations of a place to prepare for *jihad*. The term also came to be used to denote retreats and monasteries (Phillip Chiviges Naylor, *Historical Dictionary of Algeria*, 4th ed., Historical Dictionaries of Africa [Lanham, MD: Rowman & Littlefield Publishers, 2015], 584).

[18] Père blanc Claude Rault was later bishop of Laghouat (the Sahara). McGlynn suggests that the idea of the Ribât arose from conversations between Christian, Rault, and others (Donald McGlynn, "Atlas Martyrs," CSQ 32, no. 2 [1997]: 171). In a letter to Maurice Borrmans (February 20, 1979) Christian is adamant that the initiative was not his own but suggests that the need for such an association emerged, providentially, among a number of religious living in Algeria (Christian de Chergé, *Lettres à un ami fraternel. Correspondance avec Maurice Borrmans* [Paris: Bayard, 2015], 134).

[19] Chergé, *Lettres à un ami fraternel*, 134. Moines de Tibhirine, *Heureux ceux qui espèrent*, 419.

place. The community diary records the monks' commitments to the Ribât:

> We carry them in our prayer united with all who pray to the One God (*Dieu-Unique*);
>
> We will continue to welcome Muslims who come to rejuvenate their faith alongside us;
>
> We agree that the place where they can meet and take stock is Tibhirine.[20]

Christian was an enthusiastic participant in the Ribât. Its establishment gave him hope at a time when he was still struggling with the fit between his own vocation and his monastic community. Christian had an affinity with the members of the Ribât, even though they lived and worked in different situations, in their shared commitment to "living together" (*vivre ensemble*) with Algerian Muslims—a commitment that they embraced with intentional optimism and hope. For Christian this constituted a real link or bond (*lien*).[21]

In fact the Ribât became a place of significant exchange between Christians and Muslims, with the possibility of "encounter in prayer" taking on an unexpected form. After meeting Fr. Jean-Pierre in Médéa on Christmas Eve 1979, a member of a local Sufi fraternity, the 'Alawiyines of Médéa, formally wrote to the community expressing their desire to meet with the brothers. So in February 1980 eight members of their fraternity came to the monastery to pray with the monks.[22]

[20] Moines de Tibhirine, *Heureux ceux qui espèrent*, 422.

[21] At the end of 1979 Christian gave considerable thought to the Ribât during a long retreat at Assekrem, the hermitage of Charles de Foucauld in southern Algeria (Moines de Tibhirine, *Heureux ceux qui espèrent*, 427).

[22] Moines de Tibhirine, *Heureux ceux qui espèrent*, 431. This Sufi fraternity followed the teaching of Ahmad al-'Alawi (1869–1934). It should not be confused with the predominantly Syrian sect of Alawites.

To pray, not to debate. As Christian recounted to the Cistercian general chapter at Poyo, Spain, in 1993, their Sufi friends had made this intention very clear:

> We do not want to engage in a theological dialogue with you . . . because it has often erected barriers that are the work of men. Yet we feel called by God to unity. We must therefore let God invent something new between us. This can only be done in prayer.[23]

The Sufis understood that few Muslims, or Christians, would comprehend their approach, but they emphasized that it was the sharing of prayer that "we felt called to do with you."[24]

It was the beginning of a long-lasting friendship between the two groups of brothers, and a significant development for the Ribât: reflection and prayer together became a lived reality. At each of the gatherings of the Ribât, after sharing their reflections on a chosen theme, the participants, Christian and Muslim, would pray in silence for thirty minutes "around the flame of a candle, a sign, for both [*les uns et les autres*], of the divine presence."[25] After the deaths of the seven monks of his community Jean-Pierre wrote,

> We are, here, at the heart or summit of the true meaning of a monastic presence in the land of Islam. This profound and true experience of prayer in silence, together, before God, gives rise to a fraternal communion that goes beyond confessional differences. We all feel equal, all loved, children of God. So much so that one of the Sufis asked

[23] Chergé, "Confèrence du frère Christian du chapitre général 1993," 91–92.

[24] Chergé, "Confèrence du frère Christian du chapitre général 1993," 92.

[25] Jean-Paul Schumacher, "Les frères de Notre-Dame de l'Atlas dans la societé algérienne, à Tibhirine," in Moines de Tibhirine, *Heureux ceux qui espèrent*, 24.

> us one day the following question: "If we continue like this, where will it take us?"[26]

After their shared silent prayer the participants of the Ribât would together choose a "divine word" or "dhikr," taken from either the Muslim or the Christian tradition, with which they would live and pray until their next gathering. The Atlas community's annual circulars regularly report on meetings of the Ribât, sharing the themes that had been the focus of the gathering and of their ongoing prayer, and offering glimpses of the fruitfulness of the meetings. For example, during the meeting on All Saints' Day 1990 around the theme "Lord, what do you want me to do?"[27] one of the Sufi participants, Mohammed M., asks "What if this 'I' were 'us,' all together?"[28] The question inspired the prayer and theme adopted in preparation for their next meeting: "Gather together, Lord, your scattered people!"[29]

While only Christian and Michel (and later Christophe) were formally involved, the Ribât did indeed find its place at Tibhirine, and the relationships formed as a result were very important to the community. Members of the Ribât were among the priests and religious killed in the escalating violence after the ultimatum of October 1993: Br. Henri Vergès, killed with Sr. Paul-Hélène Saint-Raymond in May 1994, Fr. Christian Chessel in December 1994, Sr. Odette Prévost in November 1995. Their deaths were felt deeply by the Atlas community: these brothers and sisters were their friends. The Ribât continued to meet (though after 1992 not always at Tibhirine nor, understandably, with their Sufi friends). Indeed, members of the Ribât had gathered at Tibhirine on March 26, 1996, the day before the seven monks' abduction from the monastery. The theme, set the previous year, was "you are my (our) hope in

[26] Schumacher, "Les frères de Notre-Dame de l'Atlas," 24.

[27] "Seigneur, que veux-tu que je fasse?"

[28] "Et si ce 'JE', c'était 'nous', tous ensemble."

[29] "Rassemble, Seigneur, ton peuple dispersé" (Moines de Tibhirine, "Lettres circulaires de la communauté Notre-Dame de l'Atlas Tibhirine-Fès [1990]," 719).

the face [*visage*] of all the living."[30] *All* the living—the echo of Christian's testament, written two years earlier, is clear. There he dared to see the divine likeness in the face of his killer: "in God's face I see yours."[31]

The significance of the sharing between Muslims and Christians in the Ribât extended well beyond its participants. As Henri Teissier notes, it was a sign to the whole Christian community in Algeria that it was indeed possible to fulfill its vocation "to be close, spiritually, to their Muslim partners and neighbors."[32]

. . . And a Busy Gate

If the monastery door was open wide to guests who came and went, it was the door opened to the monks' local Muslim neighbors that most enriched, and sometimes challenged, the community. As was noted in chapter 2, ensuring a balance between enclosure and hospitality—guarding the community's life of prayer while also attending to relationships with its neighbors—was never straightforward. Further, after independence, a progressive, conscious shift occurred in the nature of the relationships between the monks and their neighbors. Before independence the monastery had been essentially a colonial employer. After independence there was a period when the monks provided services to the village (a school, a maternal health program in addition to Br. Luc's dispensary), but the overall trajectory moved toward collaboration and friendship.

In his account of his community's place in Algeria Fr. Jean-Pierre Schumacher, one of the two Tibhirine monks to survive, offers examples of this deliberate shift in the relationship with

[30] Moines de Tibhirine, *Heureux ceux qui espèrent*, 484: "Tu es mon (notre) espérance à la face (au visage) de tous les vivants."

[31] Bernardo Olivera, *How Far to Follow: The Martyrs of Atlas*, CS 197 (Kalamazoo, MI: Cistercian Publications, 1997), 129; Chergé, "Testament spiritual du frère Christian (1 décembre 1993; 1 janvier 1994)."

[32] Teissier, "Le monastère de Tibhirine et l'Église d'Algérie," 33.

villagers. In 1988 the monastic community made a room with direct access to the road available for use as a prayer room and Qur'anic school for the local children, pending the construction of a mosque in Tibhirine. In 1991 the community voted to formally cede a water source to the village and to divest itself of land near the monastery that former monastery workers inhabited. The villagers also continued to enjoy access to the park within the monastic enclosure as a quiet recreation space.[33]

However, it was in the management of the vegetable plots, key to the monastic economy, that this shift to collaboration was most visible. In late 1986 the community decided to form a cooperative with some of their neighbors (Ali, Ben'Ali, Ben'Aissa, Boualam, Moussa, and Mohammed) to jointly work the monastery's remaining eight hectares of arable land. The associates were allocated their own plots, while the community provided seed, fertilizer, water, and tools. Expertise, experience, and profits were equitably shared. Produce was sold locally and at the markets in Médéa, including tomatoes, beans, zucchini, potatoes, turnips, apples, plums, persimmons, strawberries, lime blossom, and lavender. The cooperative arrangement benefited both parties: it enabled the brothers to continue their small-scale agricultural enterprise and provided work and income for their associates. They often shared other produce from the orchards—grapes, figs, walnuts, quinces, and honey—with neighbors and friends.[34]

The annual circular letters offer glimpses of this shared life in the garden. Ali, the long-serving gardener, had begun working for the monastery as a young agricultural laborer before independence and was technically due to retire at the end of 1992, as he had turned sixty. Living with his family in a house

[33] Nuno de São José, "Notre-Dame de l'Atlas, mystère d'une secrète fécondité: histoire de la communauté depuis sa fondation jusqu'en 1996," *Collectanea Cisterciensia* 83 (2021): 301; Schumacher, "Les frères de Notre-Dame de l'Atlas," 20.

[34] São José, "Notre-Dame de l'Atlas, mystère d'une secrète fécondité," 300; Schumacher, "Les frères de Notre-Dame de l'Atlas," 21–22.

planted "between two ends of the garden," Ali was considered an honored elder (cf. RB 63.12) and teacher: "So many things that he knows that are not in books."[35] In the 1995 circular (the last) Mohammed the *gardien* (caretaker) is now called *gîrâ* (manager) and happily plowing "while a paint job awaits him inside." Moussa impresses the community with his "bias of joy," Ben'Ali is called "Maradona" as he speedily weeds his onions, and Ben'Aissa dreams of jets of water soaking the gardens, a dream shared with Br. Paul, "master of the waters."[36] Fraternal friendship now orders their relationships.

After Fr. Roland's departure to Fez in 1987, Christophe took on oversight of the work of the gardens. His last prayer journal is scattered with references to the challenges, joys, and spiritual nourishment that came from this work and from the associates.

The monastery gate itself (the *porterie*) was a focus of intensive interaction between the monks and their neighbors as news was exchanged and assistance rendered. The neighbors' requests were diverse: use of the telephone, assistance with reading letters or preparing paperwork, directions to the dispensary, the loan of tools, goods for sale or barter, repairs; eggs![37] The Rule of Benedict recognizes the significance of the porter or gatekeeper as the outward face of the monastery, specifying that this role should be given to "a sensible old man" with the maturity to greet visitors with "gentleness" and "the warmth of love" (RB 66). At Tibhirine the porter was the primary mediator of relationships with their neighbors.

[35] Moines de Tibhirine, "Lettres circulaires . . . ," 1992; 731.

[36] Moines de Tibhirine, "Lettres circulaires . . . ," 1995; 742.

[37] Moines de Tibhirine, *Heureux ceux qui accueillent*, 110; Schumacher, "Les frères de Notre-Dame de l'Atlas," 21. In 1968 the introduction of a mini-bus linking Tibhirine and Médéa increased the traffic around the monastery gate. São José notes that sometimes "the atmosphere at the gates of the monastery is like a small souk," leading to complaints by retreatants (São José, "Notre-Dame de l'Atlas, mystère d'une secrète fécondité," 291).

In 1984 the unexpected death of Fr. Aubin, the principal porter, was met with an outpouring of grief from villagers. The much-loved monk had lived at Tibhirine for twenty years. A steady stream of men, women, and children came to honor his body laid in the entrance to the chapel. Neighbors helped to dig his grave, almost a hundred fifty men and fifty children attended the funeral, and neighbors insisted on taking turns in carrying the stretcher bearing his body. Christian saw it as an occasion that "increased mutual trust" and "faith in the what-is-to-come-from-God [*l'à-venir de Dieu*]."[38] Fr. Amédée became principal porter in 1987 and served in this role until March 1996. Like Fr. Aubin, he was a fluent Arabic speaker, a crucial skill for this mediating role.

Notes made by Christian from a community discussion in 1986 offer an insight into the ongoing challenge of balancing the demands of the gate with the monastic commitment to communal prayer, that it is never a matter of choosing one over the other. Christian considers "door," signifying "hospitality, welcome," and "Offices," signifying "praise," as twin facets of their call—"two services of our particular ecclesial task." In fact, he observes, the door and the Offices are simply "two dimensions of the one commandment"—clearly a reference to the great commandment to love God and neighbor (Mark 12:30-31). How is it possible to fulfill both when they appear to compete? "How to be here and there?"

Christian's notes set out some possible lines of thinking. First, it was not only the neighbors who demanded attention: "God called . . . he rang too." This need to attend to God was understood by guests, but the real challenge concerned those arriving or passing, or those who did not understand the priority of the Offices. Second, in Islam if prayer were to be interrupted it must be begun again. But *salât* is significantly shorter than most monastic Offices. Third, it is God who had sent the poor to the door: "what is the use of saying Lord, Lord . . . if

[38] Letter quoted in São José, "Notre-Dame de l'Atlas, mystère d'une secrète fécondité," 297.

one doesn't respond" (see Matt 25:44). There was an evangelical imperative that demanded a response. Finally, there was the example of Jesus. Though the gospels rarely show him praying in community, the twelve-year-old Jesus rebukes his parents for disturbing his time in the temple (Luke 2:46-49), and in one case his disciples interrupt his solitary prayer: "Everyone is searching for you" (Mark 3:35-37).[39] Jesus was not immune from interruptions to his prayer.

There were no easy answers to the practical difficulties—and a variety of strategies had been tried and new ones proposed—but a core principle was reiterated. There was a desire to hold the door and the Offices closely together:

> Through prayer, we show that we are not of this world.
>
> Through welcome, we show that we remain in the world.[40]

Alongside the garden and the gate, it is impossible to overestimate the significance of the dispensary where Luc offered his services as a doctor, the *toubib*, freely for fifty years. As well as primary medical care, Luc dispensed clothes, shoes, and schoolbooks (donated by his network of friends in France) and provided a listening ear to the ordinary, often poor, people of Tibhirine and beyond. It was a form of hospitality, a sharing, that had a lasting impact on the local population. Indeed his listening ear grew in importance with the escalation of violence after the failed elections of 1992.

Over the final two years at Tibhirine the relationships with neighbors via the dispensary, garden, and gate deepened in significance. The November 1995 report prepared for the USMDA notes the value of the community's everyday work as offering "a good diversion from anxiety," but also the greater

[39] Moines de Tibhirine, *Heureux ceux qui accueillent*, 110–12.

[40] Moines de Tibhirine, *Heureux ceux qui accueillent*, 111. "Par la prière, nous montrons que nous ne sommes pas du monde. Par l'accueil, nous montrons que nous restons dans le monde."

risks associated with some of tasks—especially the gate and the dispensary, and the shopping that necessitated trips to Médéa. But there was also gift:

> Working together with neighbors is the expression of a lived solidarity and a sharing of life, in a climate of friendship that defuses fear. People are not afraid to hang out with us as in the past, and further—we trust each other.[41]

By then the guesthouse was effectively closed, so the gate became the focus of a more intense form of hospitality. As well as assisting with material needs and services, the monks listened to the pain of their neighbors—their "hopes, worries, anxieties, family dramas"—as they together faced violence and uncertainty. They met their neighbors' concerns with "solicitude, understanding, compassion."[42] Ultimately, it was primarily for their neighbors that the monks stayed at Tibhirine.

Looking back, after the deaths of his seven brothers, Jean-Pierre pondered the remarkable distance that the Tibhirine community had traveled from their near closure in 1964 to the "life together [*vivre ensemble*] based on cooperation, esteem, and mutual respect" that characterized the community in 1996.[43]

"A sign on the mountain": The Prophetic Witness of Monasticism

Why is this lived sharing, this *vivre ensemble*, important? The welcome at the "door"—the careful, costly practice of hospitality that was foundational to the tiny Atlas community—had

[41] "Comment, dans la situation présente, rejoignons-nous le charisme de notre Order? (21 novembre 1995)," in *Sept vies pour Dieu et l'Algérie*, ed. Bruno Chenu (Paris: Bayard, 1996), 182.

[42] Chergé, "Comment, dans la situation présente," 182–83.

[43] Schumacher, "Les frères de Notre-Dame de l'Atlas," 24.

its source in the welcome each monk had experienced in the "house of God," in divine encounter. And divine encounter invites encounter with the other. The call of Christ, to communion, is never separate from the call to communion with others. The Atlas monks would have been in full agreement with the words (and practice) of Pope Francis in *Evangelii Gaudium* (EG):

> the Gospel tells us constantly to run the risk of a face-to-face encounter with others, with their physical presence which challenges us, with their pain and their pleas, with their joy which infects us in our close and continuous interaction. True faith in the incarnate Son of God is inseparable from self-giving, from membership in the community, from service, from reconciliation with others. The Son of God, by becoming flesh, summoned us to the revolution of tenderness. (EG 88)[44]

The call to "encounter with others" is the consequence of the incarnation—the encounter with the fullness of God's love revealed in the life, death, and resurrection of Jesus—inviting us to risk encounter with all others, with the loved children of God. Jesus is both the model and the means of this revolutionary path. From this perspective we are all, in the words of Pope Francis, "missionary disciples" (EG 119).

The historic separation of apostolic (missionary) and monastic (contemplative) vocations did not accurately reflect the realities of the post-colonial Algerian church, and especially the significance of contemplative life to the Christian presence in a Muslim land. Henri Teissier understood this well. On his installation as archbishop of Algiers in 1988 he addressed those called to contemplative life in his diocese:

[44] https://www.vatican.va/content/dam/francesco/pdf/apost_exhortations/documents/papa-francesco_esortazione-ap_20131124_evangelii-gaudium_en.pdf. I am indebted to New Testament scholar Micah D. Kiel for this reference and for his suggestion that the word *encounter* summarizes the whole ministry of Pope Francis.

> Together we are in communion with each other in that center of our vocation that you make visible, which is to pass from death to life, through obedience to the will of God and fraternal communion. This witness, in which the strength of the Christian community is renewed, is also perceived by many non-Christian brothers and sisters in the country. In this way you participate doubly in the mission of our Church, supporting her apostolic work and her diaconal service, but also by placing a sign on the mountain, so that whoever seeks God may feel comforted in his ascent towards the summit.[45]

The small community at Tibhirine was one such sign on the mountain. Indeed *Signum in montibus* had been its motto since 1953,[46] and the prophetic nature of this particular sign had become clearer over the years. By 1988 the Ribât had been meeting, along with the 'Alawiyines of Médéa, at Tibhirine for almost ten years, while the monastic community continued to build warm relationships with Muslim neighbors and friends. The community had grown in confidence in their shared vocation. An invitation to address the 17th Journées Romaines in September 1989 enabled Christian to draw attention both to the prophetic witness of monastic life, hidden to most of the world, and to the place of monasticism in interreligious dialogue.[47]

[45] Moines de Tibhirine, "Lettres circulaires de la communauté Notre-Dame de l'Atlas Tibhirine-Fès (1988)," 705.

[46] See Isa 18:3. São José, "Notre-Dame de l'Atlas, mystère d'une secrète fécondité," 271, n2.

[47] The Journées Romaines was a meeting of Christian leaders committed to Muslim-Christian dialogue sponsored by the Pontifical Institute for Arabic Studies (PISAI), where Christian had studied and maintained links via his friendship with his teacher, Maurice Borrmans. Christian revised his Journées Romaines address for publication. The first two parts were published in the *Bulletin* of the Pontifical Council for Non-Christians (73 [1990/1991]) and the third part in *Lettre de Ligugé* (256 [1991/1992]). They were published as a whole after Christian's death (Christian de Chergé, "L'échelle mystique du dialogue," *Islamochristiana*

Vatican II: Opening the Way for Encounter

A brief pause before we consider Christian's Journées Romaines talk. It is important here to note the significance of Vatican II (1962–1965) and subsequent developments both on Christian's formation and thinking and on the Atlas community as a whole. Paul VI set the direction in his encyclical *Ecclesiam Suam*, with its strong emphasis on dialogue. The Dogmatic Constitution on the Church (*Lumen Gentium* [LG]), proclaimed in 1964, declared that "the plan of salvation also includes those who acknowledge the Creator" and that "amongst these there are the Muslims, who, professing to hold the faith of Abraham, along with us adore the one and merciful God" (LG 16).[48] In 1965 the Declaration on the Relation of the Church to non-Christian Religions (*Nostra Aetate*) formally opened the way for dialogue. In 1964 Paul VI established the Secretariat for Non-Christians, later called the Pontifical Council for Interreligious Dialogue (PCID).[49] Algerian-born Pierre Claverie, bishop of Oran (1981–1996), became a member of the PCID in 1987, although he had little time for "conference dialogue."[50]

Catholic leaders from the Maghreb embraced these developments. In 1974 Cardinal Léon Duval, then archbishop of Algiers, and Msg. Henri Teissier, then bishop of Oran, as well as Mouloud Qâcim, the Algerian Minister of Religious Affairs, joined Muslims in the cathedral of Cordoba in Spain, built originally as a mosque, to celebrate Friday prayers—held there

---

23 [1997]). For an English translation see Christian de Chergé, *Christian de Chergé: Spiritual Writings*, ed. and trans. Christian Krokus and Habib Zanzana, Modern Spiritual Masters series (Maryknoll, NY: Orbis Books, 2025), 115–57.

[48] https://www.vatican.va/archive/hist_councils/ii_vatican_council/documents/vat-ii_const_19641121_lumen-gentium_en.html.

[49] Now the Dicastery for Interreligious Dialogue (DID).

[50] Claverie contributed to production of the important PCID document "Dialogue and Proclamation" (1991) (*Dictionary of African Christian Biography*, accessed May 16, 2025, https://dacb.org/stories/algeria/claverie-pierre/). Claverie was killed by a bomb in Oran on August 1, 1996, alongside his driver and friend Mohammed Bouchikhi.

for the first time since the *Reconquista* of 1236. The following day Muslims were invited to participate in the Mass, where Duval presided. At the time Christian rightly deemed this a "revolutionary initiative in terms of prayer" and a challenge to his own monastic community. He expresses the desire that their eucharistic thanksgiving "join in this common approach, and to seek a part of its expression in the spiritual treasure directly inspired by the love of the One God." He continues, "Would anyone have dreamed, only ten years ago, of singing the introductory Sura of the Qur'an as an introit? Saying things like this still scandalizes."[51]

In 1979 the conference of bishops of North Africa prepared a pastoral letter, *Chrétiens au Maghreb: le sens de nos rencontres*, which carefully considered the nature and vocation of the minority Christian presence in their post-colonial contexts; Duval and Teissier were both signatories. Two years earlier, in 1977, a group of priests from the diocese of Algiers, meeting in Constantine, had articulated the new path that had opened up:

> The years that have passed since independence have made us discover another way by which, within the limited and modest framework of our relations, the Kingdom of God—which we believe overflows us on all sides—can be signified and put into practice: fraternal friendship. Purified, humble, disinterested friendship. Not communion and encounter in the ritualized sacrament, but nevertheless a sign and reality of God's favor, a sacrament that belongs neither to Christians nor to Muslims, but to both, perceived by each according to his or her own way, a path traveled together bearing each other's burdens, helping us mutually to understand, to transform us, to serve, to be faithful.[52]

[51] Moines de Tibhirine, *Heureux ceux qui espèrent*, 359. In recent years there has been resistance to permitting Muslim prayer in the cathedral.

[52] Quoted in Henri Teissier and Jean-Jacques Pérennès, Introduction to Moines de Tibhirine, *Heureux ceux qui osent la rencontre: des moines en*

The tide was not all one way however, as Christian's published writing indicates. In 1982, for example, he responded passionately to an article by "a missionary priest in North Africa" published in *Tychique,* a journal dedicated to the formation of those in charismatic prayer groups that had advocated the evangelistic conversion of Muslims. Christian believed the article to be completely out of sync with the spirit of Vatican II and indeed with the bishops of the Maghreb.[53] The case for respect and openness to Islam still needed to be prosecuted.

Christian's 1989 contribution to the Journées Romaines, then, has a rich pedigree. And while the monastic contribution to inter-religious dialogue, beginning with Thomas Merton and Henri Le Saux, had focused on Asian religions, Christian's particular contribution was to draw attention to the fertile ground monastic life offered in relation to Christian-Muslim relations.

Priants parmi d'autre priants: Existential Dialogue

Christian began his Journées Romaines address with the phrase that had come to characterize the monastic community since 1976: *Priants parmi d'autre priants.* I have generally translated it as "praying among others who pray," but English translations struggle to capture the simplicity and directness of this resonant phrase. The present participle *priant,* "praying" (from the verb *prier* to pray), has here become a plural noun meaning "those who pray." The equivalent word in English is the rather awkward "pray-ers." In the visual arts the word *priants* is sometimes used to describe kneeling figures, figures at prayer, in funerary sculpture. Perhaps the resonances of this posture are at play here—and I am reminded of the card Br. Michel sent to his cousin Joseph showing a Muslim at prayer, with

---

pays d'Islam, ed. Marie-Dominique Minassian, Les écrits de Tibhirine (Paris: Bayard-Cerf-Bellefontaine, 2022), 32.

[53] Christian de Chergé, "Prier en Église à l'écoute de l'Islam (1982)," *Chemins de dialogue* 27 (2009): 17.

the inscription "A free man can pray on his knees."[54] Regardless, the phrase *priants parmi d'autre priants* speaks of equality before God: the monks are simply pray-ers among other pray-ers, people who share this common call to seek God in prayer.[55]

This shared call to prayer[56] had a tangible outworking in Tibhirine at this time. With villagers using a large room of the monastery as a temporary mosque, the bell calling the monks to prayer and the muezzin calling their neighbors to prayer came from "inside the same enclosure." Christian remarks: "It is difficult not to welcome the call to prayer, wherever it comes from, as a reminder of the communion that prevails in the heart of the One towards whom we turn with the same abandonment."[57]

Visiting Tibhirine from Tamié for the first time in 1990, Philippe Hémon experienced this same sense of communion in the side-by-side prayers of the monks and their neighbors:

> About six o'clock in the morning, I opened my window, which looked out on the Tamesguida mountains. The day that was dawning was promising to be fine. After the storms of the previous day, the sky was clear, and it was somewhat fresh. Soon there would be the office of Lauds; I was preparing for it when, suddenly—and to this day,

[54] Moines de Tibhirine, *Heureux ceux qui espèrent*, 144 n1. The card is not dated, but it is probably from September or October 1980—before Michel became a Cistercian monk.

[55] In her translation of Salenson's book Nada Conic has translated the phrase as "those who pray among others who pray" which offers a helpful sense of the side-by-side nature intended in the French (Salenson, *Christian de Chergé: A Theology of Hope*, 181). Jennifer Rushworth opts for "praying among other people at prayer"; see Christian de Chergé, *God for All Days: The Final Monastic Chapters of Christian de Chergé*, trans. Jennifer Rushworth, ed. Matthew Cheung Salisbury, MW 73 (Collegeville, MN: Cistercian Publications, 2025), 151. My translation, "Praying among other people who pray" is an attempt to capture the verbal, active emphasis of the French.

[56] Chergé, "L'échelle mystique du dialogue," 19.

[57] Chergé, "L'échelle mystique du dialogue," 19–20.

> it is perhaps one of the most overwhelming emotions of my life—I heard, rising in the silence and the blue sky, the natural voice of a muezzin, a fine voice, prayerful and pacific. I thought at that moment that truly God is present when his people praise him.[58]

Hémon's vivid description of this moment reminds us that encounter takes place in space and time, in the here and now. For Christian dialogue is necessarily located in the daily, the quotidian, and, importantly, is grounded in a community committed to stability, to a place. In fact, Christian stresses, his own testimony at the Journées Romaines regarding this fruitful dialogue is the testimony of a community: "Nothing can be explained outside a constant, communal presence, and the faithfulness of each to the humble reality of daily life, from the gate to the garden, from the kitchen to the 'lectio divina.'"[59]

Christian describes the dialogue that arises in this context as "existential." The monks "never take the initiative," he stresses; rather, dialogue is "the fruit of a 'living together' [*vivre ensemble*], of shared worries, often very concrete." He admits that it can seldom be classed as dialogue of a "strictly theological order"—but that is of little interest to them. (In fact Christian considers "games of this kind" to be "narrow-minded.") But neither does he see this existential dialogue as a purely human transaction. Rather, it is founded in the monks' shared identity as children of God: "the man or woman who comes to us can

[58] Philippe Hémon, "An En-Visaged Good-By-E," CSQ 34, no. 2 (1999): 209. Sadly, this sense of peaceful co-existence was challenged following the ascendency of Islamists in local elections, and the construction of a new mosque provocatively located opposite the monastery gates. A loudspeaker was installed in a tree opposite the monastery. Hémon, on a later visit to the monastery, observed its noisy broadcast drowning out the monks' voices at the end of Vespers: "at times I read on their faces something more than consternation" (210).

[59] Chergé, "L'échelle mystique du dialogue," 2. "Rien ne saurait s'expliquer en dehors d'une présence commune constante, et de la fidélité de chacun à l'humble réalité quotidienne, de la porte au jardin, de la cuisine à la 'lectio divina.'"

only be welcomed in their concrete and mysterious reality as children of God, 'created beforehand in Christ' (Eph 2:10)." So dialogue is unavoidably spiritual (and thus, I would argue, contrary to Christian's view, theological in its deepest sense): "We would cease to be Christians and even simply men if we happened to mutilate the other in his hidden dimension, supposedly to meet him only 'man to man,' that is, in a humility purged of any reference to God, of any personal and therefore unique relationship with the All-Other."[60] Existential dialogue encompasses both the "manual and spiritual," the "everyday and eternal." It has, Christian suggests, "its feet on the ground (and even in the manure), but with a searching head."[61]

Christian does not hesitate to name this work of existential dialogue as prophetic. Indeed he suggests that the monastic vocation is aligned closely with the prophetic role of the church and that the dialogue that the Atlas community lived out at Tibhirine was precisely the bridge-building work required of churches "buried in the 'House of Islam'" that had been advocated by Pope Jean-Paul II during his 1985 visit to Casablanca, Morocco.[62] They were to be "a light on the mountain."

But it is a modest light. There is a necessary humility in this: dialogue at the level of the daily, the quotidian, has an inescapably grounded quality. One is indeed exposed to the concrete realities of the everyday and to the mud, even manure, of ordinary human existence.

Well, Horizon, Ladder: The Poetry of Encounter

When Christian comes to speak about the monastic community's understanding and experience of "existential

[60] Chergé, "L'échelle mystique du dialogue," 2. "Nous cesserions d'être chrétiens et tout simplement hommes, s'il nous arrivait de mutiler l'autre dans sa dimension cachée, pour ne le rencontrer soi-disant que 'd'homme à homme,' entendez dans une humilité expurgée de toute référence à Dieu, de toute relation personnelle et donc unique avec le Tout-Autre."

[61] Chergé, "L'échelle mystique du dialogue," 2.

[62] Chergé, "L'échelle mystique du dialogue," 2.

dialogue," he turns to metaphor. Their experience of dialogue cannot be tied down in propositional terms. Metaphors—some with long, rich histories—allow space, possibilities. I think here of liturgical theologian Aidan Kavanagh's wisdom on the centrality of symbol to the liturgy: "Symbols coax one into a swamp of meaning and require one to frolic in it."[63] Metaphors work in a similar way. Just as the mystery of God's being is both revealed and protected by the use of metaphorical language, so too the nature of encounter, dialogue, and friendship are best explored through metaphor. As Kavanagh suggests, "One resorts to symbol when reality swamps all other forms of discourse. This happens regularly when one approaches God with others . . . ."[64] It is worth noting here that Christian, and indeed the group of priests speaking in Constantine in 1977, finds it necessary to introduce the language of sacramentality to describe "fraternal friendship" with "the other," with "difference." Metaphor, symbol, sacrament all open, rather than closing, possibilities and meanings. They all require one to "frolic."[65]

At the Bottom of the Well: The Water of God

Some of the metaphors that Christian shares are in fact the gift of the community's Muslim friends. So, for example, Christian tells how a young neighbor, M., had unexpectedly approached him for instruction on prayer and had subsequently sought him out for regular conversation. When too much time had lapsed between their meetings (the consequence of Christian's guesthouse responsibilities), M. invented a metaphor that signaled the desire for an "in-depth exchange": "It's been a long time since we have dug our well." These words became the signal that a meeting was due. Once too Christian asked,

[63] Aidan Kavanagh, *Elements of Rite: A Handbook of Liturgical Style* (New York: Pueblo Publishing Company, 1982), 5.

[64] Kavanagh, *Elements of Rite*, 103.

[65] See Henri Teissier and Jean-Jacques Pérennès, Introduction to Moines de Tibhirine, *Heureux ceux qui osent la rencontre*, 32.

jokingly, "And in the bottom of our well, what will we find? Muslim water or Christian water?" M. looked at Christian "half-laughing, half-sorrowfully": "We have been walking together all this time, and you are still asking yourself this question! . . . you know, at the bottom of that well, what we find, it is the water of God."[66]

As Salenson suggests, the parable of the well "speaks of the need each has of the other": we dig more effectively together, and "by the fact of his or her difference, the other is always inviting us to go deeper," beyond the limits of all religious traditions, to "the water of God."[67] We can embark on the "exodus towards the other" with confidence because, as Christian says elsewhere, "our paths converge when the same thirst draws us to the same well."[68]

Pilgrims of the Horizon

The monks' Sufi friends also gave them rich metaphors. In their letter seeking to meet for prayer with the monks the 'Alawiyines wrote,

> Let us show that our religions should not be opposed, but that they are a magnificent pearl connected to other magnificent pearls by the divine thread . . . all different apparently, but each contributing to enhance the incomparable brilliance of the necklace that God has given to humanity.[69]

When the Sufis joined the Ribât for the first time on the feast of All Saints in 1980 they brought with them a verse from the Qur'an:

[66] Chergé, "L'échelle mystique du dialogue," 15–16.

[67] Salenson, *Christian de Chergé: A Theology of Hope*, 50.

[68] Chergé, "Venons-en à une parole commune: Chrétiens et musulmans, témoins et pèlerins de la miséricorde (1983)," 73–74.

[69] Chergé, "Chrétiens et musulmans: nos différences ont-elles le sens d'une communion? (1984)," 112.

> We will show them our Signs,
> on the horizon and within themselves . . . (Qur'an 41:53)

This was an invitation to walk together with openness and hope, an invitation that Christian and the Altas community embraced.

In his Journées Romaines address Christian takes up the metaphor of the horizon: Muslims and Christians are, together, "pilgrims of the horizon." And that horizon, he says, always invites us to go further: "it is always from beyond the horizon of our reason that God comes to us, whatever our respective faiths." We can "expect something new," he suggests, by making the effort to "decipher" the "*signs* at the *horizons* of worlds and hearts," through an openness to listening and learning in "the school of the other."[70] (Christian is, of course, intentionally echoing RB Prologue 45, "the school for the Lord's service.") Embarking on such a journey is not without risk. Like Abraham, we are invited on a "spiritual adventure," "leaving home without knowing where we are going, because God leads us."[71]

However, while the route remains an unfolding adventure, there is a goal, a *telos*. Monastic life has an eschatological orientation, that is, it is oriented toward an end, to hope.[72] For Christian this orientation constitutes monasticism's primary gift to the world: "If a monk thinks he has anything to say here, it is less in the role of an efficient builder of the human city (even though he might do much on this level . . .) than as a resolute adherent of a way of being in the world that is senseless apart from what we call the 'ultimate ends' [*fins dernières*]—

[70] Chergé, "L'échelle mystique du dialogue," 7.

[71] Chergé, "L'échelle mystique du dialogue," 8. Here Christian is quoting from the 1977 pastoral letter of the conference of North African bishops.

[72] This orientation is expressed paradigmatically in RB 72.11: "Let them prefer nothing whatever to Christ, and may he bring us all together to everlasting life."

the eschatology—of hope."[73] With a secure trust in this end in God, it was possible to live with openness and hope.

The Mystical Ladder of Dialogue

Christian deepens this sense of journey or pilgrimage by drawing on the metaphor of the ladder—an image that has its roots in the Hebrew Scriptures and a long pedigree in the Christian monastic tradition, including the Rule of Benedict.[74] He imagines the two faiths, Islam and Christianity, as "two parallel posts" with their "point of meeting in the infinite": both are made in the earth, "fertilized by the same dung, suffering, sickness, death," and both are oriented towards the same hope, pointed "towards the heavens." Here he evokes Jacob, who "on a beautiful Oriental night" set his bed on the earth and "nose in the air" and dreamed of a ladder "whose top touched the heavens [*le ciel*]" (see Gen 28:12). All existence points towards this horizon. The dream of climbing the ladder is shared by all human beings: "Man is not a monkey who would be satisfied with a perch. He has been created from above; he invents the ladder [*scala*] to support his climb; with two uprights, precisely, and the crossings [*passage*] from one to another [*l'un à l'autre*] for support, at more or less regular intervals. Why not imagine climbing them in two lines, this common ladder whose uprights could be our respective faiths?"[75]

Christian is insistent too that the ladder must be anchored "in our common clay." He suggests that "top-down theology" would generally start with securing "the eschatological

[73] Chergé, "L'échelle mystique du dialogue," 3.

[74] For an extended discussion of Christian's reimagining of Benedict's ladder (RB 7.5), see Jane Foulcher, *Reclaiming Humility: Four Studies in the Monastic Tradition*, CS 255 (Collegeville, MN: Cistercian Publications, 2015), 268–80.

[75] Chergé, "L'échelle mystique du dialogue," 8–9. Christian had developed these ideas in the context of his chapter talks on humility in the Rule of Benedict. See Foulcher, *Reclaiming Humility*, 268–72.

anchorage" in the beyond for which we reach. But this would be to neglect the sequence we find in Jacob's vision, where the angels begin by ascending, not descending. The same sequence is found in Jesus' declaration to Nathaniel: "you will see heaven opened and the angels of God ascending and descending upon the Son of Man" (John 1:51). We start from where we have been placed, in the clay of life.

For Christian this eschatological anchor, this "end of hope," was a gift he had received though concrete experience: by the witness, indeed the martyrdom, of Mohammed, who had saved his life in 1959 during his national service. For Christian this expression of love, of the paschal mystery, placed Mohammed firmly in the communion of saints:

> To go further, in direct relationship to my faith in Christ, I must evoke here a Muslim friend I knew at the time when I found myself confronted, with my whole generation, with the harsh reality of what has been called the *Algerian War.* He was a mature man, deeply religious and seemingly united in himself; he taught me to speak of God without concern for human opinion, and to go to Him with simplicity and trust. A deep affection was born . . . This illiterate man did not mince words. One felt that he was torn between his brothers and his friends, incapable of betraying one for another, thus putting his life and the care of his ten children at risk. He was to express this gift concretely by paying with his life for the protection he had sought to give, during a skirmish with his brothers, to a friend more exposed than himself.
>
> Since then, I have known that I can fix at the end of my hope, in the communion of all the elect with Christ, this beloved brother who lived, even in his death, the commandment of perfect love. This beyond of the communion of saints, where Christians and Muslims, and so many others with them, share the same filial joy, it is up to us to signify it visibly, like all the other mysteries of the Kingdom. And how else can we go about it than by

> loving now, freely, those who, by a mysterious plan of God, are being prepared and sanctified through the way of Islam, and by living with them the eucharistic sharing of all the quotidian, of daily life? Further, it seems to me that by entering into the urgency of the incarnation of this reality of communion that is so far beyond us, we exorcise as best we can the stench of proselytism and this fixed idea that tends to reduce conversion to the journey [*passage*] from one religion to another. When there is actually a *passage*, it is that God has intervened further than human mediations, and this too commands respect.[76]

The Visitation: The Feast of Encounter

Finally, one singular Gospel story offers a dynamic image of encounter with the other, an image that opens just such a God-given "passage": the story of the visit of Mary to her cousin Elizabeth, known as the visitation (Luke 1:39-56). Indeed, the Feast of the Visitation, celebrated on May 31, was the "quasi-patronal" festival of the Atlas community—an association perhaps inspired by Charles de Foucauld's commitment "to carrying the hidden Jesus, like Mary."[77] In a retreat talk given to the Petites Soeurs de Jésus in 1990 Christian stresses the importance of the "mystery of the Visitation" for the whole of the church in the Maghreb: it should be given a privileged place in a church that lives alongside Islam.[78] In fact the story of the visitation had long been used as a way of imaging Christian-Muslim relations: it inspired Charles de Foucauld and is found in the work of the French Catholic

[76] Chergé, "L'échelle mystique du dialogue," 18.

[77] Christian de Chergé, *L'AUTRE que nous attendons: homélies de Père Christian de Chergé (1970–1996)* (Montjoyer: Abbaye Notre-Dame d'Aiguebelle, 2006), 394; May 31, 1993.

[78] Christian de Chergé, *Retraite sur le Cantique des cantiques*, ed. Christian Salenson, Spiritualité (Bruyères-le-Châtel: Nouvelle Cité, 2013), 74. An English translation of excerpts from these retreat talks can be found in Chergé, *Christian de Chergé: Spiritual Writings*, 58–62.

scholar of Islam Louis Massignon (1883–1962), who influenced Vatican II and *Nostra Aetate*.[79]

We can add here Fr. Jean-Mohammed Abd-el-Jali (1904–1979), a Moroccan-born convert to Christianity and among the pioneers of interreligious dialogue. Br. Luc quoted Abd-el-Jali in a 1953 lecture given to medical colleagues in Algiers on the social, medical, and religious condition of the peasant population around Tibhirine. In his conclusion he drew attention to the mission of Mary, to which he was himself deeply committed: "I would like to remind you of the approach of the Virgin Mary, who, although Mother of God, did not avail herself of this title and hastily went to her cousin Elizabeth to bring her both the material help of her hands and the spiritual help of Him who in her was the light of the world." Luc then quotes from Abd-el-Jali's book, *Marie et l'Islam* (1950): "The Marian mystery par excellence that must be lived among the Muslim populations is that of the Visitation."[80]

Luc lived out this Marian mystery of the visitation: the dispensary at Tibhirine was dedicated in the name of Notre-Dame des Meskines—*meskine* (Arabic: *miskin*) is a term often denoting the poor, the vulnerable or helpless. The dispensary became a place of perpetual visitation. The image of the visitation is implicit in the thoughts Luc shared in a letter to his friend and colleague George Guillemin during Advent 1991:

> We believe we are searching for God, but it is He who is searching for us. Our only work is to welcome him. Each of my days is an Advent, and it is each day that we must welcome the Lord. In this world of violence, we must hasten the coming of the Kingdom of God by acts of love to break the Kingdom of Violence. These 45 years of presence at Tibhirine, after having given at least 600,000 con-

[79] See Salenson's introduction to the retreat addresses (Chergé, *Retraite sur le Cantique des cantiques*, 73). See also Christian Krokus, "Healing and Creating in Christian-Muslim History: Charles de Foucauld, Louis Massignon, Christian de Chergé," *Theological Studies* 85, no. 3 (2024).

[80] Moines de Tibhirine, *Heureux ceux qui espèrent*, 94.

> sultations, in all sincerity, I can say, that among those, or those that I have received, I have found more things to admire than to fault.[81]

For Luc each consultation was an invitation to welcome the Lord and to participate in building the kingdom of love. Each held the mystery of the visitation. This approach extended to his treatment of those one might deem to be enemies. After the visit of Sayah Attiya and his men on Christmas Eve 1993, Luc continued to treat the "men from the mountains" as well as "the men from the plains." Christophe records one such instance in his journal: "Tuesday: one of their visits. Three of them, plus another wounded one who was brought on a donkey. Brother Luc receives them as if they were You. Everyone around us notices. In the evening it's the army's turn."[82]

The story of the visitation continued to be a reference point and source of nourishment for the monastic community. In what Salenson rightly describes as a text of "rare intensity," Christian offered a meditation on the visitation as part of his 1990 retreat for the Petites Soeurs.[83] The story spoke to the context that the monks and the sisters shared as Christians living in a Muslim country: "I can well imagine that we are in the position of Mary, who goes to see her cousin Elizabeth and who carries within her a living secret—the same one that we can carry ourselves, a living Good News."[84]

[81] Frère Luc, *Tu verras éclater le printemps: Lettres de Tibhirine*, Les Écrits de Tibhirine - Lettres 1 (Paris: Bayard-Cerf-Bellefontaine, 2021), 106; December 3, 1991.

[82] Christophe Lebreton, *Born from the Gaze of God: The Tibhirine Journal of a Martyr Monk (1993–1996)*, trans. Mette Louise Nygård and Edith Scholl, MW 37 (Collegeville, MN: Cistercian Publications, 2014), 105; September 15, 1994.

[83] Chergé, *Retraite sur le Cantique des cantiques*, 73.

[84] Chergé, *Retraite sur le Cantique des cantiques*, 74. The translations here and below draw on Salenson, *Christian de Chergé: A Theology of Hope*, 149–51.

Their encounter invites careful reflection. It is not a matter of Mary simply delivering a piece of news to her cousin; it is news that she had received from an angel. The "living secret" cannot be reduced to bare facts, a transaction.[85] Christian imagines Mary's hesitation: "It must be that she does not know how to go about delivering this secret. Is she going to say something to Elizabeth? Can she say it? How does she say it? How to go about it? Should it be hidden? And yet, everything in her is overflowing, but she does not know."[86] Here, of course, Christian is articulating the questions, and hesitations, that occupy the monks as "bearers of the Good News," the Gospel, in a Muslim context.

Christian continues, "In the first instance it is God's secret." The sharing of this "living secret" does not depend on Mary's comprehension, which is limited at this point. Elizabeth also bears an unborn child, but Mary does not understand the significance of this:

> what Mary doesn't really grasp is the link [*lien*], the connection, between this child she is carrying and the child Elizabeth is carrying. And it would be easier for her to express herself if she knew about this link. But on this particular point, she has not had a revelation: regarding the mutual dependence between the two children. She simply knows that there is a link since this is the sign that was given to her: her cousin Elizabeth.[87]

[85] Salenson offers a helpful discussion of how the visitation helps us re-think mission, including an astute observation: "Defining revelation as the self-communication of God in the present to each person and in each culture is undoubtedly quite different from considering it essentially as a message to be transmitted, whose transmission is incumbent upon the Church, or, a fortiori, thinking of revelation as a compendium of truths to be believed [. . .] depending on where the emphasis is placed [. . .] very different missionary attitudes will result" (Salenson, *Christian de Chergé: A Theology of Hope*, 143).

[86] Chergé, *Retraite sur le Cantique des cantiques*, 74.

[87] Chergé, *Retraite sur le Cantique des cantiques*, 74.

Elizabeth is a sign because she too is the "bearer of a message that comes from God." This is precisely the situation in which the church finds itself:

> And so it is with our Church, which carries within it the Good News—and our Church is each one of us—and we have come a little like Mary, first of all to be of service (in the end, this is her primary ambition) . . . But also, in bringing this Good News, how we are going to go about speaking it . . . And we know that those we have come to meet, they are a bit like Elizabeth, they are bearers of a message that comes from God. And our Church does not tell us or know what the exact link is between the Good News that we carry and this message that gives life to the other. In the end, my Church does not tell me what the link is between Christ and Islam. And I go towards Muslims without knowing what this link is.[88]

We are constrained, because we do not (and cannot) know the full picture. A level of existential humility is needed in our approach to one another.

But as the story of the visitation unfolds there is hope—of encounter at a deeper level. When Mary greets Elizabeth the child in her cousin's womb leaps. Christian proposes that Mary's greeting, though not specified in the text, is one of peace (*As-salam alaikum*! Peace be upon you), and that this "simple greeting made something vibrate, someone in Elizabeth. And in this vibration, something was said . . . Which was the Good News." This greeting of peace, which Christian stresses is "something we can do," makes possible the sharing of Good News—"not the whole of the Good News, but what could be glimpsed in the moment." So, he implies, approached in the spirit of peace, our meeting with those of a different faith can, and does, reveal the Gospel.

[88] Chergé, *Retraite sur le Cantique des cantiques*, 74–75.

He continues to press into the text: Elizabeth ponders, "why has this happened to me that . . . the child who is in me has leapt?" Christian speculates: "presumably the child that was inside Mary leapt first."[89] The encounter is, in the first place, between the two children. Thus, the visitation is more than an encounter between two women; it is an encounter between two unborn children. Salenson neatly summarizes the dynamic at play here: "What the one is carrying has come to meet what the other is carrying."[90] Each bears a word of God.

Importantly, Christian notes, it is Elizabeth who "released the *Magnificat* of Mary"—through her initiative, through her words. He continues:

> if we are attentive and if we understand our encounter with the other in a similar way, in terms of our attentiveness to them and our desire to connect with them, and also our need for the other and what they have to say to us, we can reasonably expect the other to say something that will connect with what we are carrying, revealing a tacit agreement between us . . . And allowing us to broaden our Eucharist, because in the end, the *Magnificat* that is given to us to sing, the one that we are capable of singing, is the Eucharist. The Church's first Eucharist was Mary's *Magnificat*. What this points to is our need of the other in order to celebrate Eucharist: for you and for the many . . .[91]

[89] Chergé, *Retraite sur le Cantique des cantiques*, 75.

[90] Salenson, *Christian de Chergé: A Theology of Hope*, 151.

[91] Chergé, *Retraite sur le Cantique des cantiques*, 75; Salenson, *Christian de Chergé: A Theology of Hope*, 151 (translation modified): "si nous sommes attentifs et si nous situons à ce niveau-là notre rencontre avec l'autre, dans une attention et une volonté de le rejoindre, et aussi dans un besoin de ce qu'il est et de ce qu'il a à nous dire, vraisemblablement, il va nous dire quelque chose qui va rejoindre ce que nous portons, montrant qu'il est de connivence . . . Et nous permettant d'élargir notre Eucharistie, car finalement le *Magnificat* que nous pouvons, qu'il nous est donné, de chanter, c'est l'Eucharistie. La première Eucharistie de l'Église, c'était le

Situating the encounter with the other within the dynamics of the visitation opens the possibility of inhabiting a more generous yet mysterious space—pointing towards a fuller expression of the joyful thanksgiving that is the essence of the Eucharist.

In a text of equal density, Christian presses in the same direction in his 1993 homily for the Feast of the Visitation. In their situation, he notes, it is "the other" who often takes "the initiative of salvation [*du salut*]," and, just as Elizabeth's words were spoken "in the freedom of the spirit," the same spirit can "unveil deep communion, beyond all borders and differences." When this communion occurs,

> Then something is freed in us too, an irresistible word, those of a Magnificat, a canticle with two voices and One face [*visage Unique*], a prelude to Reconciliation that is Sacrifice and Gift of self, a prelude to the Eucharist that is the mystery of faith, and a Viaticum for humanity on pilgrimage to this God who never ceases to work wonders: HOLY is HIS NAME![92]

Christian's writing here is dense, loaded with theological shorthand, because ultimately this is sacred ground—one can only joyfully frolic.

Embracing the Risk of Encounter

The understanding that the visitation invites not only careful attention to the other but the possibility of sacred encounter,

---

Magnificat de Marie. Ce qui veut dire le besoin où nous sommes de l'autre pour faire Eucharistie: pour vous et pour la multitude . . . "

[92] Chergé, *L'AUTRE que nous attendons*, 395; May 31, 1993. "Alors quelque chose se libère en nous aussi, une parole irrésistible, celles d'un Magnificat, un cantique à deux voix et à visage Unique, prélude à la Réconciliation qui est Sacrifice et Don de soi, prélude à l'Eucharistie qui est mystère de la foi, et Viatique pour l'humanité en pèlerinage vers ce Dieu qui n'en finit pas de faire merveille: SAINT est son NOM!"

of communion, inspired the community to articulate a new practice (or, in monastic language, a customary), which was adopted on the Feast of the Visitation in 1991. It was called *"garde du silence et usage de la parole,"* custody of silence and speech. The community's annual circular offered this rationale:

> Conscious of our place as silent ones in the proclamation of the Good News, we recognize the necessity of an opening to the world . . . the simplicity of our relations with the neighborhood preserves us from worldliness . . . the face of the poor can dispose our hearts to the grace of contemplation, to the experience of the tenderness of the Father.[93]

The practices of silence and of care around speech were already normative for Cistercian monks living in community (CST 24), but here is a very conscious extension of this climate of attentiveness to include their interactions with their neighbors, their "opening to the world." It affirms both their prophetic role as silent witnesses of the Gospel and their receptivity to the gift of the other. Approaching their neighborly relations in the spirit of the visitation required the cultivation of space where a deeper exchange between each might be possible—where "what the one is carrying has come to meet what the other is carrying,"[94] where they might hear the Word carried by the other.

One glimpses the power of this intentionality around the interactions with their neighbors in Christophe's journal. An entry in July 1994, for example, echoes the language of their customary:

[93] Moines de Tibhirine, "Lettres circulaires de la communauté Notre-Dame de l'Atlas Tibhirine-Fès (1991)," 727.

[94] Salenson, *Christian de Chergé: A Theology of Hope*, 151.

> Before Lauds, Mohammed asks me for hoes to dig up the potatoes. With a great desire for the WORD [PAROLE], I want to remember [*garde*] this in connection with our work together in the gardens: "You know: it is as if the same blood runs through us, irrigates us together."
>
> Thus, for him, blood speaks first of all of LIFE, of a shared, common life.[95]

On this particular day it is Mohammed who brings the Word.

For the monks of Atlas, opening the door to God and opening the door to the other were of a piece. God could equally be welcomed in the other at the gate, in the garden, or in the dispensary, as received through word and sacrament in the chapel. The monks understood themselves to be guests at God's table. Each had sat at that table and tasted the divine presence—each had his own, different, "night of fire." They understood that ultimately God is the host who invites us to participate in a divine adventure that is both the beginning and end of human life—an adventure that requires courage, humility, and trust. Courage—because hospitality, opening the door and welcoming God (the wholly Other) and the other (whose face bears the divine imprint), always involves risk. Humility—because the mystery of divine encounter can never be fully known or understood, it will always be at least partly hidden, beyond words or concepts. And finally trust—because when we taste the mystery of divine encounter (in meeting, in friendship, in fraternity, in love) we are given a gift to embrace that comes from beyond the horizon of our limited human understanding.

[95] Lebreton, *Born from the Gaze of God*, 93; July 22, 1994; Christophe Lebreton, *Le souffle du don: Journal de Frère Christophe, moine de Tibhirine, 8 août 1993–19 mars 1996* (Paris: Bayard-Centurion, 1999), 119.

Part IV

Loving to the End
Aimer jusqu'à l'extrême

Chapter 7

Given

The order has more need of monks than of martyrs.
—Bernardo Olivera

There is no contradiction.
—Christian de Chergé

On the Day of Pentecost 1993 Brother Michel made an "Act of Self-Offering." The text, written in pencil on a postcard and dotted with abbreviations and additions, was found slipped into a book.

Holy Spirit Creator,
Let me enter—as soon as possible . . .
not my will but yours—the Paschal
Mystery of Jesus-Xrist our Lord in
the ways which You want—I am certain that You,
Lord [J], You will live it in me—and for
whatever purpose you may want. [In the i. of M^{y} and of the
Apo.] Deign to receive this poor offering
of your unworthy servant [Jn 15:12-16 and "friend" M.].
[for the p(rai)se of your glory]
and to consume it in the fire of your Love.
You, who live in the cmn of the F. and of the S.,
praise and glory to you for all the ages.
given on this blessed day of Pentecost May 30, 1993

br. M. the m.
[N.B. Vigil of the feast of Visitation and of the feast of the Aïd-el-Kbir][1]

In 1993 three feast days sat side by side: Pentecost on May 30, and then on the following day, May 31, the feast of the Visitation and the Muslim feast of the Sacrifice, Eid el-Adha (Aïd-el-Kébir). Pentecost, the feast fifty days after Easter Day, celebrates the gift of the Spirit to Jesus' disciples. The feast of the Visitation, as we have seen in chapter 6, was par excellence the feast that spoke of the monastic community's commitment to encounter with Muslims. Eid el-Adha recalls the willingness of Abraham to sacrifice his son (Ishmael in Islamic tradition) in obedience to God.[2] For Michel, 1993 marked ten years since his first monastic profession, and his ninth year at Tibhirine. It was also a year of escalating violence within Algeria. The political and social context of Michel's "Act of Offering" is important for understanding its sense of urgency and the shy signature at the end of this prayer: "br. M. the m."—Brother Michel the martyr.[3]

[1] Moines de Tibhirine, *Heureux ceux qui se donnent: la vie donnée plus forte que la mort*, ed. Marie-Dominique Minassian, Les écrits de Tibhirine 2 (Paris: Bayard-Cerf-Bellefontaine, 2020), 34–35. The text in brackets appears to have been added later (Bernardo Olivera, trans., "Tibhirine Today: Circular Letter to the Members of the Order on the 10th Anniversary of the Passage of Our Brothers of Our Lady of Atlas," *Ordo Cisterciensis S.O.*, no. Prot. No. 01/AG/06 [May 21, 2006]).

[2] Known as the *Akedah* (the binding) in the Jewish tradition (Gen 22:1-19). In fact, Christian at the Eucharist of the day preached on this correlation of feast days (Christian de Chergé, *L'AUTRE que nous attendons: homélies de Père Christian de Chergé [1970–1996]* [Montjoyer: Abbaye Notre-Dame d'Aiguebelle, 2006], 394–95; May 31, 1993).

[3] Olivera, "Tibhirine Today," 6.2.2 (Moines de Tibhirine, *Heureux ceux qui se donnent*, 36). While the meaning of this "m." cannot be known for certain, Michel annotated a published conference on the Lyon Martyrs using the same abbreviation.

This chapter begins with an outline of the deteriorating situation in Algeria in the period up to 1993, the backdrop to the final years of the monastic community at Tibhirine. We then turn to a small selection of Christian de Chergé's writings to witness his concern, in view of an increasingly dangerous situation and the deaths of other religious, to address the possibility of their own deaths. While he directly addresses the question of martyrdom, his primary concern is to clarify the meaning of their shared contemplative vocation in the here and now, the *hic et nunc*. What emerges is an affirmation of life, freely offered, and the priority of love over violence.

Into the Abyss

After independence in 1962 Algeria faced huge economic challenges, and increasing social and political instability. The nationalization of agriculture and industry by its socialist-inspired government failed to deliver economic growth. Algeria's dependence on oil revenues made it vulnerable to the oil shocks of the 1980s—foreign debt increased exponentially, and austerity measures implemented to address this debt exacerbated a downward economic spiral, resulting in significant hardship for many Algerians. The population had doubled to 23 million between 1966 and 1987 with over two-thirds under the age of 25. Young people bore the brunt of the mass unemployment that dogged the country: by the mid-1980s those under 25 constituted 72 percent of those looking for work. Adolescent youths were often referred to as *hittistes* (from the Arabic *heta*, 'walls') for the way they loitered around neighborhood walls. As Martin Evans and John Phillips observe, "these unemployed young men defined 1980s Algeria."[4]

Survival often meant turning to the black market or to petty crime, so interactions with police increased tensions on the streets. Despair, hopelessness, and resentment towards those

[4] Martin Evans and John Phillips, *Algeria: Anger of the Dispossessed* (New Haven, CT: Yale University Press, 2007), 106–9.

in power (*le pouvoir*) intensified—and poor, urban neighborhoods became seedbeds for the growth of Islamist ideology. Spread via street mosques and popular preachers, fundamentalist teaching, hostile to non-Islamic religion and culture, offered certainty and a ready-made identity to alienated youth, especially young men.[5]

Power was tightly held by political elites supported by the military. Corruption and nepotism were endemic at all levels of government and administration. After independence, the FLN was the only legal political party, but the adoption of a revised constitution in 1989 allowed for the formation of other political parties. While technically ineligible, the newly formed fundamentalist FIS was also officially recognized, perhaps in an attempt to incorporate rather than repress Islamism. In reality, as Evans and Phillips suggest, the FIS was an "umbrella movement" rather than a conventional political party—with a "tidal wave of religious fervor" driving its Islamist social and political agenda. Committed to the destruction of the existing political system, it found a ready "bedrock" of support amongst unemployed youth.[6]

In the municipal elections of June 1990, the first free elections since independence, the FIS won 54% of votes, gaining control of more than half of Algeria's communes and the majority of its administrative regions, or *wilaya*. The polarization of Algerian society became more pronounced: Berber culture against Arab culture, secular society against Islamism, Arabist against francophone. Middle-class francophone professionals—doctors, lawyers, academics—began to flee the country.[7] In FIS-dominated areas, previously enjoyed freedoms around alcohol, music, and sexual relations were often curtailed, women faced increasing restrictions, and in some areas *sharia* was imposed. The dramatic rise of the FIS as a political force threatened *le pouvoir*, but with the FLN politically weakened

[5] Evans and Phillips, *Algeria: Anger of the Dispossessed*, 131–34.
[6] Evans and Phillips, *Algeria: Anger of the Dispossessed*, 147–51.
[7] Evans and Phillips, *Algeria: Anger of the Dispossessed*, 157–58.

it was the military that acted—in June 1991 ordering the removal of Islamic slogans from town halls and the arrest of two key FIS leaders.[8]

In the national election held on December 26, 1991, the first of two planned rounds, the FIS won 188 out of 231 seats. In January 1992, as Algerians debated the implications of this landslide, and the consequent prospect of a FIS victory and implementation of a hardline Islamic state, *le pouvoir* took action. In what was essentially a coup d'état, the National Assembly was dissolved, the president resigned, the elections were canceled, and power was handed over to a hastily convened Haut Conseil de Sécurité (High Council of Security), dominated by the military.[9] In the same month Mohammed Boudiaf, one of the founders of the FLN, was invited to return from his long post-independence exile to accept the position of president of the newly created Haut Comité d'État (High Council of State). In February violent clashes between angry FIS militants and the army resulted in the declaration of a state of emergency and the repression of the FIS—including the detention of over eight thousand people suspected of being members in camps in the Sahara Desert.[10]

In June 1992, just six months after his appointment, Boudiaf was assassinated while giving a televised public speech. There had been a moment of hope: Boudiaf had embarked on a program of reform and national unity, seeking to address the nepotism and corruption that continued to cripple the economy.[11] In the Atlas community's annual circular letter for 1992 Christian wrote that Boudiaf's "voice rang true when he gave his program the names of probity, work, participation, national unity." Boudiaf's agenda resonated with ordinary Algerians, and "young people were sensitive to his direct style." With his assassination, Christian lamented, "they are

[8] Evans and Phillips, *Algeria: Anger of the Dispossessed*, 165.
[9] Evans and Phillips, *Algeria: Anger of the Dispossessed*, 169–72.
[10] Evans and Phillips, *Algeria: Anger of the Dispossessed*, 171–73.
[11] Evans and Phillips, *Algeria: Anger of the Dispossessed*, 174–76.

again in a wasteland."[12] It was from that wasteland that violent opposition now erupted. Boudiaf's assassination, probably initiated from inside a regime resistant to his anti-corruption moves, marked a point of no return as the country plunged into an abyss of violence.

By the time Michel wrote his "Act of Self-Offering" at the end of May 1993, the level of violence had escalated further. Rural guerrilla warfare had been replaced by a campaign of urban terrorism conducted through a fluid network of grass-roots cells led by local commanders collectively known as the Groupe Islamique Armé (GIA). It found ready recruits among disenfranchised urban youth. Bombings and executions targeted military and political leaders, army personnel, intellectuals, journalists, and, increasingly, ordinary Algerians, as what Evans and Phillips call "puritanical prohibitions" were enforced in the name of Islam.[13] A counter-terrorist force created in April 1993 added its own set of tools to the "pitiless cycle of violence and counter-violence."[14] As Phillip Naylor observes, "the insurgency was not merely between two sides but among many sides," with "cruelty and brutality" shared, so that the term "civil war" does not really fit. Increasingly the question was "who is killing whom" (*qui tue qui*).[15]

[12] Moines de Tibhirine, "Lettres circulaires de la communauté Notre-Dame de l'Atlas Tibhirine-Fès (1992)," in *Heureux ceux qui espèrent: Autobiographies spirituelles*, Les écrits de Tibhirine 1 (Paris: Bayard-Cerf-Bellefontaine, 2018), 733.

[13] In GIS-controlled areas these included, for example, prohibitions on women consulting male doctors, the prohibition of satellite dishes' giving access to Western films, the closure of shops selling alcohol, videos, and raï music, and the closure of women's bathhouses and hair dressing salons (Evans and Phillips, *Algeria: Anger of the Dispossessed*, 187).

[14] Evans and Phillips, *Algeria: Anger of the Dispossessed*, 188–89.

[15] Phillip Chiviges Naylor, *Historical Dictionary of Algeria*, 4th ed., Historical Dictionaries of Africa (Lanham, MD: Rowman & Littlefield Publishers, 2015), 153–56. This complexity is very much part of the story of the deaths of the seven monks and was considered in the French judicial enquiry that commenced in 2004. The 2018 report of the inquiry cast

All this must have been on Michel's mind as he wrote his short prayer. He, like his brother monks, was aware of the possible loss of his own life in this increasingly unstable environment. He alludes in an abridged quotation—"not my will but yours" (see Luke 22:42)—to Jesus' own prayer of self-offering, born out of his struggle in the Garden of Gethsemane on the night before he died. Michel's desire to be identified with the paschal mystery is a desire to walk in the way of Jesus, whatever its cost. His "Act of Self-Offering" is both an expression of trust in God and a plea for that trust to be realized.

More lay ahead: the GIA ultimatum to foreigners (October 30, 1993), the massacre of the twelve Croatians working at Tamesguida (December 15, 1993), and the first visit of armed insurgents to the monastery at Tibhirine (December 24, 1993). By July 1994 fifty-one foreigners had been killed, including the first religious to lose their lives: Br. Henri Vergès and Sr. Paul-Hélène Saint Raymonde (May 8, 1994).[16]

In August 1994 Michel wrote to his cousin, Joseph Crand,

> Algeria . . . a vision of the Apocalypse (through the window of our study, there is nothing but smoke, fire in the valley, in the hills, in the mountains), until when?
>
> "Martyr" is such an ambiguous word here . . .
>
> If something happens to us—I don't wish for it—we want to live it here in solidarity with all those Algerians who have already paid with their lives, united with all these unknowns, innocents. . . [17]

---

doubt on the accounts of both the Algerian government and the GIA. See also Olivera, "Tibhirine Today," 3–4.

[16] Evans and Phillips, *Algeria: Anger of the Dispossessed*, 195–96.

[17] Moines de Tibhirine, *Heureux ceux qui espèrent: Autobiographies spirituelles*, ed. Marie-Dominique Minassian, Les écrits de Tibhirine 1 (Paris: Bayard-Cerf-Bellefontaine, 2018), 174.

Christian de Chergé on "Martyrdom"

"'Martyr' is such an ambiguous word here." The word *martyr* comes directly from the Greek μάρτυς, meaning simply "witness," but as Christians faced persecution in the early centuries of the church, the meaning of *martyr* narrowed, coming to designate those who had suffered death for the faith—it became a title. The Tibhirine monks understood the dangers around the language of martyrdom: "All those who have died a violent death are considered *chouhada* [martyrs] in this country," Christian remarked in an address to a gathering of lay Christians in Algiers in early March 1996.[18] He promised to clarify the question of martyrdom, but warned his audience, "let's leave it, it does not concern us, it is dangerous."[19] The word *martyr* is still fraught in our contemporary world: the title is regularly claimed in relation to those killed, both combatants and civilians, in situations of violent conflict—claims often made in the name of God. It is dangerous language.

Christian was right to advise caution. However, in order to place martyrdom in its proper place (not our focus, not our concern), it was necessary to clarify its meaning in a context where violent death was an ever-present reality. As prior of Notre-Dame de l'Atlas, Christian did not shy away from this responsibility. It is possible to observe how he developed his thinking in a number of surviving texts, including his 1994 and 1995 Holy Week homilies, and his last series of chapter talks, delivered between November 1995 and March 1996. He shared some of this thinking in his address to lay Christians in Algiers on March 8, 1996, three weeks before he and six other brothers were kidnapped from the monastery at Tibhirine. What is particularly compelling about this material is that it is lived theology: Christian was working out his theology while living its reality. It is not mere theory.

[18] Christian de Chergé, "'L'Église, c'est l'Incarnation continuée': Récollection de carême, 8 mars 1996," in *L'invincible espérance*, ed. Bruno Chenu (Paris: Bayard, 2010), 311.

[19] Chergé, "'L'Église, c'est l'Incarnation continuée,'" 299.

The "Martyrdom" of Love: The Homily for Holy Thursday

Christian's homilies for the great three days of the Paschal Triduum in 1994—just a few months after the slaughter of the Croatians and the Christmas Eve visit—take "martyrdom" as their theme: the "martyrdom" of charity on Holy Thursday, the "martyrdom" of innocence on Good Friday, and the "martyrdom" of hope at the Easter Vigil.[20] They are an extraordinary set of homilies—clarifying, honest, challenging—delivered to a community that had been marked by the events of the previous months. It is notable that in the titles of each, *martyrdom* is placed in quotation marks. Christian uses the language of martyrdom with caution. The first of this series forms the foundation of Christian's thinking.

In his homily for Holy Thursday Christian carefully grounds his understanding of martyrdom in love. He observes that by the end of the twentieth century there had been an important shift in emphasis in the church's understanding of martyrdom: from "a witness to faith" to a "witness of supreme charity" (notably in the case of Maximilian Kolbe[21]). He notes that the Arabic word for martyr, *shahîd* (plural: *shouhada*), shares the same root as *shahâda*, the Islamic declaration of faith, and that Christianity had similarly traditionally understood martyrdom as directly related to the profession of faith—in Christ and in "Christian dogma." However, Christian suggests, such an understanding presents difficulties. First, faith now admits "doubt and questioning," so that the stories of the assured faith of the early Christian martyrs "astonish us." Second, in the "acts of the martyrs," some features of these early texts

[20] For English translations of these homilies see Christian de Chergé, *Christian de Chergé: Spiritual Writings*, ed. and trans. Christian Krokus and Habib Zanzana, Modern Spiritual Masters series (Maryknoll, NY: Orbis Books, 2025), 76–91.

[21] Maximilian Kolbe (1894–1941), a Franciscan, offered his life for another Polish prisoner at Auschwitz. He was canonized as a "martyr of charity" by John Paul II in 1982.

now "confuse and offend us": particularly "the harshness of these witnesses of the faith towards their judges, their awareness of being 'pure', this expressed certainty that their persecutor will go straight to hell." We are not far from fundamentalism, Christian suggests.[22]

Yet Jesus offers a different starting place: love, a love that is radically inclusive and forgiving. The words of the Gospel of John, read on Holy Thursday, signal the extent of this love: "Having loved his own who were in the world, he loved them to the end" (John 13:1). Around the table, on the night before he died, Jesus shared bread with *all* who were gathered, even his betrayer. He washes *all* their feet. He calls them *all* friends:

> The witness of Jesus unto death, his "martyrdom," is a martyrdom of love, of love for man, for all men, even for thieves, even for assassins and executioners, those who act in the darkness, ready to treat you as *an animal for slaughter* (Ps 49), or to torture you to death because one of your own has become one of "theirs." Yet he had warned: *If you only love your friends, what are you doing there that is extraordinary? Even the pagans* [. . .] *do the same*! [see Matt 5:46-47] For [Jesus], friends and enemies have a mutual source in the same Father: *You are all brothers*!
>
> That is because the martyrdom of love includes forgiveness. This is the perfect gift, that which God gives without reserve. So much so that washing feet, sharing bread, giving oneself over to death, and forgiveness, are all one and for all: *for you, and for the multitude, for the forgiveness of sins.* [see Matt 26:28] [23]

Jesus' demonstration of love "to the end, to the extreme" (*jusqu'à la fin, jusqu'à l'extrême*), can be seen in each of his actions: in the washing of feet, even of his betrayer, the sharing of bread with all, the laying down of his life, and his offering

[22] Chergé, *L'AUTRE que nous attendons*, 419; March 31, 1994.
[23] Chergé, *L'AUTRE que nous attendons*, 419–20; March 31, 1994.

of forgiveness to his killers. There is freedom here, Christian says, because "the Son's choice coincides completely with the Father's choice of love." So Jesus is able to say, "My life, no one takes it, but it is I who give it" [see John 10:18].[24]

Given. Christian reminds his community that this same self-offering, the giving of oneself to love, underpins the monastic vocation: "Giving one's life for the love of God, in advance, unconditionally, this is what we have done . . . or at least what we believed we were doing. We did not ask then why or how. We relied on God to use this gift, to its destination, day after day, to the last."[25]

Of course the reality is that even monks are unable to fulfill this vow of self-offering: "it is impossible for us to do everything for love, and therefore to pretend that our life is a testimony of love, a 'martyrdom' of love."[26] Christian returns here to the daily, the quotidian, as he does so often. It is in the daily that one is most tested. This is not about grand gestures. Washing a brother's feet on Holy Thursday is relatively easy, but what if this were daily, and for all comers? It is often easier to give to one person than another—but the call is to love all. This commitment is costly; it does not come without struggle. Christian holds up the example of Luc, living out his vocation as a doctor, which "leads him to care for all the sick, 'even the devil,'" as Br. Luc would add.[27]

It is the same commitment, to love, that underpinned the monks' decision not to take sides in the violence engulfing Algeria: not as "a neutrality that washes its hands," but rather "to remain free to love all, because that is our choice, in the name of Jesus and with his grace." Christian then speaks more personally:

> If I have given my life to all Algerians, I have also given it to the "emir" S. A. [Sayat Attiya]. He will not take it

[24] Chergé, *L'AUTRE que nous attendons*, 419–20; March 31, 1994.
[25] Chergé, *L'AUTRE que nous attendons*, 420; March 31, 1994.
[26] Chergé, *L'AUTRE que nous attendons*, 420; March 31, 1994.
[27] Chergé, *L'AUTRE que nous attendons*, 420; March 31, 1994.

> from me, even if he decides to inflict the same treatment on me as on our Croatian friends. Yet I sincerely hope that he will respect it, in the name of the love that God has also inscribed in his vocation as a man. Jesus could not wish for the betrayal of Judas. Still calling him "friend," he addresses buried love. He seeks his Father in this man. I even believe that he found him.[28]

Framing martyrdom in this way, as the consequence of love, allows one to move beyond religious and confessional boundaries—it becomes the "gift of the Spirit." So Christian names as martyrs of love a man who had recently saved the life of a wounded policeman near the Basilica of Notre-Dame d'Afrique in Algiers and who was then killed a few days later for his act of charity, together with the Bosnian Muslim worker who risked his life to save others at Tamesguida. And from his own history Christian names Mohammed, who had similarly paid with this own life at the hand of his brother Muslims for protecting his young friend.[29] Where there is charity and love, God

[28] Chergé, *L'AUTRE que nous attendons*, 420; March 31, 1994.

[29] I am grateful to Christian Krokus and Habib Zanzana for clarifying this reference. Chergé, *Christian de Chergé: Spiritual Writings*, 77. In his homily for Holy Thursday 1995, delivered to the small community in Fez, Christian speaks personally and poetically of the gift of life given freely:

> He loved me to the end, to the end of me, to the end of him . . .
> He loved me in his way, which is not mine.
> He loved me graciously, gratuitously . . . I might perhaps have liked it to be more discreet, less solemn.
> He loved me as I do not know how to love: this simplicity, this self-forgetting, this humble service without self-gratification, without any self-regard.
> He loved me with the benevolent but inexorable authority of a father, and also with the indulgent and somewhat nervous tenderness of a mother.

As Christian Salenson observes, it is impossible to tell if Christian is speaking of Mohammed, Christ, or both (Christian Salenson, *Christian de Chergé: A Theology of Hope*, trans. Nada Conic, CS 247 [Collegeville,

is there—Christian quotes the words of the antiphon sung for the washing of the feet on Holy Thursday: *ubi caritas et amor Deus ibi est*. He returns to the radical challenge of Jesus' own martyrdom: "no greater love than to lay down one's life for one's friends . . . You are, all, my friends!" [see John 15:13]. Even the devil, we might add with Luc. This challenge is beyond our own capacities, Christian concludes, but in the gift of the Eucharist, given on this same Holy Thursday, we are given "his flesh to eat, to assimilate, as the Bread of our witness"—the nourishment that enables us to become witnesses to love.[30]

"No One Should Run Towards Martyrdom"

The commitment to the priority of love has significant consequences for how one approaches the possibility of martyrdom. After the Christmas Eve visit of Sayat Attiya to the monastery, Christian naturally sought the advice of both the Cistercian abbot general, Bernardo Olivera, and their local bishop, Henri Teissier. When Christian met the abbot general at Timadeuc in early 1994, Olivera said, "The Order needs monks more than it needs martyrs." He continued, "So you must do everything you can to avoid a dramatic end that would be of no use to anybody." Teissier had similarly advised that "the hardest thing for everyone would be for you to meet with the same fate as the Croatians. We cannot run this risk."[31] Underpinning their advice, Christian suggests, is a principle

---

MN: Cistercian Publications, 2012], 26). Chergé, *L'AUTRE que nous attendons*, 455–56; April 13, 1995 (trans. Salenson).

[30] Chergé, *L'AUTRE que nous attendons*, 420–21; March 31, 1994.

[31] Christian de Chergé, *God for All Days: The Final Monastic Chapters of Christian de Chergé*, trans. Jennifer Rushworth, ed. Matthew Cheung Salisbury, MW 73 (Collegeville, MN: Cistercian Publications, 2025), 184; November 7, 1995. Christian's final two series of chapter talks have been translated into English. For the original French publication of all surviving chapter talks see Christian de Chergé, *Dieu pour tout jour: chapitres de Père Christian de Chergé à la communauté de Tibhirine (1985–1996)*, 2nd ed. (Montjoyer: Abbaye Notre-Dame d'Aiguebelle, 2006). For simplicity, I

that he believes "to be profoundly true" and part of the tradition of the church, especially in North Africa: "we do not have the right to hasten our own deaths, including through 'martyrdom.' We could not, without committing a sin, place our neighbors in the position of being tempted to kill by confronting them directly on their own ground, where temporary blindness encloses them."[32] We must not cause our neighbor to sin. This, as Christian Salenson confirms, is very much the traditional teaching of the church. The third-century North African saint and martyr Cyprian, to whom Christian alludes in his words, had taught that "no one should run toward martyrdom."[33]

Charism and "Martyrdom": The Final Chapter Talks

To focus on martyrdom is to be diverted from the business of living. Christian considers Olivera's comment, "the Order needs monks more than it needs martyrs," to be a distraction from the real question, "which is that of knowing whether the Order needs us in this country, at the present time . . . If our Church, our surroundings need us?"[34] The answer that the community had discerned, more than once, was "Yes": the call still stands. Christian's final series of chapter talks, delivered between November 4, 1995, and March 16, 1996, focus on the nature of this call, the community's charism, in the *hic et nunc,* the here and now—in the midst of civil unrest and violence.

The chapter talks have been grouped for publication under a title taken from the title of the first talk in the series: "The Charism of the Martyr." There is a subtle difference in the titles, though: for his chapter talk Christian places the word *martyr* in quotation marks, as he does in his earlier homily, but these quotation marks are missing in the series title. How would

---

have only cited the French publication when I have departed substantially from Rushworth's translations.

[32] Chergé, *God for All Days*, 184; November 7, 1995.

[33] Salenson, *Christian de Chergé: A Theology of Hope*, 159.

[34] Chergé, *God for All Days*, 185; November 7, 1995.

Christian have titled this series? I am not convinced that the word *martyr* would have appeared at all. His immediate concern was to help the community consider how their Cistercian charism could be lived out in the situation in which they now found themselves—the question that had been posed to each of the religious congregations remaining in Algeria by the Union des Supérieurs Majeurs d'Algeria (USMDA).[35] This situation necessitated a careful reflection on the meaning of the lives already lost and on the possibility of their own deaths. Hence death, martyrdom, the paschal mystery were all on the agenda—but in the service of a more important question, one that all religious, and indeed all Christians in Algeria faced. For his Algiers talk in March 1996 Christian reframed the question inclusively: "what is our call, the grace that is given to us to live?"[36] The emphasis is always on living.

Christian's final series of chapter talks begins in the wake of the deaths of Sisters Bibiane Leclerq and Angèline-Marie Littlejohn, on September 3, 1995. Sister Odette Prévost was killed on November 10, 1995, a week after Christian's first talk, "the charism of the 'martyr.'" Eleven religious and priests had now been killed. The title and the direction of this first talk was inspired by the papal legate, Msgr. Francisco Javier Errázuriz. Speaking in relation to the deaths of Sisters Bibiane and Angèline, Errázuriz had quoted extracts from the constitutions of their order, the Sœurs missionaires de Notre-Dame des Apôtres, which simply drew attention to the continuity between the sisters' vowed lives and their deaths.[37] In his own talk, Christian says, "it is indeed this consistency between their fundamental vocation [*ideal de vie*] and their concrete existence, lived out in their daily lives (for more than thirty years), and not only at the last minute, that struck us, just as it struck the

[35] The report prepared by the community for the meeting of USMDA on November 21, 1995, is discussed in the Introduction to this book. It is notable that the word *martyr* does not appear in the report.

[36] Chergé, "'L'Église, c'est l'Incarnation continuée,'" 291.

[37] The Sœurs missionaires de Notre-Dame des Apôtres (Missionary Sisters of Our Lady of the Apostles) were founded in 1876 in Lyon.

legate."[38] They had faithfully lived out their charism to the end of their lives. Their deaths needed to be viewed in the context of their call. What might help the monks to live out their own charism, with its contemplative rather than missionary focus?

Among the extracts from the sisters' constitution quoted by the papal legate and shared by Christian with his community was a clear statement of the connection between the sisters' daily lives and the paschal mystery: "By accepting the self-denial [*dépouillement*] and difficulties of each day, we enter, following Christ, into the paschal mystery of death and resurrection inseparable from all apostolic life (article 11)."[39] Inspired by this example, Christian began a search within their own Cistercian heritage, embarking on "a few mini-chapters on the place of the paschal mystery of death and life in the Rule of Saint Benedict and in our Constitutions."[40] In fact, over the course of the series Christian ranges widely across this heritage. He begins by reading the "Declaration of the General Chapter of 1969 on the Cistercian Life," then turns to the 1969 "Statute on Unity and Pluralism," which articulates a series of guidelines on the essentials of the Cistercian charism. He rereads the Cistercian Constitutions and the guidelines on formation, *Ratio Institutionis*, as well as the Rule of Benedict, and trawls through various papal documents, including *Lumen Gentium*, *Perfectae Caritatis*, *Ad Gentes*, and *Gaudium et Spes*. Often he expresses disappointment with how little he finds that directly addresses his quest.

What he does find in these documents he often makes implicit rather than explicit. The chapter talks themselves meander somewhat—unlike earlier series, they never seem as tightly resolved—perhaps indicating the extraordinary pressure that the community was under. Nevertheless, Christian expresses a sustained confidence in the gift of the community's contem-

[38] Chergé, *God for All Days*, 182; November 4, 1995. Translation modified.

[39] Chergé, *God for All Days*, 182; November 4, 1995. Translation modified.

[40] Chergé, *God for All Days*, 182; November 4, 1995.

plative charism for the here and now, the *hic et nunc*. He is faced with an almost impossible task as prior of the community: both preparing the brothers for the very real possibility of their deaths and encouraging them to continue to live, and to live well. What is noticeable in the chapter talks, however, is the way Christian returns again and again to the quotidian, to the monks' daily living out of their vocation and, as we will see, the way he grounds this living theologically through an understanding of the incarnation and the paschal mystery as both dynamic and coextensive.

Monasticism and Martyrdom

Martyrdom, understood as "dying for the faith," is exceptional for Cistercians, as it is for most Christians. However, what monks understand, Christian reiterates, is that their lives are already given:

> [The monk] knows that his life does not belong to him, that it is definitively linked to the love of God that his faith inspires in him. He knows that the GIFT of his life becomes currency day by day, humbly and tenaciously. Because he wishes to be a friend of the whole of humankind, he cannot imagine a death that would injure another person, whoever they are, making him a murderer of his brother. If such a situation presents itself, God ALONE provides the lamb for the sacrifice![41]

Christian finds confirmation too in the writing of Jeanne-Françoise de Chantel (1572–1641), who noted that few of the church fathers were martyrs but that there is a "martyrdom of love" that consists in the unending giving of oneself to God,

[41] Chergé, *Dieu pour tout jour*, 535; December 12, 1995. The "lamb for the sacrifice" is a dual reference to the provision of the ram in the story of the *Akedah* (Gen 22:1-19) and to Jesus, understood as the lamb of God (John 1:29).

until death. This is no easy route. Indeed, de Chantel styles it a form of madness! "Love is as MAD [*FOU*] as death," she says, playing with the familiar words of the Song of Songs, "love is strong as death" (Song 8:6). She suggests that "the martyrs of love suffer infinitely more in preserving their life to do the will of God than if they laid it down as a testimony of their faith, their love, and their constancy."[42] Christian sees here a note of encouragement for the path that they have chosen as a community—the same "madness" of risking both love and death.

In fact, this form of martyrdom is to be found in the story of Christian monasticism. The rise of monasticism in the fourth century was in part a reaction to the too-settled position of Christianity after the conversion of Constantine (312 CE). Persecution, and hence martyrdom, had begun to recede, and the idea of monasticism as a form of martyrdom soon emerged.[43] Christian draws attention to this development and to the example of Anthony fleeing to the deserts of Egypt (the locale of the first Passover), not only to "lose his life" but also to do battle with "the traditional Enemy of the human race." That was a different sort of martyrdom. The interior combat takes place not just once, but over decades—"passing over" is a long, slow, iterative process. For Christian this process is at the heart of the monastic vocation: "It is this shedding of flesh and blood drop by drop in the desert to which we must constantly return in order to adhere to the specific fecundity of our lives *hic et nunc*."[44] The monastery is indeed a desert, or, as André Louf

[42] Chergé, *God for All Days*, 193; December 14, 1995 (translation modified).

[43] Andrew Louth, *The Origins of the Christian Mystical Tradition: From Plato to Denys*, 2nd ed. (Oxford: Oxford University Press, 2007), 98–99. This struggle is often referred to as "white martyrdom," as opposed to "red martyrdom," where blood is shed.

[44] Chergé, *God for All Days*, 195–96; December 16, 1995.

suggests, "a crucible" where one is painfully but beautifully remade.[45]

Christian had found a commitment to this long "passing over" in the Cistercian "Statute on Unity and Pluralism" (SUP), a precis of the key elements of Cistercian life. Each of its eleven guidelines articulating the Cistercian essentials, Christian suggests, is the site of "something like a perpetual Passover [*Pâques*] [. . .] the site of a death to oneself in view of a life for and with God, for and with the community in its mission here and now."[46] The paschal mystery of dying and rising underpins the whole monastic journey.

Christian uses the SUP as a sort of checklist and is able to confirm that the community's practice continues to sit well with the guidelines. Some elements of the SUP guidelines particularly resonate with the monks' experiences. The monastery has been visited three times by groups of insurgents, each time at nightfall.[47] So the commitment to nocturnal prayer (guideline 4), especially the timing of the Office of Vigils, offers both an antidote to "the fear of the night that is inhabited by 'others'" and the promise of resurrection as the monks "watch for the coming of the Lord." Christian notes that this watching in anticipation is a "rare" allusion in the guidelines to the paschal mystery—so that the night becomes "the time of resurrection (and not only a place of death)." The commitment to "continual prayer" (guideline 5) has a particular urgency "when the end seems to be nearing"—the presence of "the one who waits for us" eases this endeavor. Similarly, the long-practiced "atmosphere of recollection and silence" (guideline 6), including the "great silence" between Compline and Vigils, plays a significant

[45] André Louf, *In the School of Contemplation*, trans. Paul Rowe, MW 48 (Collegeville, MN: Cistercian Publications, 2015), 73.

[46] Chergé, *God for All Days*, 187; November 14, 1995. For the SUP see https://ocso.org/wp-content/uploads/2021/06/Statute-Unity-and-Pluralism-EN.pdf.

[47] December 24, 1993; September 30 and December 30, 1994 (Chergé, *God for All Days*, 189; November 18, 1995).

role in helping the community deal with the emotional toll of its situation:

> A degree of agitation and anxiety linked to events can harm this atmosphere, which is always delicate. Each one of us must face up to these new difficulties. We confirm that the "great silence," which has passed into our habits and our reflexes, has had a beneficial role, as the renewer of serenity . . . in the measure that it is lived together, as an appropriate language of compassion, hope, and communion in spite of everything, with EVERYONE if possible.[48]

The practice of silence should not lead to isolation. It is not about each monk being abandoned to struggle alone. Silence is grounded in the commitment to fraternal community; it is shared.

The community's monastic practices, then, provide not just tools but habits, deeply embedded through their long commitment to the "desert," helping them to live this "perpetual *Pâques*." Christian offers encouragement that living ever more deeply into their monastic tradition, into their charism, remains their shared call.

Incarnation: The *premier visage* of the Paschal Mystery

As Christian proceeds with his search "for the traces of the 'paschal mystery' in the Cistercian charism"[49] he bumps into Christmas. This is simply the playing out of the rhythm of the liturgical year, but it causes him to pause to consider the significance of the incarnation for thinking about the paschal mystery. It proves to be a decisive and productive move. In his chapter talk for December 23, 1995, with the second anniver-

[48] Chergé, *God for All Days*, 189; November 18, 1995.
[49] Chergé, *God for All Days*, 210; February 1, 1996.

sary of the Christmas Eve visit not far from consciousness, Christian sets out in this new direction.

What has become clear to Christian is that the paschal mystery must be imagined more expansively—beyond a narrow focus on the passion, death, and resurrection of Jesus. He finds the foundation for such "an all-encompassing vision" in the incarnation: "Everything is *Pâque,* passage, in the life of the Lord among mortals, God's passing down to earth, God's participation in human finitude, and the progressive introduction of humankind into the glory of God."[50] The word *Pâque,* in French, denotes both the Jewish festival of Passover and Easter, the Christian celebration of the resurrection of Jesus, his passing over from death to life. The double resonance is important in understanding *Pâque* as a *passage,* a way, a crossing. Christian understands *Pâque* not as a singular event but as coextensive with the incarnation. Everything is Passover, everything is Easter. The paschal mystery and the mystery of Christmas are interwoven, in a way that signals God's participation in human life and invites and makes possible our participation in the life of God.

It is worth pausing here to observe Christian's theological method. He begins with an insight or intuition or nudge from his own spiritual experience, then begins to unwrap and explore it, drawing on Scripture, the teaching of the church, and the wisdom of his long monastic tradition—reaching back to the fathers—always looking to resource and respond to the community's experience of the *hic et nunc*. Christian offers his community theology crafted not in the academy but in midst of the quotidian: it is monastic, not Scholastic. In later talks Christian mentions the Dominican theologian Marie-Dominique Chenu (1895–1990) and Jesuit Pierre Teilhard de Chardin (1881–1955) and their influence on key conciliar documents,

[50] Chergé, *God for All Days*, 197; December 23, 1995 (translation modified). "Tout est Pâque, passage, dans la vie du Seigneur parmi les hommes, passage de Dieu sur la terre, participation de Dieu à la finitude de l'homme et introduction progressive de l'homme dans la gloire de Dieu" (Chergé, *Dieu pour tout jour*, 537; December 23, 1995).

but in this instance he finds little to assist him in exploring this interweaving of incarnation and the paschal.

Returning then to Christian's reflection on the meeting of Christmas and Easter, we find him turning to Scripture. The ancient hymn of Philippians 2:5-11 places Jesus' obedience to the Father, even "to the point of death," in the same context—"the abasement of the incarnation":

> Let the same mind be in you that was in Christ Jesus,
> who, though he was in the form of God,
> did not regard equality with God
> as something to be exploited,
> but emptied himself,
> taking the form of a slave,
> being born in human likeness.
> And being found in human form,
> he humbled himself
> and became obedient to the point of death—
> even death on a cross. (Phil 2:5-8)

The "Son's obedience," Christian says, is "the dynamic principle of this *Pâque*"; it is what makes the passing over, the movement from death to life, possible. Obedience here is understood, with the Philippians text, as self-emptying (*kenosis*)—that unending giving of oneself to God. So, he continues, "Christmas is to be deciphered entirely in pascal light." Indeed it is clear from the gospels that the mystery of Christmas was only understood in retrospect.[51]

So the celebration of Christmas, preceded by the waiting time of Advent, offers a particular gift to the monastic community: "this very first face [*premier visage*] of the paschal mystery."[52] That first face is the face of the child, Jesus. The

[51] Chergé, *God for All Days*, 197; December 23, 1995.

[52] Chergé, *Dieu pour tout jour*, 537; December 23, 1995 (my translation). "ce tout premier visage du mystère pascal." The French word *visage* also connotes appearance or manifestation. Christian almost certainly has in mind Emmanuel Levinas's use of the language of "face." For a late col-

paschal mystery is first manifest in a child. The gift is twofold. First, the monks are reminded of the continuity, indeed the necessary unity, of the incarnation and the paschal mystery. Christian says, "we must constantly return" to the incarnation, that "*premier visage* [. . .], to be sure of properly interpreting the Passion, the Cross, and Resurrection." When we do so we find "The face of a small human, being formed in his mother's womb, then growing in a family, modestly, laboriously, and with joy, in the simplicity of a daily life, a quotidian, like all others, with all others."[53]

Second, this picture of Jesus' human life, his long formation in the context of ordinary daily existence, speaks directly to the monks' own formation as monks—formation that is intended to shape them, day by day, into the likeness of Christ so that they too might be "sons of the Father." Monastic consecration is an agreement to this formation, over a lifetime. If monastic life is understood as "waiting, desire, a perpetual ADVENT," it is also "a permanent nativity"[54]—birth is iterative, ongoing. Christian finds confirmation of this idea in the Cistercian constitutions: "The monastery is a school of the Lord's service where Christ is FORMED in the hearts of the brothers through the liturgy, the abbot's teaching, and the fraternal way of life" (CST 3.2). Christian pushes further: this being formed in, or into, Christ is in fact something that they share with Jesus of Nazareth. He too was being formed into Christ: it "will 'come to pass' that in him too 'Christ will be FORMED'" (see Gal 4:19).[55]

---

lection of writings demonstrating the development of Levinas's thought, see Emmanuel Levinas, *Entre Nous: Essays on Thinking-of-the-Other*, trans. Michael B. Smith and Barbara Harshav (New York: Columbia University Press, 1998).

[53] Chergé, *Dieu pour tout jour*, 537–38; December 23, 1995 (my translation).

[54] Chergé, *God for All Days*, 198; December 23, 1995.

[55] Cf. Heb 5:8-9: "Although he was a Son, he learned obedience through what he suffered; and having been made perfect, he became the source of eternal salvation for all who obey him" (Chergé, *God for All Days*, 198;

This is what incarnation looks like. In this short chapter talk, delivered the day before the Vigil of Christmas, Christian had found the key to unlocking the meaning of the community's continued presence in Tibhirine and its relationship to the paschal mystery: incarnation. And incarnation is paschal, a perpetual dying and rising.

Here too Christian has touched on "the spirituality of Nazareth," which had come to prominence in the twentieth century, particularly in response to the choice of Charles de Foucauld to live a "hidden life" in Nazareth, initially literally but later symbolically, on the edge of the Sahara. *Nazareth* signaled Jesus' first thirty years of "hidden life," before his final three years of public ministry, and Christian is surprised that this understanding had not found its way explicitly into Cistercian thinking, given that monastic life is precisely about this "slow maturing of the Word [*le Verbe*] made flesh."[56]

Christian now has an answer to Olivera's comment: "In response to our abbot general's quip that our Order needs monks more than it needs martyrs, our answer must therefore be that we are truly monks by continuing to live, here, the very mystery of Christmas, of GOD LIVING among men . . . and exposing himself in this way, from the cradle to the massacre

December 23, 1995). As Salenson observes, like Teilhard de Chardin, Christian embraced "a Christology of the incarnate Word," allowing him to imagine a "greater Christ." De Chardin's work in the context of the science of evolution led him to develop his Christology of the "cosmic Christ." Christian's engagement with Islam led him along a similar path. The incarnation of the Word in Jesus of Nazareth is not an end in itself, but rather the means of our own participation in the life of God. In Christian's words, "The goal and meaning of the incarnation is not primarily that the Word should become flesh, but that our flesh should be brought into the divine milieu of the Word." Trans. Salenson, *Christian de Chergé: A Theology of Hope*, 88–90. For the French text see Chergé, *Dieu pour tout jour*, 499; July 19, 1994 (erroneously cited by Salenson as a homily).

[56] Chergé, *God for All Days*, 199; December 30, 1995. For a recent Anglican reclamation of the significance of Nazareth for ethics, see Samuel Wells, *A Nazareth Manifesto: Being with God* (Chichester: Wiley Blackwell, 2015).

of Innocents."[57] Incarnation means vulnerability, openness to all that human existence delivers. So, Christian observes, the story of the "massacre of innocents," part of the birth narrative in the gospel of Matthew (2:16-18), precedes the cross. Christian extends this phrase, "massacre of Innocents," to include "the multitudes" who have been massacred both before and after the crucifixion of Jesus—numbered among them are the Croatian workers at Tamesguida. Christian acknowledges too their own exposure to the violence engulfing Algeria. Passion and death are woven into the story of Christmas—the *premier visage* of the paschal mystery.

Over the following weeks Christian's chapter talks circle around the same themes. He continues to explore this interrelationship of Christmas and Easter (*Pâques*), the "constant interpenetration, over more than thirty years of Jesus' earthly life, of the mysteries of the Incarnation and the Redemption."[58] The tendency is to think of these sequentially, as steps in the unfolding story of revelation, but they are actually coextensive. So if the "first face" of the paschal mystery is found in the incarnate life of Jesus, incarnation is also found in his passion and death. Importantly, Christian draws out the significance of this for humanity:

> What took place during the hours of the passion was continual Incarnation: the Word [*le Verbe*] became human flesh and bone then as in the days of his birth and upbringing. He came to inhabit suffering and death like all the other realities shared by all people in this world. But he did so in order to bring the great dynamism of incarnation to its conclusion by enabling it to establish a foothold in the glory that he has from his Father from the very beginning. For the fulfillment of the Redemption is indeed this Incarnation of a humanity like ours in the very same glory of God . . . and thereby, the coming of

[57] Chergé, *God for All Days*, 203; January 4, 1996 (translation modified).
[58] Chergé, *God for All Days*, 202; January 4, 1996.

God into human community through the communion of saints.[59]

The intertwining of incarnation and the pascal mystery is purposeful. The foothold in the eternal makes it possible to live with hope: the incarnate Word teaches us "to taste this new combination of joy and suffering, of death and life" that actually satisfies the human thirst for God.[60] Indeed, Christian argues, "this is why the paschal mystery must be held to be as extensive as the Incarnation, that is, as extensive as human LIFE and vice versa." Incarnation is the very fabric of our redemption or, as Christian expresses it, "in Christ's Passover [*Pâque*] Incarnation is the method, and Redemption is the motive."[61] Incarnation and redemption are both active, both dynamic movements of the Spirit: so, he suggests, one should speak not simply of the redeeming Word, but also of the *incarnating* Word.[62]

When Christian came to speak in March 1996 in Algiers, to a retreat for lay Christians, he was able to articulate these ideas with confidence and clarity. It was Lent, but Christian chose to speak about the incarnation:

[59] Chergé, *God for All Days*, 210; January 30, 1996 (translation modified). "Ce qui s'est passé aux heures de la Passion, c'est de l'Incarnation continuée: le Verbe y prend chair et consistance humaines comme aux jours de sa naissance et de sa croissance. Il est venu habiter la souffrance et la mort comme toutes les autres réalités partagées par tous les hommes de ce monde. Mais c'est pour conduire à son terme ce grand dynamisme d'incarnation en lui donnant de prendre pied dans la gloire qu'il tient de son Père depuis les origines. Car l'aboutissement même de la Rédemption, c'est bien cette Incarnation d'une humanité semblable à la nôtre dans la gloire même de Dieu . . . et par là même, l'entrée de Dieu en communauté humaine par la communion des saints." Chergé, *Dieu pour tout jours*, 542.

[60] Chergé, *God for All Days*, 211; February 1, 1996 (translation modified).

[61] Chergé, *God for All Days*, 211; February 1, 1996.

[62] Chergé, *God for All Days*, 208; January 9, 1996. Christian coins the word *INCARNATEUR* to make the point that we normally use the effectively passive "Incarnate Word," but the active "redeeming Word."

One might tell oneself this is not the time. We are in the middle of Lent! The mystery of the moment is the paschal mystery, and when we think of the paschal mystery we think of the mystery of the Redemption. Yes, but is there a paschal mystery without incarnation? Is the incarnation only the birth and public life of Jesus? Are not this death and resurrection part of the mystery of the incarnation? But yes! insofar as it is indeed a question of the Son of God taking a humanity similar to ours and leading it to its end, which is to enter into the life of God. The Incarnation continues in the glory of Jesus living with his Father.

For Christmas, Gilles Nicolas, our parish priest, said, "We must find in the mystery of the incarnation our true reasons for staying despite the threats and the turmoil. Christmas is Emmanuel, God silently present, the presence of love itself, which alone is revolutionary, which alone transforms one another's hearts [*les cœurs des uns et des autres*]." What was true at Christmas must be true at Easter. The mystery of the incarnation remains that which we have to live, and, it seems to me, it is there that the deepest of our reasons for staying, our reasons for being here, are rooted.

We must have a very broad vision of the paschal mystery. Everything is paschal in the life of the Christ. Easter [*Pâque*] begins with God's participation in the finitude of man, in what we are.[63]

Death . . . and the Tree of Life

The Christian journey, then, is a living out of the interwoven realities of incarnation and the paschal mystery, an invitation to participation—in the life of God. In his chapter talks, when Christian comes to speak more directly about death it is within

[63] Chergé, "'L'Église, c'est l'Incarnation continuée,'" 293.

this larger frame. He observes that in the Cistercian constitutions physical death is "hardly mentioned."[64] He draws attention to the vows made at a monk's solemn profession and the formula specified in the constitutions: "I, Brother N, promise my stability, my fidelity to the monastic way of life, and obedience until death in accordance with the Rule of Saint Benedict. I do this before God and all his saints, in this monastery of N . . . " (CST 56.3). Physical death is simply "the natural endpoint" of monastic consecration. The emphasis, Christian stresses, is on "LIFE."

The three vows shape both the life and the death of the monk and are not negated by the form that death might take. In fact, the monk's death has already been offered to God as part of this monastic consecration, in the context of a monastic community: "our DEATH is included in our gift, [. . .] it does not belong to us, and so can only be risked in the same Gospel atmosphere as all our other moments offered to God in this monastic community to which we are united through love 'in life as in death' or 'for better and for worse.'"[65] Here Christian uses words from the marriage vows to emphasize that the locus of this offering, this consecration, is the monastic community.

And this is where the monk experiences death most keenly. Christian notes that the word *death* appears in the constitutions in relation to the obedience of the monk: "In thus renouncing his own will he follows the example of Christ, who was obedient until death, and commits himself to the school of the Lord's service" (CST 11). The model for monastic obedience is Jesus' obedience to the Father, his loving "to the end" [*jusqu'à la fin, jusqu'à l'extrême,* see John 13:1]. It is a difficult journey, experienced as death: "our death, which is a slow and difficult death, is that of our own will." This has a paschal quality: "The paschal mystery, which is continually implicit in our Constitutions as in the Rule, is this slow passage of obedience that renounces

[64] Chergé, *God for All Days,* 227; February 20, 1996.
[65] Chergé, *God for All Days,* 221; February 15, 1996.

one's own will in order to appreciate LIFE only in the life of God. Gethsemane is our place."[66] We join Jesus in the painful struggle he experienced in the Garden of Gethsemane before his arrest. Again, this is a "shedding of flesh and blood drop by drop in the desert."[67]

Suffering is inevitable, but Christian warns against the "morbid" traditions that would have one "digging one's grave every day."[68] He is grateful for the "SOBER," moderate language of the Rule of Benedict, which draws back from the often harsh language of the earlier Rule of the Master, which speaks of the "martyrdom" of the will (drawn to his attention by Br. Christophe). Instead, taking his cue from Benedict, Christian reframes *passion* as patience and the *cross* as obedience when speaking of the monastic path as a "participation in the sufferings of Christ."[69]

What grounds this hard journey, however, is an eschatological vision. Monastic life is oriented to its end in Christ, toward hope: "While dwelling on earth, their minds are occupied with heavenly things, desiring eternal life with all spiritual longing" (CST 22). A foothold in the eternal. Christian offers a vivid picture of this orientation toward hope, overlaying the metaphor of the ladder, with which he has played many times over the years, with that of the tree of life—drawing on the deep biblical tradition culminating in the vision of Revelation 22:

> It is thus a matter of "dwelling on earth," of keeping one's feet on the ground, all the while having the "heavens" in

[66] Chergé, *God for All Days*, 222; February 15, 1996. Christian refers to the French philosopher and writer Gustav Thibon here but does not specify a particular work.

[67] Chergé, *God for All Days*, 196; December 16, 1995.

[68] Chergé, *God for All Days*, 222; February 15, 1996.

[69] Chergé, *God for All Days*, 225–26; February 20, 1996. The Rule of the Master is generally considered to be a key source for the Rule of Benedict. Benedict's modifications to the Rule of the Master reveal a more moderate and optimistic vision of monastic life.

> view and never losing sight of the aim, the endpoint: treetops do not point towards their roots. There is no reason for us to be exempt from this law of creation that aspires "to the things above" [see Col 3:2]. It is up to us to turn this into an orientation towards the choice of freedom and of perpetually renewed desire, whose sap irrigates all our impulses without ceasing to be drawn from the fertile ground of the quotidian.[70]

Christian then puts the metaphor of the tree (a vision of incarnating life) together with the cross (the pascal mystery) to create a vision of abundant, flourishing life:

> The tree of the cross enables this comparison. It reveals all human dimensions, both vertical and horizontal in its outstretched arms. And if we contemplate it tirelessly, it is indeed because the true CROSS is not the wood of torture that causes death, but the tree of life, which is similar to us in all aspects, whose head touches the sky and where everyone can make his nest in the breach of an open heart.[71]

He then presses into the transformation bought about by Jesus' death and resurrection, the paschal mystery:

> Because the Incarnation of the Son of God passed through this [death] in order to declare, in the fullness of human communion, the meaning of death, our death, has henceforth been changed. It is not a site of decay. It is no longer an uprooting, but rather a definitive taking root there where the head has gained a foothold.[72]

[70] Chergé, *God for All Days*, 218; February 13, 1996. Translation modified.

[71] Chergé, *God for All Days*, 218–19; February 13, 1996.

[72] Chergé, *God for All Days*, 219; February 13, 1996 (translation modified). "Parce que l'Incarnation du Fils de Dieu est passée par là pour se dire, en plénitude de communion humaine, la mort, notre mort désormais

With hope secured, the human journey continues as a perpetual incarnating and redeeming movement—a movement that always requires letting go rather than clinging to a particular point or stage of the journey. Death is simply the final, trusting, letting go:

> The great movement of the Incarnation is that of Jacob's ladder, where there is no end of descending and reascending in order to embrace everything relating to the human condition, which is thus accomplished as "spiritual ardor": death, no doubt, means not clinging onto the rungs of the ladder, no more on the first than on the last of them![73]

As he concludes this series of talks on "the paschal mystery and our founding texts," Christian remarks that "it is perhaps good that the reality of even physical death should be hardly mentioned in our Constitutions, if not as if in passing . . . while both death to oneself and the desire for life consummated in God are permanently at stake in everything we commit to together."[74] With hope secured in "the heavens," physical death is gathered into a larger frame, that of the paschal mystery, the passing from death to life—lived out through costly yet ultimately joyful self-offering, day by day, in the quotidian.

This final series of chapter talks takes us on a serious journey alongside monks who had freely chosen to continue living out their monastic consecration at Tibhirine, fully aware of its probable end. The monks understood their lives to have been given, in response to the love of God, for love. They sought to be witnesses (martyrs) of love and hope, knowing that the choice for love must be made again and again, that this commitment

---

change de sens. Elle n'est pas le lieu d'une désintégration. Elle n'est plus déracinement, mais enracinement définitif là où la tête a pris pied."

[73] Chergé, *God for All Days*, 219; February 13, 1996 (translation modified).

[74] Chergé, *God for All Days*, 227; February 20, 1996.

is costly, a life-long struggle, and that love is itself a grace, a gift of God. Christian's insightful exploration of the interweaving of the dual mysteries of the incarnation and *Pâques* offered to the community both an affirmation of their experience of living, ever more deeply, the paschal mystery of death and resurrection, and a challenge to continue in this way of the life-giving cross ("the tree of life") with confidence in the foothold in the eternal, opened through Christ, that each had tasted.

Running towards the Kingdom: The Last Chapter Talk

In early March 1996 Christian, with the community, began preparations for the forthcoming general chapter. The theme, "The Community, School of Charity," sent him back to the Rule of Benedict. Inspired by the abbot general's letter announcing this theme, Christian's last documented chapter talk revisits the fundamentals of the community's monastic vocation, drawing on the bookends of the Rule: the Prologue and chapter 72. The talk also recapitulates the territory that Christian has been exploring over the previous weeks and months. Indeed, he was intending to step down as prior at the election planned for the end of March, so this talk forms his own bookend to all that he has learned and shared with his brother monks. And for this he gives Benedict center stage.

Benedict's Prologue famously declares the monastery to be "a school for the Lord's service" (*Dominici schola servitii*), reframed in the Cistercian tradition as a "school of charity" (*schola caritatis*). However, Christian suggests, the Prologue culminates in a passage that comes just after the word *caritas* (charity) first appears. Christian simply picks out some the key phrases from this passage, but it is worth quoting the text from the Rule in full:

> as we progress in this way of life and in faith, we shall run on the path of God's commandments, our hearts overflowing with the inexpressible delight of love. Never swerving

> from his instructions then, but faithfully observing his teaching in the monastery until death, we shall through patience share in the sufferings of Christ that we may deserve also to share in his kingdom. (RB Prol.49–50)

Christian, as was his habit, capitalizes the key words that he had pulled from the text, words the monks had been pondering over the previous weeks, words which speak of joy: "CHARITY, the DELIGHT OF LOVE, the OVERFLOWING of the heart." All of this arises, he says, "in the PATIENCE of stability and perseverance," which is the monastic way of "sharing in the sufferings of Christ." The commitment is always to the daily, the quotidian, in this place, at this time, the *hic et nunc*. This, he continues, "is our 'MARTYRDOM,' which should thus be a 'martyrdom of love,' and just as well a 'martyrdom of HOPE,' since this passage [of the Rule] is all about movement, about walking and running towards the kingdom of which the community is the image, but not yet the full reality."[75] Running towards the kingdom, not running toward martyrdom. Christian reiterates the optimistic vision of the Rule and of monastic life. The kingdom towards which they run is both now and not yet.

Christian closes this last chapter talk by inviting the community to read together, in full, the penultimate chapter of the Rule, "The Good Zeal of Monks" (RB 72). It is a chapter, Christian says, that "says EVERYTHING, in fact, about what we want to be." And this "good zeal," we should note, leads to love, not violence. The final words of Benedict's chapter speak of the path that the monks of Notre-Dame de l'Atlas chose, each day, to run: "Let them prefer nothing whatever to Christ, and may he bring us all together to everlasting life" (RB 72.12).

[75] Chergé, *God for All Days*, 232; March 16, 1996.

Given . . . to Love

Brother Luc was a man of few words, but his last two letters to Geneviève Guillemin, the widow of his friend Georges, reveal the good zeal that continued to motivate him. He was tired and old, surprised to still be alive, yet he expressed gratitude and joy in the timely receipt of a money order from Geneviève that would enable him to continue to assist "the poor, the unfortunate, the desperate" who came to the monastery at Tibhirine. Georges and Luc had maintained a deep friendship since their days in medical school in Lyon, and the Guillemin family were generous supporters of the dispensary. Georges died in 1994, and yet, eighteen months after his death, Luc addresses his letters to both. Luc "is convinced that those who have left us are not in the hole that we dig for them, but elsewhere."[76] Like Christian, Luc carries a vivid sense of the communion of saints and of living towards the open heavens. His final letter, written on March 24, 1996, just two days before the abduction of the brothers, very simply speaks of his commitment to the way of Christ, the way of love.

> Chère Geneviève, Cher Georges
>
> With what gratitude, and what joy, I received your money order of 11–03 . . . Thanks to you, I can continue on the road.
>
> The Remembrance of Georges does not leave me. I loved him very much, and I think it was reciprocated.
>
> Here the violence is still at the same level, although censorship wants to hide it. How to get out of it. I do not think that violence can root out violence. We can only exist as men by agreeing to make ourselves the image of

[76] Frère Luc, *Tu verras éclater le printemps: Lettres de Tibhirine,* Les Écrits de Tibhirine - Lettres 1 (Paris: Bayard-Cerf-Bellefontaine, 2021), 154; February 6, 1996.

Love, as it is manifested in Christ, who simply chose to suffer an unjust Fate. I have not forgotten you. I often think of you. Fond greetings to François and all his family. I hope you are doing well. May the Lord bless you and fill your heart. Happy Easter. With my great gratitude, fraternally yours, I embrace you with what strength I have left.

Br. Luc[77]

[77] Luc, *Tu verras éclater le printemps*, 155; March 24, 1996.

Chapter 8

Choosing Life

ce qu'il nous restait à faire, c'était à vivre;
et la première chose à vivre.

what remained for us to do was to live;
and the first thing, to live.
—Christian de Chergé

On habite ensemble une terre d'espérance. On la travaille. On est les habitants de ta maison. On y vit. On y prie. On y demeure jusqu'à l'heure de mourir. Ensemble, on habite ta main. De ce bonheur ouvert qui pourrait nous déloger?

We live together in a land of hope. We cultivate it. We are dwellers in your house. We live there. We pray there. We abide there until it's time to die. Together, we live in your hand. Who could dislodge us from this manifest happiness?
—Christophe Lebreton

During the 1993 Christmas Eve visit of Sayah Attiya and his men, Christophe had hidden for two hours in the cellar imagining that his brother monks "were in the hands of the 'visitors.'"[1] On this occasion Christian had persuaded them to

[1] Christophe Lebreton, *Born from the Gaze of God: The Tibhirine Journal of a Martyr Monk (1993–1996)*, trans. Mette Louise Nygård and Edith Scholl, MW 37 (Collegeville, MN: Cistercian Publications, 2014), 46; February 4, 1994. Originally published as Christophe Lebreton, *Le souffle du don: Journal de Frère Christophe, moine de Tibhirine, 8 août 1993–19 mars 1996* (Paris: Bayard-Centurion, 1999). All quotations in English are from the Nygård and Scholl translation unless otherwise noted.

leave peacefully. For Christophe these "two hours of Vigils" were a descent to "the abyss"—a night of painful struggle, a Gethsemane.[2] The following week, on the Feast of the Epiphany, Christophe wrote in his prayer journal of the impact of this event on the community, its "shock" and the difficulty of the "return" from this experience:

> I myself was led to an extreme, an excessive point. A point of gravity whose weight continues to weigh on my shoulders. I am like everyone here and like our neighbors: tired, weighed down. Indeed, the story of man is a heavy thing. You carry the responsibility for it, you who had nowhere to lay your head, you who go on working unceasingly as you see your Father does.[3]

Christophe understands that it is ultimately Jesus, the one who declared that "the Son of Man has nowhere to lay his head" (Matt 8:20), who carries the weight of human violence. Christophe then reflects on his vocation as a monk, and on the work and place to which he is committed. It is in the shared labor in the garden and his friendship with neighbors that he finds a way back from the abyss. It is here too that he finds God—incarnate in the present, in the body of Christ, in the church:

> The work of God is the true labor of the monk. I love performing it here. With Mohammed this afternoon, we talked about manure, about ploughing . . . W. and Moussa were pruning an apple tree. Ammi Ali came by with his grandson Amin—just to see us with his anxious eyes. This place is holy. A place of true adoration in the Breath of the Nazarene. Here, where the little child is,

[2] Lebreton, *Born from the Gaze of God*, 35, 39; January 16, 23, 1994.
[3] Lebreton, *Born from the Gaze of God*, 28; January 2, 1994.

> his *I am* as the Beloved is enacted in the body of Mother Church.[4]

Christophe here evokes Nazareth as an image of their hidden life, where the ordinary, the quotidian, is embraced as the place where the loving presence of God is to be found.

Christophe later speaks of the "two hours of Vigils" on Christmas Eve as a new birth: "you drew me from the pit and made me climb up from the abyss," he writes, "in order to LIVE through you, with you, for YOU, and in YOU toward the Father."[5] For Christophe the imprint of this Christmas Eve experience formed a second reference point in his relationship with God, alongside the transformative encounter when he was a young student in Tours, his own "Night of Fire"—when he had profoundly experienced God's "I love you."[6] It was a renewed invitation to choose life.

This final chapter steps into the intimate space of Christophe's prayer journal, shifting in focus from the monastic community as a whole to the experience of one of its members. Each of the monks carried the weight of their situation differently, each of them experienced struggle differently. Christophe's journal maps one monk's experience. On the Feast Day of Saint Christopher, July 25, 1993, Christophe had been given a notebook that became his prayer journal over the last two and a half years of his life, the same period that saw the rapid escalation of violence in Algeria. The journal offers a privileged insight into Christophe's interior life, how he responded emotionally and spiritually to this situation of insecurity and threat. Insight too into the impact of this situation on the monastic community and their neighbors. Above all, the journal bears witness to his courageous and hard-won commitment to life—to choosing life, day by day.

[4] Lebreton, *Born from the Gaze of God*, 28; January 2, 1994 (translation modified).

[5] Lebreton, *Born from the Gaze of God*, 51; February 19, 1994.

[6] Lebreton, *Born from the Gaze of God*, 39; January 23, 1994.

The Prayer Journal

When Christophe first wrote in his new journal on August 8, 1993, he imagined it as an enclosure (*un clôture*), a walled garden perhaps, or a cloister within the monastic cloister, a place where he could meet intimately with his Beloved. It begins poetically, drawing on the love language of the Song of Songs, so deeply treasured in the Cistercian tradition. But in the first few entries one can sense Christophe struggling to find a voice, his authentic voice for this space. If this is indeed a place of meeting with God, how can this be spoken?

> You present the page to me. How can I utter you? A great desire devours the words that write themselves: to see you.[7]

Christophe was a poet. His legacy of writings includes several hundred poems, as well as homilies and this last prayer journal. In the early journal entries Christophe is preoccupied with the interplay between writing, the self, and God. His poetic self takes charge as he begins to write on the blank pages: how to make this "a notebook of prayer"? He conceives of God as both the audience and the source for this writing; he is merely the "servant-scribe."[8]

> To transcribe a kiss. What an adventure.
> My writing is all
> stirred up at the thought.
> The one holding my hand
> draws it beyond words.
> I shall write your silence. Without translating.
> If anyone has ears, let him hear.
> I shall write from above, thus escaping any ambitious project
> I have no ambition,

[7] Lebreton, *Born from the Gaze of God*, 5; August 9, 1993.
[8] Lebreton, *Born from the Gaze of God*, 5; August 8, 10, 1993.

I speak softly
I shall say what comes to me
from you
and writes itself in me.[9]

There is a self-consciousness in these initial poetic entries of which Christophe himself is only too aware: "Above all no soaring," he reminds himself on August 15, and then, in the next entry, declares "it's no trifle to keep a journal." Christophe is aware that the act of writing can deceive as well as illuminate. On August 20 he writes, finally in simple prose, about the disjunction between his preaching and his own sense of distance from the sentiments of his homily. He knows that writing does not necessarily lead to God: "For your sake to stop writing and set off for the ineffable."[10] Later, having found a way ahead with the journal, he remarks, "sometimes I can actually write without (too much) glancing at myself."[11]

There is, though, an important shift that allows Christophe to definitively inhabit the space offered by the journal. In the poetic entry of August 10 he had ventured that "this writing detaches me from the world."[12] However, in the evening of August 22 he adds a note to that day's entry: "Assassinations in Algiers. After so many others. This journal cannot remain sheltered from this violence. It pierces me."[13] The journal cannot function as *un clôture*, a secluded enclosure; his writing cannot be detached from the realities of the world.[14] If self and God are to meet here, if this is to be a "notebook of prayer," then the world must be admitted too. Bringing oneself into this space means admitting the whole of oneself: the self that

[9] Lebreton, *Born from the Gaze of God*, 5–6; August 10, 1993.

[10] Lebreton, *Born from the Gaze of God*, 6–7; August 15, 18, 20, 1993.

[11] Lebreton, *Born from the Gaze of God*, 9; August 28, 1993.

[12] Lebreton, *Born from the Gaze of God*, 6; August 10, 1993.

[13] Lebreton, *Born from the Gaze of God*, 8; August 22, 1993.

[14] There is a necessary and healthy form of detachment that Christophe considers elsewhere in the journal.

is pierced by the violence of the world, as well as the self that has experienced the kiss of the Beloved.

What makes Christophe's journal of enduring value is precisely his embrace of this unbounded space. He brings to the journal the self that is being written into being, in the particularity of his existence. He brings to the prayer of its pages his brother monks, his family and friends, the church in Algeria, the village of Tibhirine, the garden where he worked alongside his Muslim neighbors, the suffering people of Algeria, the violence that has overwhelmed the country, the rhythm and fruit of the community's liturgical life, the nourishment of his reading, and his hopes and fears, often intertwined—all in the presence of the one whom he knows as "I love you." The journal becomes exactly what he hopes for, "a space to test my existence as being a word in the process of writing itself here. In order so to utter you."[15]

A School of Peace

"Tonight the monastery is revealed to me as a school of peace," Christophe writes early in 1995.[16] This insight sits, as it turns out, almost at the midpoint of the journal. From this point, looking back and looking forward, it is possible to view both the landscape of violence that had surrounded the monastic community and Christophe's ongoing prayerful engagement with this situation.

A conversation with his dentist inspired this journal entry. The dentist tells Christophe, "It's important that you exist." Christophe's initial response is to object: "we're practically nothing at all and can be swept away." This objection may be true, but for the dentist the existence of "religious men," both Christian and Muslim, offers, Christophe senses, a "bulwark," "something strong against Evil," resistance to "the chaos that seems about to engulf everything." Christophe accepts this

[15] Lebreton, *Born from the Gaze of God*, 10; September 5, 1993.

[16] Lebreton, *Born from the Gaze of God*, 132; January 16, 1994.

external confirmation of their vocation: "The exigency persists: to become monk(s) here, in your crucified truth."[17]

"To become" (*devenir*), not "to be"; the choice of this verb is significant. There is no arrival. The monastery is not an *oasis* of peace, but a *school* of peace. It is a place of lifelong learning. Benedict's programmatic phrase, "school for the Lord's service" (*dominici schola servitii*), together with the Cistercian understanding of the monastery as a "school of charity" (*schola caritatis*), is undoubtedly in Christophe's thoughts here. "There is so much to learn from you," Christophe adds immediately after articulating his insight. God is the teacher. Still, the monastery is the school, and Christophe had committed to its particular pedagogy. Across the journal one can observe Christophe's lived experience of monastic practices—prayer, *lectio divina*, work, fraternal community, hospitality, stability. Moreover, one can see how these monastic practices enabled the community to live faithfully in the midst of violence. What is abundantly clear is that these commitments proved to be both robust and life-giving. What is also clear is that these are commitments, not givens, and hence the focus of continued work and struggle. As Christian reminded the community: "Gethsemane is our place."[18]

The Struggle to Disarm

Violence, Christophe understood, is the antithesis of peace. There was no time when Christophe was unaware of the ultimate source of violence, the human heart, and of his own violence. In the journal, reflections on the violence "without" and the violence "within," the external and the internal, are often interwoven. On October 20, 1993, the day following the

[17] Lebreton, *Born from the Gaze of God*, 132; January 16, 1994; Lebreton, *Le souffle du don*, 158–59.

[18] Christian de Chergé, *God for All Days: The Final Monastic Chapters of Christian de Chergé*, trans. Jennifer Rushworth, ed. Matthew Cheung Salisbury, MW 73 (Collegeville, MN: Cistercian Publications, 2025), 222; February 15, 1996.

stabbing of a young journalist, he writes, "I have to win the battle for PEACE within myself. Receive it from your pierced hands."[19] On January 13, 1994, he notes the assassination of a *wali* (provincial governor) and his bodyguards, and the killing of policemen in Algiers, and ponders the story of the primal murder, Cain killing Abel, read that morning during Vigils (Gen 4:1-16). He prays, "Jesus, heal me of the violence lurking inside me: the beast. Make me human according to your beatitudes."[20]

The battle for interior peace is ongoing, and for Christophe it manifests itself in outbursts of anger, usually in the context of strained fraternal relationships. On July 15 he writes,

> To hear myself rehearse my tiresome and unseemly violence again this morning, sends me far away from the community, excludes me radically from this protected place. One question has shaken me: Should I join the violent? No, nothing attracts me to their battle; but do I truly belong among those people, as that brother said to me who was incensed by my violence and convinced that he was completely free of it? Difficult to preside at the Eucharist in this state of mind. I haven't been able to free myself of this bad humor in me . . . Will my bitter bitterness lead me to PEACE?[21]

The journal entries thin significantly for the next fortnight, and Christophe spends the next two Sundays "apart." He needs solitude and rest to find his way back. His distress continues: the forest is burning, and their well is running dry.[22] Fatigue, arising from the trauma of the Christmas Eve visit and the unrelenting stress of living under threat, is clearly weighing heavily on Christophe and the whole community:

[19] Lebreton, *Born from the Gaze of God*, 14; October 20, 1993.
[20] Lebreton, *Born from the Gaze of God*, 32; January 13, 1994.
[21] Lebreton, *Born from the Gaze of God*, 92; July 15, 1994.
[22] Lebreton, *Born from the Gaze of God*, 93; July 29, 1994.

> Last Sunday I was at the end of my rope. I could have empathized with my brothers' fatigue, with the despair of the Algerians, muted in their heart. But there was the ego I couldn't get around: exasperated in choir, distressed over the scarcity of water.[23]

He had written a long confessional lament and thrown it in the wastebin, but he retrieves it later and copies it into his journal to both "face it and not be completely defeated." The psalms, with their daring expression of the full range of human emotions, have taught him well. The lament expresses his sense of failure and self-loathing ("I feel after Lauds on this day of the Lord / like a clot of bad blood obstructing the fountainhead / and blocking all possibility of a happy offering") and his anger at God ("you who are to blame for this messy existence"). And, like a psalmist, he reminds God of their plight:

> PS The mail hardly ever arrives here any more, the bridge
> has been blown up
> the forest is burning there is no water
> and it is hot
> and then here you know
> killing happens here a lot

The lament concludes in the place that normally brings him consolation, the cross. But here he struggles with its power to redeem:

> A glance at history shows that failure obviously dominates
> unless from your cross
> your hand

[23] Lebreton, *Born from the Gaze of God*, 94; August 4, 1994 (translation modified).

writes

in us

in me too

illegible love.[24]

If love is present, Christophe cannot read it.

In a later journal entry he recognizes that his fears and violence are nourished by a "lack of self-confidence" that he understands not as a psychological deficit but as the failure to allow oneself to "be seen" and loved by God: "that lack comes from not being present to the Gaze that gives birth to me." He continues,

> I must believe that You love to look at who I am becoming. I must believe your eyes: the nakedness of your *I love you*, that strips me naked. Just like Jesus on the cross: surrendered to your gaze, alone and trusting desperately. Certain he's being sought, certain he's being found even in this wretched place of perdition.[25]

Christophe was not alone in his struggles with violence. On the eve of Ash Wednesday 1995 the community, in chapter, had engaged in "a real dialogue about violence and non-violence" that moved from ideas to the personal. The brothers acknowledged "the need for patience with annoying and perplexing behaviors"—needful in all human communities, but under pressure even more critical. One of the brothers had asked for forgiveness. The prayer that Christian began after his Christmas Eve meeting with Sayah Attiya—"Disarm them!"—had become their own prayer: "Disarm me, disarm

[24] Lebreton, *Born from the Gaze of God*, 95–96; August 4, 1994. Christophe's prose often drifts towards the poetic, using lineation and deliberate spaces.

[25] Lebreton, *Born from the Gaze of God*, 122; December 6, 1994.

us."[26] Luc's intercession, in the wake of the same visit, continued to resonate: "Lord, give us the grace to die without hatred in our heart."[27]

Christophe understood too that the places where his own violence broke out, damaging his relations with others, were the very places where he "might little by little experience conversion": "in the liturgy, where song and word want to be prayer; in work, where much energy is given and spent; in community life, by the exercise of charity."[28] Prayer, work, community—it is no accident that these places of potential conversion are core components of monastic life. The monastery is indeed a school of peace.

At the Foot of the Cross

In these last years Christophe lived, as did his brother monks, with a deep attentiveness to the paschal mystery, of life overcoming death, that lies at the heart of the Christian faith. The community celebration of the Eucharist brought this into awareness each day, but in the face of so much suffering and death they had a deepening sense of living this mystery.

In his journal Christophe often revisits the passion narrative. He has a sense of participation in the passion, not as some sort of saint, but simply as one of the disciples following Jesus. His emphasis is resolutely on the *we*—not the *I*. He finds authorization for this emphasis in the Gospel of Matthew, where the path to the cross begins with Jesus addressing the twelve: "Behold, we are going up to Jerusalem" (Matt 20:18). The "we" includes "us," he says, "in the drama of what happened afterwards."[29]

[26] Lebreton, *Born from the Gaze of God*, 141; March 1, 1995.

[27] Lebreton, *Born from the Gaze of God*, 25; December 31, 1993.

[28] Lebreton, *Born from the Gaze of God*, 141; March 1, 1995.

[29] Lebreton, *Born from the Gaze of God*, 58; March 4, 1994. Christophe states this idea more confidently after the deaths of Sister Esther and Caridad: "After Vigils, I read the account of your Passion—which is happening to us" (113; October 28, 1994).

For Christophe, the cross is ever present in the violence overtaking Algeria: the cross is the "epicenter" of the "terrible oppression."[30] The Algerians are "a crucified people."[31] The slaughter reveals the cosmic nature of the battle for peace:

> The world is a war zone. It isn't ideas, principles, abstractions confronting one [an]other; it's Good against Evil, Life against Death, etc. There are two forces present, two antagonistic energies: two powers in competition. The power of Death is the decision to kill. The power of the Father is the decision to live. Love that begets the Son. On the Cross, the Son triumphs definitively. The Letter to the Hebrews says that by his death he reduces to impotence him who wielded the power of death. Standing firmly there, the Church is invested with the LIFE of the Son: "Woman, behold your Son."[32]

The cross becomes, paradoxically, not the end but the source of life. And it is the church that has now been given the responsibility of bearing this life. Christophe is referring here to the Gospel of John (19:25-27), to the moment when the dying Jesus speaks to his mother Mary ("Woman, here is your son") and to the beloved disciple ("Here is your mother"). Christophe is also drawing on the long tradition that sees Mary as representing the church and the unnamed "beloved disciple" as representing the Christian disciple. In the Gospel of John the birth of the church is situated in these final moments of Jesus' life. His work has finished; the work of the church begins—it is to be the bearer of his life.

It is "at the foot of the cross" that Christophe finds both healing for his own alienation and hope for a world shattered by human violence. And it is here that he finally finds his way home after the interior storms of July and August 1994: "Par-

[30] Lebreton, *Born from the Gaze of God*, 79; May 6, 1994.

[31] Lebreton, *Born from the Gaze of God*, 134; January 30, 1995.

[32] Lebreton, *Born from the Gaze of God*, 131; January 11, 1995.

don and Peace from you, in the Breath: this comes to me at the foot of the Cross."[33]

The metaphor of "the Breath" (*le souffle*) is Christophe's most frequently used designation for God—a metaphor that elegantly draws attention to the unity of the risen Christ and the gift of the Holy Spirit. When the risen Jesus appears to his fear-filled disciples he greets them with a salutation of peace and then breathes on them: "Receive the Holy Spirit" (John 20:19-23). For Christophe to accept this gift of the Breath is to receive both forgiveness and peace—the two are always linked. However, accepting the gift is not simply a matter of personal healing; it also means participation in the *missio Dei*—"As the Father has sent me, so I send you." This necessarily includes the work of forgiveness. Not long after the 1993 Christmas visitation Christophe writes,

> You are the master of the battle, You impose on us the rules of crucified Love.
> You deliver our enemies
> into our open praying hands.
>
> You entrust Forgiveness to us, in the power of your Breath of truth
> in order to insert it here into the history of Algeria
> in order to inscribe it as our Christ-like contribution to its recovery.[34]

They have been given, Christophe writes the following day, "a mission to breathe."[35]

So standing at the foot of the cross means standing at the birth of the mission of the church. After the deaths of Sisters Esther and Caridad, Christophe again reads the passion and finds himself "drawn to this spot where your Cross is raised: a little group of believers standing about you has formed,

[33] Lebreton, *Born from the Gaze of God*, 101; August 19, 1994.
[34] Lebreton, *Born from the Gaze of God*, 37–38; January 19, 1994.
[35] Lebreton, *Born from the Gaze of God*, 38; January 20, 1994.

emerging from you and from your Breath, ushering in 'the age of faith.'"[36] Christophe's particular affinity with Mary, the mother of Jesus, finds its strongest expression in this same locus. If Mary represents the church, to stand with Mary at the foot of the cross is to stand with "the communion of the living, in the bond of LIFE with YOU, crucified Love."[37] To stand "at the foot of the cross" is to participate, in communion with all the saints, in the life that flows from the paschal mystery. One does not stand alone.

However, standing in this space does not result in instant clarity—the paschal mystery remains a mystery. Christophe is reminded of the image of Mary and the beloved disciple standing near the cross as he ponders the words of a sister and a priest he has overheard at the Maison Saint-Augustin: "I don't know" and "Oh, I don't know any more . . . ." For Christophe, standing at the foot of the cross enables "another kind of knowledge." He finds nourishment in the words of Thomas Merton: "The monk, he says, does not exist in order to preserve anything at all, not even contemplation, not even religion. [. . .] On the contrary, the function of the monk in our time is TO KEEP HIMSELF ALIVE THROUGH HIS CONTACT WITH GOD."[38] The foot of the cross is the place of access to that life.

Christophe's commitment to "standing at the foot of the Cross" is not a glorification of suffering. The cross is the source of life precisely because it is not a terminus: it is the place where love endures, overcomes, because the cross is illuminated by the light of the Resurrection. The cross opens a space that makes possible "the decision to live." Standing there, with Jesus, the disciple discovers that he or she is loved, forgiven. "On the Cross," Christophe says, "you open the time for healing."[39]

[36] Lebreton, *Born from the Gaze of God*, 113; October 28, 1994.
[37] Lebreton, *Born from the Gaze of God*, 187; September 1, 1995.
[38] Lebreton, *Born from the Gaze of God*, 188–89; September 15, 1995.
[39] Lebreton, *Born from the Gaze of God*, 101; August 15, 1994.

Choosing Life

In a long journal entry, written at the end of May 1995 while he was staying at the monastery in Fez, Christophe explored, in conversation with John Paul II's encyclical *The Gospel of Life* (*Evangelium Vitae*), what it means to live the paschal mystery. He appreciated that their choice "to live" was itself a "pascal experience," expressed clearly in the celebration of the Eucharist but also in their work of loving service:

> In each Eucharist we *celebrate* LIFE: the victory of the Living One over against those who kill. This celebration overflows into a *service of charity*, exercised by each one according to the measure of his gift of faith [. . .] this is a task lived out at the dispensary, at the gate, in the kitchen, or in the garden.[40]

In his reflections Christophe articulates and affirms the community's continuing choice to embrace the gift of resurrection life:

> A community that is alive—and that has resolutely decided for life. In spite of, and even by virtue of, the signs of our aging, I sense that each one of us is truly alive, and using our freedom in order to live—until we die. [. . .]
>
> A community facing Evil: we experience that something within us puts up resistance: someone in our midst confronts the aggression, offering his face of peace and open hands. [. . .]
>
> A fighting community, yes: but unarmed and affirming a true space of lived fraternal peace, where the Prayer of the risen Jesus takes place, creating a locus of PEACE. This, in turn, demands from us a great concern for the

[40] Lebreton, *Born from the Gaze of God*, 158; May 29, 1995.

> truth: without smugness and without complicity with the murderous Lie.
>
> A Marian community, close to the Cross, attentive to the life that is about to be (re)born.[41]

In different hands such words might have constituted a manifesto for this monastic school of peace. But for Christophe and his brother monks the commitment to the way of peace was simply lived out in the quotidian, day by day, with all its attendant struggles, within and without. There is a sense of hope, but not of arrival: the pursuit of peace is a commitment that needs to be constantly renewed, a desire that needs to be constantly awakened, a gift to be opened and received. Its reality, though, is confirmed in the foretaste that comes always and only from the source of peace, as a Gift (*un don*) of the Breath (*le souffle*). In one of his last entries in the journal Christophe speaks of such a foretaste:

> Moussa says: "Fear of R.?! One shouldn't be afraid except of God." "So was that father happy here?" "Yes." "So he saw with his own eyes that there's peace here." (We could hear shots of a semi-automatic, and two helicopters hovering over the mountains, and Brother Paul in Médéa barely escaped an operation by the armed forces that is said to have left five dead . . .). Moussa was talking of peace not as the world gives it (which is so precarious!) but of another peace that he savors and shares because he lives of it in his own depths.[42]

In this school of peace it is the Spirit of the risen Christ who breathes: "Peace I leave with you; my peace I give to you. I do

[41] Lebreton, *Born from the Gaze of God*, 158–59; May 29, 1995.

[42] Lebreton, *Born from the Gaze of God*, 209; March 3, 1996. Moussa's reference to "that father" was to Fr. Bernard Rérolle, who had conducted the community's Lent retreat.

not give to you as the world gives. Do not let your hearts be troubled, and do not let them be afraid" (John 14:27).

Living in the Garden

Finally, the garden. The monastery garden and its modest cooperative agricultural enterprise was the location of much of Christophe's work and the source of both joy and frustration. But the garden was more than his workplace. It was woven into the very fabric of his life and vocation.

In a journal entry at the end of November 1994, Christophe takes stock after the difficult year since the Christmas Eve visit. He knows God's intention for him: "You put me back on my feet to walk, to run, upright, toward you who are coming."[43] It is the beginning of Advent, the time of longing for the coming of Christ. Christophe knows that to tread this path does not mean escaping the realities of the here and now:

> To say to you "come" is irreconcilable with a flight
> from the world
> which would be something other than coming
> and living on this covenanted earth.[44]

So he prays, "May I say to you 'come,' as long as you want me to remain here." This prayer "stabilizes" in him as "a single desire." Not a pure desire, of course; he recognizes that it competes with other desires, "including the desire to be finished with it all." Nevertheless his deepest desire is "To live at Tibhirine—to dwell in your gardens: with reference to You who are coming."[45]

The garden is both a physical and an imaginative space—and this interweaving can be seen in Christophe's journal. The gardens of the Hebrew and Christian Scriptures are never far

[43] Lebreton, *Born from the Gaze of God*, 117; November 26, 1994.
[44] Lebreton, *Born from the Gaze of God*, 118; November 26, 1994.
[45] Lebreton, *Born from the Gaze of God*, 118; November 28, 1994.

from his consciousness: the paradisical garden of Eden and the Garden of Gethsemane, as well as the rich imagery so often used by Jesus—of vineyards, of sowing, planting, and pruning. Christophe found the image of the garden in the Qur'an too: "Those who adhere and are upright are among the Companions of the Garden, they are there forever" (Qur'an II:82).[46] His Muslim co-workers and neighbors were his "Companions of the Garden," and it was among them that Christophe so often found God's presence. The garden was a place of meeting and encounter, a place of listening and sharing.

On a day that he had struggled with the realities of walking in the way of the cross and had shared Br. Luc's anger over the mutilation of a fifteen-year-old girl in Médéa for failing to wear a hijab, he also notes a precious encounter in the garden:

> This afternoon: Amin, four years old (as he tells me), stayed alone with me in the garden a good while because his grandfather Ali forgot him. We toiled at your Work. It makes me feel younger to hear him say "my brother."[47]

My brother—one glimpses here the depth of trust and friendship between Christophe and his fellow workers and their families. The garden is a place of both receiving and giving.

> Before Vespers I met Ali in Your garden, ensconced in this space of greenery and air. He talks to me about what has happened to him, what he has seen, heard, touched. No ideological or even plain conceptual reflex. I don't understand all the words. I hear his deep emotion, his interior upheaval and immense distress: "It's as if you're out in the ocean with waves. First you are thrown one way, then the other. You're at the mercy of it. . . ."[48]

[46] Lebreton, *Born from the Gaze of God*, 19; December 22, 1993.
[47] Lebreton, *Born from the Gaze of God*, 57; March 2, 1994.
[48] Lebreton, *Born from the Gaze of God*, 64; March 15, 1994.

In the spring of 1994, Christophe notes in his journal the welcome return of Christian to the monastery and then the unsettling receipt of a letter to the papal nuncio from the Ministry of Foreign Affairs, again raising questions about their continued existence. At the end of the entry Christophe writes,

> We have sown tomatoes, eggplants, peppers and
> flowers for your GARDEN.
> When will you come down, FRIEND, into your
> garden?[49]

There is an air of gentle, almost humorous, defiance here: we have sown our (humble) lives here, the garden is not ours anyhow, we await the Lord of the garden. The garden is a microcosm of the whole of Algeria and, indeed, of the whole human project set in motion in the garden of Eden.

The garden, as a place of friendship between God and humanity, and between Christians and Muslims, is also woven through Christophe's reflections during Holy Week of 1994. On Palm (Passion) Sunday he notices that in the Gospel of Mark, as Jesus faces the growing threat of violence, his "way of confronting it is to make us sit down at table," opening up "a space that resists and holds out: a place of essential conviviality, exchange, sharing."[50] While Christophe does not name it directly, the monastery garden is such a space—it has been his table.

On Tuesday of Holy Week Christophe notes that he had written to his bishop in response to a proposed communication project of the African Synod: "A mission for the Church: to promote evangelical relations with Muslims." Christophe is ambivalent about this language, likening it to promoting "values, products, ideas, systems, morals" to an untrustworthy marketplace—"an enterprise doomed to fail." He is clear that

[49] Lebreton, *Born from the Gaze of God*, 61; March 12, 1994.
[50] Lebreton, *Born from the Gaze of God*, 68; March 27, 1994.

their mission is an existential one, focused on living in the here and now:

> It's elsewhere I feel called to abide until your return: in the place where I can offer your Presence and receive it.
>
> Our Gospel mission: to live the Good News of our relation with Muslims. It's up to the Church to believe in Christ-like relations here today.

Then, again with a sense of defiance, "Today we're going to work in the vineyard." Christophe is working with his neighbors, tying pruned branches. It is in their living, day by day, working side by side at Tibhirine that the Gospel mission is located. He continues:

> I am going to ponder all this: You, planted here in this land of Algeria
>
> and without you nothing can be done (that perdures)
> you: bear in us fruits of friendship.
> I pray to the Father that this may come to pass
> among us
> the GIFT
> that's stronger than murder.[51]

He resumes these reflections the next day, while his neighbors anticipate "the approaching [Easter] feast."

> My Father is the vine-dresser. Today we continue tying up the branches that have "burst." Bursts of life. Rush of Christ-sap. It's a job for believers: the lambs come out to pasture in the vineyard, and as for its future fruit: uncertainty and threats weigh it down.[52]

[51] Lebreton, *Born from the Gaze of God*, 69; March 29, 1994.
[52] Lebreton, *Born from the Gaze of God*, 70; March 30, 1994.

Working side by side, Christian and Muslim, they are like lambs—full of new life, yet vulnerable.

On Holy Saturday Christophe writes, "It was Ali I met in the garden when I went to water it, and Ali who offered me your presence there after the reading of your Passion."[53] Earlier he had written, "What a joy to meet Mohammed, Ali, or Moussa. In them, the Mystery flowers with simplicity and purity. It's a quality of presence: peaceful, tender, nourishing."[54]

The garden, however, is no paradise. In the midst of the liturgical demands of the Octave of Easter Christophe finds himself tired and irritable:

> Saturday there was the fit of anger against our neighbor and his sheep, then against Mohammed. Where was then the good news of fraternal relations? When I manage to go beyond such angry reactions, then I can sense this Gospel thrust all the stronger which allows me to look at Mohammed and receive his honest gaze. He doesn't judge me. "You know, I didn't notice a thing." My explanations, my reasons have their place, but they fall so short of the essence of what transpired between us out there—something given. I do believe it came from you.[55]

The "Presence" is both offered and received in the garden. On this occasion it is Christophe who receives the gift of forgiveness.

The garden, both physical and metaphorical, is the site of on-going work.

> Yesterday we started to prune the vines. Today, I am on retreat close by you, the true vine. In order to dwell in you as you dwell in me, and to produce fruit that the Father expects of me. This morning I tasted great joy—so very

[53] Lebreton, *Born from the Gaze of God*, 71; April 2, 1994.
[54] Lebreton, *Born from the Gaze of God*, 50; February 12, 1994.
[55] Lebreton, *Born from the Gaze of God*, 74; April 11, 1994.

> undeserved!—of being your beloved disciple. [. . .] The only thing necessary for the branch that has been pruned by the Word is to obey the divine sap completely.[56]

Christophe is aware that pruning will be needed again. The work never stops. But this is worthwhile work.

Christophe's last prayer journal opens a privileged window into the joys and struggles of the demanding journey he shared with his brother monks over his last two and a half years. Oriented toward the God whom he had encountered as love, it was a journey that was both hard and fruitful, a journey of ultimate value. So Christophe declares, "Onward! Today: to the VINEYARD."[57]

A Time for Sowing

On June 4, 1996, on a "wet and overcast" day, when "all nature seemed to be weeping for sorrow," the remains of the seven brothers were buried in the gardens at Tibhirine.[58]

More accurately, in the monastery's cemetery, where each monk had imagined being buried. In a sense this was simply the outworking of their commitment to monastic stability. In 1991, after the community had voted unanimously to welcome his solemn profession, Brother Paul had written to his mother, "Since then, I have been going down to the cemetery to ask the cypresses to see if there is one who will be willing to watch over me when the time comes!"[59]

The seven coffins were lowered into the ground, and the first spadefuls of earth were cast into the graves by their arch-

[56] Lebreton, *Born from the Gaze of God*, 136; February 8, 1995.

[57] Lebreton, *Born from the Gaze of God*, 77; April 23, 1994.

[58] Bernardo Olivera, *How Far to Follow: The Martyrs of Atlas*, CS 197 (Kalamazoo, MI: Cistercian Publications, 1997), 43.

[59] Moines de Tibhirine, *Heureux ceux qui espèrent: Autobiographies spirituelles*, ed. Marie-Dominique Minassian, Les écrits de Tibhirine 1 (Paris: Bayard-Cerf-Bellefontaine, 2018), 68.

bishop, Msgr. Henri Tessier, and their abbot general, Dom Bernardo Olivera. Their neighbors "continued the task," and, Olivera recounts, "at that very moment the sun broke through the clouds." He continues, "The coffins disappeared under the earth, and we disappeared beneath the embraces, kisses, and condolences of countless neighbors of the monastery, who at the same time thanked us for having buried the monks here."[60]

The monks' graves, and the small patch of earth in the Atlas Mountains that had hosted the Cistercian monastery of Notre-Dame de l'Atlas, have become a place of pilgrimage for Muslims as well as Christians, honoring the monks and remembering all those who lost their lives in Algeria's black decade.

A little over a month before the monks' abduction Christophe had written in his journal, "I sowed my second cross somewhere in the garden." The cross had been a gift, crafted in the tau shape of a Franciscan cross, and this sowing had presumably happened accidently in the course of his work. But Christophe does not think of it as lost. Instead he asks, "When will it be the hour to be sown—beloved by you—at Tibhirine?" For Christophe and all the monks death was ever present, as it was for Jesus when he entered Jerusalem, and the cross sown in the garden reminds Christophe of Jesus' words: "unless a grain of wheat falls into the earth and dies, it remains just a single grain; but if it dies, it bears much fruit" (John 12:24).

[60] Olivera, *How Far to Follow*, 44.

Epilogue

A Heritage for Us

"The pathway has been marked out, we have only to walk along it."[1] After thirty years Bernardo Olivera's call to embrace the gift left to us by the Tibhirine monks still stands. In fact the path is simple: to follow Christ, to the end. But it is this commitment to following Christ to the very end, made by each of the monks and by the community as a whole, that continues to astonish us—in part for its simplicity, its ordinariness, its doggedness as well as the courage that it represents. Of course it presses us to ask ourselves: are we capable of walking such a path? The reassuring answer that we would receive from each of the monks is "well no, neither were we!"—but, they would say, in the company of the Christ who goes before us, and together as his body, all things are possible.

In early March 1996, three weeks before the monks' abduction, Christian de Chergé gave a retreat in Algiers to ordinary lay Christians. Like the monks, they too lived amid violence and under threat. Christian spoke with sensitivity about their common situation, sharing what the Tibhirine community had experienced and learned. And he proposed five pillars of peace: patience, poverty, presence, prayer, and pardon. He was echoing the five pillars of Islam but also offering a handy mnemonic to his audience—helping them as fellow Christians to articulate and remember their shared vocation: to remain

[1] Bernardo Olivera, *How Far to Follow: The Martyrs of Atlas*, CS 197 (Kalamazoo, MI: Cistercian Publications, 1997), 103.

faithful to the Gospel of peace in a time of violence.[2] For people of faith this is *our* shared vocation—so these five pillars of peace might well function in the same way for us. Here I have used these pillars to frame some tentative reflections on the gift and challenge of journeying in the company of the Tibhirine monks. And it has been impossible to resist sitting at the feet of Christian one last time, as he speaks to people who are not monks, people like us.

Patience

There is one word I will always associate with Christian and his brother monks: the *quotidian*—the daily, the mundane, the workaday. The choices made by the monks were made day by day in the context of their ordinary lives: in their relations with one another as well as with their neighbors; in their work in the dispensary, the garden, the kitchen, at the gate, or in the guesthouse; and in their commitment to prayer, to the priority of returning again and again to God. They never embark on a heroic journey. In fact, Christian tells his retreat audience, it is in the quotidian that we require and learn patience. He remarks, "we know that it is courage for the quotidian that takes us most by surprise."[3] The quotidian is where we are most tested. Patience and passion, he points out, have the same

[2] Christian de Chergé, "'L'Église, c'est l'Incarnation continuée': Récollection de carême, 8 mars 1996," in *L'invincible espérance*, ed. Bruno Chenu (Paris: Bayard, 2010). Br. Christophe also refers to five pillars, "Patience, Prayer, Sharing [*Partage*], Pardon, and Peace," in a journal entry in which he is recounting Christian's homily at their Ash Wednesday Eucharist. The five pillars seem to have been suggested to Christian by their neighbor Mohammed in relation to Ramadan. Christian may have adapted this idea for his retreat talk (Christophe Lebreton, *Born from the Gaze of God: The Tibhirine Journal of a Martyr Monk (1993–1996)*, trans. Mette Louise Nygård and Edith Scholl, MW 37 [Collegeville, MN: Cistercian Publications, 2014], 207; February 21, 1996).

[3] Chergé, "'L'Église, c'est l'Incarnation continuée,'" 300.

etymology; both are rooted in the Latin word *pati*, meaning to suffer or endure.

Patience, Christian suggests, is "the virtue of hope."[4] Without this connection to hope, patient endurance would make no sense. On the contrary, endurance is purposeful. As Christian would say, we are creatures who long, we are pilgrims of the horizon, we are running towards the kingdom. Monastic life, indeed Christian life, has an eschatological orientation: it is life open to God's unfolding future, a future that can never be grasped or known, but that is secured in the hope found in the paschal mystery, the death and resurrection of Jesus Christ. The celebration of the Eucharist rehearses this hope, and the memorial acclamation "Christ has died, Christ has risen, Christ will come again" points us toward that hope.

But as Christian points out, this future belongs to God, and hope requires that we accept that we cannot see it. Christian speaks strongly—"to want to see or imagine the future is to make hope-fiction, and it seems to me that this somehow violates it."[5] He draws attention to the desert experience of the liberated Hebrew slaves for whom the "gift of manna" was "a daily gift"—it rotted if they tried to store it (Exod 16:19-20). Rather, hope is resolutely practiced in the quotidian, so that the eternal and the present (the here and now) converge. The orientation is never otherworldly but always located in this blessed clay.

In his series of chapter talks on humility Christian expressed this idea vividly: "Humility begins when I realize I have only this brief day, today, to give him who calls me for ALL DAYS, but how can I tell him 'yes' for always if I don't give him this little day . . . God has a thousand years to make a day; I have but one day to make eternity—today!"[6] There is strength in this convergence of the quotidian and the eternal. It resists

[4] Chergé, "'L'Église, c'est l'Incarnation continuée,'" 301.

[5] Chergé, "'L'Église, c'est l'Incarnation continuée,'" 301.

[6] Christian de Chergé, *Dieu pour tout jour: chapitres de Père Christian de Chergé à la communauté de Tibhirine (1985–1996)*, 2nd ed. (Montjoyer: Abbaye Notre-Dame d'Aiguebelle, 2006), 312–13; January 30, 1990.

both despondency and pious escapism. It requires courageous, kindly patience.

Poverty

Not knowing, Christian suggests, is a form of poverty: "Let the Holy Spirit do his work, he will go fishing."[7] Recognizing that "the future belongs to God, who, from all eternity, wants to fulfill us" is "true poverty."[8] The Tibhirine community learned to live with a permanent sense of provisionality. Politically and religiously their position in post-colonial Algeria was always precarious. Economically too—their agricultural and guesthouse businesses were marginal operations. They lived very simply, conscious of the material poverty of their neighbors, and bore with them the exigencies of Algeria's deteriorating economy.

Following Jean-Baptist Metz, Philippe Hémon rightly identifies precariousness as a signal of the "eschatological openness" that underpins religious life.[9] How many of us are willing to live with such precariousness, such trustful openness to God? Tibhirine challenges us. As Christian Salenson notes, "precariousness has not prevented this community from bearing fruit—fruit that may well indeed last."[10] There is also a challenge here for the contemporary church, particularly in the West. As Christian Salenson astutely observes, many Christian communities are in situations of precariousness, "often unacknowledged," but sadly, "such precariousness is rarely considered a form of evangelical poverty."[11]

[7] Chergé, "'L'Église, c'est l'Incarnation continuée,'" 302.

[8] Chergé, "'L'Église, c'est l'Incarnation continuée,'" 303.

[9] Philippe Hémon, "An En-Visaged Good-By-E," CSQ 34, no. 2 (1999): 208.

[10] Christian Salenson, "Monastic Life, Interreligious Dialogue, and Openness to the Ultimate: A Reflection on the Tibhirine Monks' Experience," *The Way* 45, no. 3 (2006): 25.

[11] Salenson, "Monastic Life," 25.

Radical dependence and trust in God, abandonment into the arms of God, is not easily lived, of course. The Tibhirine community shows us both its cost and its fruit. Hémon's experience is apposite: "What freedom I felt with those men, stripped of all, able to offer only that in themselves which made them day by day more human."[12] Stripping—*dépouillement*—is another word that is woven through the Tibhirine story. In fact, it is a word that characterizes the whole monastic journey wherever it is lived. Its harsh-sounding overtones might frighten those of us who live in material and imagined psychological and spiritual comfort.

The desert of the monastery is intended to be the place where over a lifetime, through self-denial, the monk becomes more Christ-like. However, at Tibhirine the stripping is less an ascetic practice than a freely embraced condition of the monks' presence in Algeria. Their exterior material and political circumstances motivated their ongoing interior conversion (*metanoia*). What Hémon, and indeed other visitors to the monastery, detected was the authenticity of the monks' way of living. This stripping, both exterior and interior, had made them more human.

I am reminded here of Dietrich Bonhoeffer's letter to his friend Eberhard Bethge, written from prison in July 1944, where Bonhoeffer awaited probable execution. His own stripping had taken him to a place that echoes the experience of the Tibhirine monks:

> In the last few years I have come to know and understand more and more the profound this-worldliness of Christianity. The Christian is not a *homo religiosus* but simply a human being, in the same way that Jesus was a human being [. . .]. I do not mean the shallow and banal this-worldliness of the enlightened, the bustling, the comfortable, or the lascivious, but the profound this-worldliness

[12] Hémon, "An En-Visaged Good-By-E," 208.

> that shows discipline and includes the ever-present knowledge of death and resurrection. [. . .]
>
> [I] am still discovering to this day, that one only learns to have faith by living in the full this-worldliness of life. If one has completely renounced making something of oneself—whether it be a saint or a converted sinner or a church leader (a so-called priestly figure!), a just or an unjust person, a sick or a healthy person—then one throws oneself completely into the arms of God, and this is what I call this-worldliness: living fully in the midst of life's tasks, questions, successes and failures, experiences, and perplexities—then one takes seriously no longer one's own sufferings but rather the suffering of God in the world. Then one stays awake with Christ in Gethsemane. And I think this is faith; this is *metanoia*. And this is how one becomes a human being, a Christian.[13]

Presence

Presence is the word that perhaps best characterizes the monastic community at Tibhirine. Present to God, to each other, and to the others among whom they lived. The community had no apostolic or missionary purpose. It was simply a presence of Christians in a predominantly Muslim country. After 1976 the community articulated this presence as *priants parmi d'autre priants*, praying among others who pray. The necessity of being such a presence, Christian understood, was simply a consequence of the incarnation. As God came to dwell among us (Emmanuel), so the baptized are called not only to witness to God's presence in the world, but to be bearers of that

[13] Dietrich Bonhoeffer, *Letters and Papers from Prison*, ed. John W. De Gruchy (Minneapolis: Fortress Press, 2010), 488–86, Letter to Eberhard Bethege, July 21, 1944.

presence. The church is the continuation of the incarnation.[14] Our presence is simply required.

Further, the quality of presence matters. The witness of the Tibhirine monks, like that of other contemplative monastic communities, offers a powerful counter story to a world of shrinking attention spans, where the human capacity to attend to the other is endangered. Cistercian monasticism places at its center a commitment to contemplation, understood as opening oneself to the presence of God. However, attending to God does not take us out of the world. It never invites flight. On the contrary, being present to God's presence enables us to be present to others.

The paradoxical consequence of attending to God is that we see all things afresh. Listening, attending, becomes a priority in our relations with others, indeed in our relations with the whole of creation. So, in the spirit of the story of the visitation, the brothers intentionally extended their contemplative practice ("custody of silence and speech") into their relationships with their neighbors, listening for God's presence in them—listening to the other, for the Other. Carmelite William McNamara's summation of contemplation as "a long loving look at the real" is pertinent here.[15] Long—because "presence" is a long-term commitment. Little can be achieved at speed. Neither do the habits of attention and the capacity to see and to love flourish without carefully prepared ground.

Prayer

Prayer and presence go hand in hand. Christian recognized that God's call to Abraham to "walk in my presence" is a shared human vocation and that prayer is simply a vehicle for

[14] Chergé, "'L'Église, c'est l'Incarnation continuée,'" 303.

[15] Quoted in Walter J. Burghardt, "Contemplation: A Long Loving Look at the Real," in *An Ignatian Spirituality Reader*, ed. George W. Traub (Chicago: Loyola Press, 2008), 91.

remembering the presence of God. The truth is that we require a lot of reminding!

Cistercian monastic life is shaped to support this remembrance of God. Prayer is not one endeavor among many, but rather it is embedded in the whole rhythm of life. The rhythm of communal prayer (the *Opus Dei*) provides a scaffold or framework for prayer, but this too is woven into the rhythms of prayer and work (*ora et labora*), solitude and community, community and hospitality. For the Atlas community this monastic rhythm of life, directed always to remembering the presence of God, proved to be robust in a time of violence.

Robust, and radical. Prayer, as attention to the presence of God, is not an activity but rather the locus of transformation. We are to pray for our enemies, Christian reminds the retreatants in Algiers: "Are we praying enough, in all directions, without borders, for all [*les uns et les autres*]?" Easily said perhaps, but then he shares something of his own journey following the Christmas Eve visit of the heavily armed Emir Sayah Attiya to the monastery: he admits that it was harder to come back from death than to accept it, that it took almost three weeks to find his feet, and that he struggled to know how to pray for the man with whom he had shared such an intense dialogue. In the struggle to pray Christian was faced with their shared humanity, their shared tendency to violence:

> I can't ask the good God: kill him. But I can ask: disarm him. Afterwards, I said to myself: Do I have the right to demand: disarm him, if I don't start by demanding: disarm me and disarm us in community. This is my daily prayer, I simply entrust it to you.

Pardon

It is the recognition of our own capacity for violence, for wrongdoing, for complicity with evil that is the foundation for Christian's final pillar of peace—pardon. It is this pillar that makes living together possible. He invites us to walk the path of forgiveness—"forgive us as we forgive"—knowing that the work of forgiveness begins with the recognition of one's own need for forgiveness.[16] In his *Testament* Christian lays this out simply:

> I would like, when the time comes,
>
> to have a moment of spiritual clarity
>
> which would allow me to beg forgiveness of God
>
> and of my fellow human beings,
>
> and at the same time forgive with all my heart
>
> the one who will strike me down.

From a human perspective, walking the path of forgiveness seems impossibly difficult. It requires God's intervention. The path to forgiveness and reconciliation begins with the gift of God's forgiveness. As Christophe writes in his journal, "Pardon and Peace from you, in the Breath: this comes to me at the foot of the Cross." However, if forgiveness is a gift received from God, it is a gift to be shared. So Christophe realizes, "You entrust Forgiveness to us." Forgiveness is to be lived—in relationships both within and beyond the monastery. Walking the path of forgiveness is incarnating, making present God's gift of forgiveness—a participation in the work of redemption.

The Tibhirine monks chose to walk this way of pardon, of costly love, aware that it is difficult and always a work in progress. In his *Testament* Christian refers to himself and his killer as "happy thieves" who are both, like the criminal dying on the cross beside Jesus, destined to be with him in paradise (Luke 23:43). The way of forgiveness is indeed the path to peace.

[16] Chergé, "'L'Église, c'est l'Incarnation continuée,'" 314.

Five pillars of peace—patience, poverty, presence, prayer, pardon. In closing his Algiers retreat address, Christian says, "I believe that, without these five pillars, peace is not possible. But peace is first and foremost a gift of God. It is given to us. Let's not say that it doesn't exist; it is there. It simply needs to be brought to light." And he observes that pardon—*ar-Rahman*, the Most Merciful—is the first of the ninety-nine names of God in Islamic tradition and that patience—*es-Sabur*, the Patient—is the last. But then he insists, "God himself is poor, God himself is present, and God is prayer. This is the peace that God gives. It is not as the world gives."[17]

The Prophetic Gift

I began this book lamenting, with David Tacey, the untethered nature of much contemporary spirituality—and the attendant risk that "the flower of spirituality might wilt and die when its day passes, unless it can find its way back to the sources from which it arose."[18] Perhaps a greater challenge for contemporary Christians is a loss of confidence in the deep wisdom of our own traditions. Institutional crises have eroded the moral credibility of a church already struggling in a secular age.

Yet what the Tibhirine monks clearly lived, faithfully and fruitfully, was a living and life-giving tradition of discipleship, a deeply integrated way of following Christ, a way that is built on two thousand years of Christian wisdom and on the rich and practical tradition of Benedictine and Cistercian monasticism; a way that is open to the mystery of God, resisting all fundamentalisms; a way that is unafraid of difference or of dialogue with other religious traditions; a costly way that is open to being tested in the deep, often turbulent, waters of real

[17] Chergé, "'L'Église, c'est l'Incarnation continuée,'" 317–18.

[18] David Tacey, "Contemporary Spirituality," in *Oxford Textbook of Spirituality in Healthcare*, ed. Mark Cobb, Christina M. Puchalski, and Bruce D. Rumbold (Oxford: Oxford University Press, 2012), 473.

life—and, in the face of hatred and violence, is resolutely committed to the love that is found in the crucified and risen Christ.

I, for one, am happy to be tethered to such a tradition, to this school of peace.

Appendix I

The *Testament* of Christian de Chergé

The *Testament* of Christian de Chergé is increasingly recognized as one of the most profound spiritual texts of the twentieth century. The text bears two dates reflecting its composition over the eventful end of 1993. December 1, 1993, was the date of the expiration of the GIA ultimatum for foreigners to leave Algeria. It was also the anniversary of the death of Charles de Foucauld, killed at Tamanrasset, in southern Algeria, in 1916. The testament was completed on January 1, 1994, a Marian feast day. By then the threatened killing of foreigners had begun, including the murder of the twelve Croatian workers on December 15, and the monastery itself had been visited by armed insurgents on Christmas Eve. Sealed and sent to Christian's younger brother and godson, Gérard, the testament was opened and read by Christian's mother and his siblings on Pentecost Sunday, May 26, 1996. Understanding its significance, they released it to the Catholic daily newspaper *La Croix*, where it was first published on May 29.[1]

[1] The English translation reproduced here is from Bernardo Olivera, *How Far to Follow: The Martyrs of Atlas*, CS 197 (Kalamazoo, MI: Cistercian Publications, 1997), 127–29. This translation retains *A-DIEU* in the title rather than using the English translation *goodbye* or *farewell*. In French *adieu* also means "to or for God," and this meaning together with Christian's hyphenation makes his intention clear—it is a farewell, but one that is taking him to God. For the French text of the *Testament* see https://ocso.org/history/saints-blesseds-martyrs/testament-of-christian-de-cherge/.

When we face an A-DIEU . . .
[*Quand un A-DIEU s'envisage*]

If it should happen one day—and it could be today—
that I become a victim of the terrorism
which now seems ready to engulf
all the foreigners living in Algeria,
I would like my community, my Church, and my family
to remember that my life was GIVEN
to God and to this country.
I ask them to accept the fact
that the One Master of all life
was not a stranger to this brutal departure.
I would ask them to pray for me:
for how could I be found worthy of such an offering?
I ask them to associate this death
with so many other equally violent ones
which are forgotten through indifference or anonymity.
My life has no more value than any other.
Nor any less value.
In any case, it has not the innocence of childhood.
I have lived long enough to know
that I am an accomplice in the evil
which seems, alas, to prevail in the world,
even in the evil which might blindly strike me down.
I would like, when the time comes,
to have a moment of spiritual clarity
which would allow me to beg forgiveness of God
and of my fellow human beings,
and at the same time forgive with all my heart
the one who will strike me down.
I could not desire such a death.

For an exegesis of the text see Bernardo Olivera, "Monk, Martyr, and Mystic: Christian de Chergé (1937–1996)," CSQ 34, no. 3 (1999): 321–38. On the interpretation (and hence translation) of the difficult phrase *envisagé de toi* as "in God's face I see yours" see also Olivera, *How Far to Follow*, 36–37.

It seems to me important to state this.
I do not see, in fact, how I could rejoice
if the people I love were indiscriminately
accused of my murder.
It would be too high a price to pay
for what will perhaps be called
the "grace of martyrdom"
to owe this to an Algerian, whoever he may be,
especially if he says he is acting in fidelity
to what he believes to be Islam.
I am aware of the scorn which can be heaped
on the Algerians indiscriminately.
I am also aware of the caricatures of Islam
which a certain Islamism fosters.
It is too easy to soothe one's conscience
by identifying this religious way with
the fundamentalist ideology of its extremists.
For me, Algeria and Islam are not that,
but rather a body and a soul.
I have proclaimed this often enough, I think,
in the light of what I have received from it.
I so often find there that true strand of the Gospel
which I learned at my mother's knee,
my very first Church,
precisely in Algeria, and already inspired
with respect for Muslim believers.
Obviously, my death will appear to confirm
those who hastily judged me naive or idealistic:
"Let him tell us now what he thinks of it!"
But these persons should know that finally
my most avid curiosity will be set free.
This is what I shall be able to do, please God:
immerse my gaze in that of the Father
to contemplate with him His children of Islam
just as he sees them, all shining with the glory of Christ,
the fruit of His Passion, filled with the Gift of the Spirit
whose secret joy will always be to establish communion
and restore the likeness, playing with the differences.

For this life lost, totally mine and totally theirs,
I thank God, who seems to have willed it entirely
for the sake of that JOY in everything
and in spite of everything.
In this THANK YOU, which is said
for everything in my life from now on,
I certainly include you, friends of yesterday and today,
and you, my friends of this place,
along with my mother and father,
my sisters and brothers and their families.
You are the hundredfold granted as was promised!
And also you, my last-minute friend,
who will not have known what you were doing:
Yes, I want this THANK YOU and this "A-DIEU"
to be for you, too,
because in God's face I see yours [*en-visagé de toi*].
May we meet again as happy thieves
in Paradise, if it please God, the Father of us both.

AMEN! INCH'ALLAH!

Algiers, December 1, 1993

Tibhirine, January 1, 1994

Christian+

Appendix II

The Brothers

Luc (Paul) Dochier 1914–1996

Brother Luc was the much-loved, undisputed elder of the Atlas community. He was eighty-two and in indifferent health at the time of his kidnapping and death. Luc's vocation as monk and doctor, lived out in service at Tibhirine for almost fifty years, gave the monastic community a particular, even unusual, character and was central to the monks' relationship to the village and surrounding region.

Luc Dochier (baptized Paul) was born on January 31, 1914, in Bourg-de-Péage, Drôme, in southeast France. In 1932 he commenced medical studies in Lyon, though towards the end of his studies he "disappeared" to the monastery of Notre-Dame d'Aiguebelle, sensing a different call on his life. While he was persuaded to return to his medical studies, their completion was interrupted in 1938 by military service. Luc was deployed as a medical auxiliary in southern Morocco, where he continued to serve after the declaration of war in 1939. It was an experience that gave him a love of the Maghreb and its people. In 1940 he returned to Lyon to defend his doctoral thesis, finally completing his medical studies.[1]

[1] Frère Luc, *Tu verras éclater le printemps: Lettres de Tibhirine*, Les Écrits de Tibhirine - Lettres 1 (Paris: Bayard-Cerf-Bellefontaine, 2021), 21–23; Moines de Tibhirine, *Heureux ceux qui espèrent: Autobiographies spirituelles*,

Following his discharge from military service in 1941 Luc once more turned to his monastic vocation. On December 28, 1941, he was clothed as a novice choir monk. By the end of the following year, however, he had changed direction, becoming a lay brother (*convers*) and taking on the name Luc. This was a decisive moment in his vocational journey. Taking a new name, that of Luke the Evangelist and doctor, and identifying as a lay brother, a worker monk, signaled the twin elements of his vocation—monk and doctor (*moine et médecin*).[2]

In 1943 war called Luc to a different kind of service. A friend from Bourg-de-Péage, a doctor with a large family, had been detained in a German prisoner-of-war camp. Luc volunteered to take his place and worked as part of the camp's medical team, caring for up to 4000 prisoners, including the harshly treated Russians, until its liberation in July 1945.[3]

After the war Luc returned to Aiguebelle and took his first, temporary, vows on August 15, 1946, just before being sent to Tibhirine with five other monks. It is clear that the plan was for him to exercise his dual vocation there. A dispensary was opened, which in its first year treated 3600 patients.[4] The dispensary operated almost continuously—from October 1946 until the night of March 26, 1996—for nearly fifty years with brother Luc, "Frélou," as the much-revered doctor, the *toubid*.

In July 1957, during the Algerian War of Independence, Luc and a fellow monk were taken hostage by armed *fellaghas*. A small group of heavily armed men had entered the monastery seeking to kidnap the monks in retaliation for the death of a pro-FLN imam in Médéa. The abbot refused, but to defuse the situation Luc, who recognized some of the men, and Fr. Mathieu, who had also had long-term contact with the *fellaghas*, volunteered to go with them. They were released, unharmed,

---

ed. Marie-Dominique Minassian, Les écrits de Tibhirine 1 (Paris: Bayard-Cerf-Bellefontaine, 2018), 85.

[2] Moines de Tibhirine, *Heureux ceux qui espèrent*, 86.

[3] Luc, *Tu verras éclater le printemps*, 25.

[4] Moines de Tibhirine, *Heureux ceux qui espèrent*, 90–91.

eight days later, eighty kilometers from the monastery. The ordeal took a significant physical and psychological toll on both brothers, and subsequently Luc was sent to France for a period of rest—cut short by an accident at Tibhirine that required the presence of a doctor.[5]

Algerian independence in 1962 marked the beginning of a period of significant instability for the monastery and for Luc himself. In 1962 and again in 1964–1965 Luc spent time at Notre-Dame des Neiges, Orval, Belgium, ostensibly for rest. Only a handful of monks remained at Tibhirine, and under a change of leadership the place of the dispensary had been questioned. Luc felt he could not remain there if he could not practice as a doctor. He pleaded his case with the then abbot general and was eventually given permission to return to Tibhirine.[6]

Luc returned to the Atlas community at the beginning of October 1965. Apart from occasional visits to France for rest or medical treatment, he remained there until the monks were kidnapped in March 1996, serving the local community as their doctor and wise confidant, and his brother monks as their cook and respected elder.

Christian de Chergé 1937–1996

Christian was born at Colmar, Alsace, northeastern France on January 18, 1937, into a family with an aristocratic and military pedigree. His father Guy served in Algeria during World War II and was afterwards promoted to the rank of general and appointed as director of studies at the École de Guerre, Paris. His mother Monique, a devout Catholic with old French noble ancestry, encouraged the faith development of her large family of eight children, of whom Christian was

[5] Luc, *Tu verras éclater le printemps*, 31; Moines de Tibhirine, *Heureux ceux qui espèrent*, 95–97.

[6] Luc, *Tu verras éclater le printemps*, 31–32; Moines de Tibhirine, *Heureux ceux qui espèrent*, 98–100.

the third son. After the three war years spent in Algeria, the family settled in the fashionable quarter of Faubourg Saint-Honoré in Paris. Christian attended a Marianist school for boys, Sainte-Marie de Monceau, where he excelled academically. He sensed a priestly vocation early in his life, and in 1956 he entered the Séminaire des Carmes in Paris, undertaking its rigorous six-year program of philosophy and theology.[7]

Christian's seminary program was interrupted by twenty-seven months of compulsory national service. In 1959, after completing officer training, he was posted to Algeria during the War of Independence. He was returning to the country where he had already lived as a child during World War II, a place where his parents had taught him a respect for the Arab population. This return proved to be a decisive experience for his future. He was appointed as an officer with the SAS to Tiaret, one of six hundred administrative districts designed to bring rural Algeria more firmly under French control.[8]

In Algeria in 1959 Christian found himself in a situation of considerable political and spiritual complexity. The fact that Algerian independence was by then firmly on the French political agenda led to a growing sense of betrayal among the European population. While the archbishop of Algiers, Léon-Étienne Duval, spoke in support of justice and self-determination for all Algerians, Christian's local parish priest vehemently opposed independence and showed little respect for Arabs or for Islam.[9] Christian met Duval and was impressed by him and, at the invitation of his commanding officer, experienced hospitality and "courteous dialogue" with a local mufti, confirming his "intuition that the antagonism between Christianity and Islam was encumbered with prejudices."[10] However, his brief friendship with a rural guard, Mohammed,

[7] John W. Kiser, *The Monks of Tibhirine: Faith, Love, and Terror in Algeria* (New York: St Martin's Griffin, 2002), 23–25; Marie-Christine Ray, *Christian de Chergé, prieur de Tibhirine*, 2nd ed. (Paris: Bayard, 1998), 15–35.

[8] Kiser, *The Monks of Tibhirine*, 9–10.

[9] Kiser, *The Monks of Tibhirine*, 9–10.

[10] Moines de Tibhirine, *Heureux ceux qui espèrent*, 310.

and this devout man's murder by the FLN on November 8, 1959, after he had defended Christian during an ambush whilst they were on patrol together, tied Christian permanently to Algeria and to prayer.

On completing his military service, Christian returned to his seminary studies and was ordained in 1964 as a priest of the archdiocese of Paris. He served as a chaplain for five years at Sacré-Coeur in Montmartre, under its conservative rector Monsignor Maxime Charles. The environment was at odds with Christian's "dream of a poor and *fraternelle* church"—he would have preferred to serve one of the working-class parishes that he could see only from the elevation of Montmartre.[11] The environment was at odds too with his own emerging theology and practice as a priest, which was strongly influenced by Vatican II (1962–1965).

Christian had confided a call to monastic life to his bishop well before his ordination but had been asked to serve as a diocesan priest for a period of three years, later extended to five years.[12] However, this ministry left him with invaluable experience and a love for preaching and spiritual direction. When he entered Aiguebelle as a postulant on the feast day of Saint Bernard of Clairvaux, August 20, 1969, he had a return to Algeria firmly in view. His choice of the Cistercians was motivated by their commitment to prayer, especially prayer in community, and to manual work, but above all by the fact that the order had a monastery in Algeria, at Tibhirine.

When Christian joined the community of Notre-Dame de l'Atlas on January 15, 1971, he was still completing his novitiate. Schedules written in his personal notebook from this period reveal his disciplined use of time, his personal pattern of prayer intentions, and an extensive program of reading, including an orientation to Islam and African culture, all this managed within the framework of Cistercian life with its demanding schedule of communal prayer, manual work, and community

[11] Ray, *Christian de Chergé*, 67–68.

[12] Moines de Tibhirine, *Heureux ceux qui espèrent*, 312.

formation.[13] Throughout his life Christian had an astonishing capacity for work and apparently needed little sleep.

Soon after his arrival at Tibhirine Christian was given leave to study at the Pontifical Institute for Arabic and Islamic Studies (IPEA) in Rome. At the end of June 1974, after two years study under Fr. Maurice Borrmans, Christian returned to Tibhirine. He was assigned to assist Fr. Placide in the guesthouse, with responsibility for providing spiritual direction to retreatants, a role for which he was eminently suited. His Islamic studies proved useful as guests brought their curiosity about living and working in a Muslim environment. Muslim guests also brought their own questions, regarding Christian attitudes to Islam and about Christian practices.[14]

Christian was due to make his solemn profession in 1976, a time of significant political upheaval and uncertainty in Algeria—the monastery had again been threatened with closure by Algerian authorities. There is no doubt that Christian's solemn profession on October 1 constituted a turning point for the whole monastic community, as it recognized a shared call to be "a presence of the Church praying with the prayer of Islam and a monastic presence in the Church of Algeria."[15] Still, this naming of a shared call did not mean plain sailing ahead. Personnel and leadership changes continued, and Christian's own strong sense of vocation did not always sit well with the rest of the community. The formation in early 1979 of the *Ribât es-Salâm*, the Bond of Peace, was deeply encouraging for him. However, by the end of the year the combination of a heavy workload in the guesthouse and the ongoing struggles over his vocation had taken a toll. Christian spent two months of rest and prayer at Asskrem, the hermitage of Charles de Foucauld on the edge of the Sahara Desert. When he returned to Tibhirine in early 1980 it was with renewed clarity: "REMAIN

[13] Moines de Tibhirine, *Heureux ceux qui espèrent*, 326–27.

[14] Moines de Tibhirine, *Heureux ceux qui espèrent*, 359–60, 372.

[15] "Profession solennelle du frère Christian 1 octobre 1976," in *Sept vies pour Dieu et l'Algérie*, ed. Bruno Chenu (Paris: Bayard, 1996), 26.

HERE and REMAIN WHAT I AM."[16] A few days after his return a further confirmation arrived in the form of a letter from a Muslim brotherhood of 'Alawiyines, seeking to meet with the monks. During this period Christian's writing reflects a growing confidence in articulating what he believed to be the place of the monastic community, and indeed the church, in a Muslim country.[17]

By late 1983, as subprior and in view of the ill health of their superior Jean de la Croix, Christian was already taking on leadership responsibilities in the community. In late 1983 and early 1984 he helped the community to resolve its irregular canonical status: while officially holding the status of an abbey, Notre-Dame de l'Atlas had since Algerian independence in 1962 been led by a *superior ad natum*, a superior appointed directly by their motherhouse, Aiguebelle, rather than by an abbot elected by the community. This was normally a temporary measure for an abbey experiencing difficulties, but this irregular arrangement had become entrenched and had undoubtedly contributed to the revolving door of leadership that had seen nine superiors in twelve years. The solution was to renounce the status of abbey, becoming instead a priory and opening the way for local leadership once more.[18] An election

[16] Moines de Tibhirine, *Heureux ceux qui espèrent*, 430.

[17] The earliest of these publications seems to be "Prier en Église à l'écoute de l'Islam," originally published in the Revue *Tychique* in 1982 and reprinted in *Chemins de dialogue* 27 (2007). Christian also contributed to *Lettre de Ligugé*, a publication of the French Benedictine abbey of Saint-Martin de Ligugé. Some of this material was reworked for different contexts. These early texts have been republished along with Christian's later writing on this subject: Christian de Chergé, "Venons-en à une parole commune: Chrétiens et musulmans, témoins et pèlerins de la miséricorde (1983)," in *L'invincible espérance*, ed. Bruno Chenu (Paris: Bayard, 2010), 67–108; Chergé, "Chrétiens et musulmans: nos différences ont-elles le sens d'une communion? (1984)," 109–66.

[18] As a priory the small community was able to function autonomously once more. Under the *Statute on Foundations* a community wishing to become an abbey needs at least twelve solemnly professed monks as well as the superior prepared to make their stability there. A priory requires

was set for March 31, 1984. The day began with Mass at 7 a.m., the voting commenced at 8 a.m., and by 8.45 a.m., after three rounds of votes, Christian had been elected prior of Notre-Dame de l'Atlas, a position he held for two six-year terms—a period of stability and renewal for the community.[19]

Christophe Lebreton 1950–1996

Christophe was the youngest member of the monastic community, and just forty-five when he was killed. A poet at heart, he was passionate, sensitive, prone to withdrawal and to occasional outbursts of anger. We are the privileged witnesses to all this in the published prayer journal of his last two and a half years.[20]

Christophe was born on October 11, 1950, in Blois, Loir-et-Cher, in central France, into a large bourgeois family, the seventh of twelve children. At his own request he attended the minor seminary in Blois for secondary school. His adolescent years, though, brought inevitable complexity and eventually a vocation to the priesthood. His world had opened up, particularly through his philosophy studies. He finished secondary school in 1968, a year of significant political ferment and civil unrest in France, sparked by the violent escalation of student protests during the spring. As for others of his generation, Christophe's faith in social and political institutions was unsettled. With no clear sense of direction, Christophe enrolled in the Faculty of Law at the University of Tours, studying political science. While a student, however, he spent summers working with the homeless and marginalized at the Emmaus camps founded by Abbé Pierre. This experience proved to be formative, giving him a passionate belief in God's solidarity

only six and can also continue to benefit from the assistance of the mother (or founding) house.

[19] Moines de Tibhirine, *Heureux ceux qui espèrent*, 445.

[20] See chapter 8.

with the poor and inspiring his later commitment to monastic poverty.[21]

A deeper encounter with God, as the source of love, turned Christophe conclusively toward a religious vocation. That encounter became a reference point throughout his life. Christophe began to consider how he might live out a vocation as a religious, in service to the poor. Impressed by the life and writings of Charles de Foucauld, he began to explore the possibility of joining the Little Brothers of Jesus but put his vocational discernment on hold while he completed his national service.[22] This service took him to Algeria.

Christophe served as a *coopérant* from September 1972 to June 1974, working in a school for disabled children located in Hussein-Dey, a working-class district of Algiers.[23] Here too he had his first contact with the monastic community of Notre-Dame de l'Atlas. Impressed by the simplicity and authenticity of the monks' lives, he soon settled on a vocation to the Cistercians. Christophe had Atlas very much in mind but, guided by the *pied-noir* parish priest Fr. Joseph Carmona, he sought to enter the Cistercian community of Tamié (rather than the motherhouse of Aiguebelle), which Carmona believed would be a good base for his formation and a refuge should Atlas ever close. This proved a good choice: Christophe found the scale and modesty of Tamié, as well as the presence of other novices of his own generation, helpful.[24]

Christophe entered the novitiate on November 1, 1974. His early experience at Tamié (1974–1975) and his first sojourn at Tibhirine (1976–1977) were hard years for him.[25] He had struggled, settling into monastic life at Tamié, but Tibhirine

[21] Christophe Lebreton, *Born from the Gaze of God: The Tibhirine Journal of a Martyr Monk (1993–1996)*, trans. Mette Louise Nygård and Edith Scholl, MW 37 (Collegeville, MN: Cistercian Publications, 2014), 120; December 1, 1994; Moines de Tibhirine, *Heureux ceux qui espèrent*, 490–98.

[22] Moines de Tibhirine, *Heureux ceux qui espèrent*, 498–503.

[23] Moines de Tibhirine, *Heureux ceux qui espèrent*, 503.

[24] Moines de Tibhirine, *Heureux ceux qui espèrent*, 509–17.

[25] See chapter 5.

proved too small and too isolated for a young man, a novice still in the early days of formation. As he settled back into life at Tamié after his return at the end of 1977, Christophe continued to ponder the shape of his dual vocation—to contemplative life and to solidarity with the poor. In the wake of Vatican II many monastic leaders were open to exploring renewed, more flexible expressions of monastic life. With preparation for the priesthood in mind, Christophe raised with his superior the possibility of another sort of formation—alongside "the working class"—an idea that eventually came to fruition in 1981 when he spent a year in Troyes as an apprentice carpenter. In the renewal of his vows in 1978 Christophe was recognized as a lay brother (even though the distinction between choir and lay brothers had technically been abolished), allowing him a simpler life of work and a reduced commitment to liturgical prayer.[26]

Christophe made his solemn profession on All Saints' Day 1980—six years after he had entered Tamié as a postulant. At the beginning of 1986 he and three other brothers were sent to the monastery of Notre-Dame des Dombes, in eastern France, to assist in the community's busy guesthouse. It was a time of consolidation and service, and here Christophe heard the call to return to the place that had given birth to his monastic vocation.[27]

Christophe returned to Tibhirine in October 1987, soon finding his place in a community that had matured into its own vocation. His formal change of stability took place on January 26, 1989. In early March his call to the priesthood was confirmed by the monastic community, and Archbishop Henry Teissier formally recognized and welcomed it on behalf of the Algerian church. He was ordained as deacon on June 3, 1989, and as a priest on New Year's Day 1990.

[26] Moines de Tibhirine, *Heureux ceux qui espèrent*, 559–86.

[27] Moines de Tibhirine, *Heureux ceux qui espèrent*, 590–604.

Michel Fleury 1944–1996

Michel "holds the saucepan in one hand and Brother Lawrence of the Resurrection in the other."[28] This is how Christian described their new chef shortly after Michel had joined the Atlas community. The comparison of Michel with Brother Lawrence, the Carmelite brother remembered for his humble kitchen service, is apposite: Michel's simplicity and his cultivation of attention to God and the people he lived alongside—his monastic brothers and their neighbors—characterized his life until its end. In his many years as a factory worker Michel had sought to integrate ordinary, daily life and his prayer. He bought this same concern to the monastery.

Michel Fleury was born and baptized on May 21, 1944, at Sainte-Anne-sur-Brivet in Loire-Atlantique in western France. He was killed, according to the GIA communique, on the same day in 1996, his fifty-second birthday. Nurtured within a devout family and inspired by Sainte-Anne's humble parish priest, Michel felt a call to the priesthood from his early teens. In 1961 he began studies at the minor seminary of Flocellière, although at the age of seventeen he was already considered a "late vocation." From 1966 to 1970 he continued studies at a major seminary but was ultimately not considered suited for the priesthood. However, a placement during his third year to work in the Joseph Paris factory in Nantes proved vocationally significant. This factory experience bought Michel into contact with construction and factory workers, many of them immigrants from the Maghreb. He fully embraced this placement, working the same hours as his fellow workers and getting to know them personally.[29]

In 1970 Michel moved to Lyon, living alongside immigrant worker communities, supporting himself by factory work.

[28] Moines de Tibhirine, *Heureux ceux qui espèrent*, 158. A popular and much translated compilation of conversations with and letters by Br. Lawrence (1614–1691) was published after his death as *The Practice of the Presence of God*.

[29] Moines de Tibhirine, *Heureux ceux qui espèrent*, 137–40.

While there he was drawn to the Prado, an association of priests and consecrated lay brothers founded by Fr. Antoine Chevrier (1826–1879) and dedicated to the evangelization of the poor. The spirituality of Chevrier and the Prado had an enduring influence on Michel's commitment to living in solidarity with the poor and marginalized. In the early 1970s Michel lived and worked with Prado brothers amongst immigrant communities in Lyon, Paris, and Marseille. He also trained as a fitter and turner (*fraiseur*) in the Alstom factory in Marseille, joining the union (*Confédération générale du travail*) and serving as treasurer.[30]

In 1979 Michel began to seriously explore the possibility of monastic life, driven by a further deepening of his attraction to prayer. After stays at the Cistercian communities of Lérins and Acey, Michel finally settled on Bellefontaine, where he had made retreats as a young seminarian. He was received as a postulant on November 17, 1980, and on the evening of the feast of the Epiphany, January 4, 1981, he "took the habit."[31]

In April 1984 Michel confided to his novice master that he sensed God calling him to join the small community of Notre-Dame de l'Atlas. Responding to a call for recruits, Michel, with his experience of working among North African migrants, was an obvious candidate, even though he had not been directly approached.[32] He departed for Algeria with fellow novice Bruno, arriving on August 28, 1984, the feast day of Saint Augustine. He was a natural fit. He settled happily into life at Tibhirine and sought to stay. When he came to renewing his temporary vows in 1985, he also changed his stability to Atlas. On August 28, 1986, two years after his arrival, Michel made his solemn profession.[33]

In Holy Week of 1989 Michel was instituted as lector along with Christophe, who was to be ordained as a deacon in June of that year. This gave Michel a formal role in the reading of

[30] Moines de Tibhirine, *Heureux ceux qui espèrent*, 140–41.
[31] Moines de Tibhirine, *Heureux ceux qui espèrent*, 146–49.
[32] Moines de Tibhirine, *Heureux ceux qui espèrent*, 152.
[33] Moines de Tibhirine, *Heureux ceux qui espèrent*, 165–66.

Scripture in the liturgical life of the community, a significant affirmation for him. Traditionally institution as a lector was a significant step in the path toward priesthood, a path that had been closed off to him in his youth.[34]

Célestin Ringeard 1933–1996

Célestin Ringeard was an unlikely candidate for monastic life. He was exuberant in his communication with people and indeed with God. Passionate and determined, Célestin spent most of his life in active priestly ministry until he formally entered Bellefontaine as a postulant in 1983 at the age of fifty.

Célestin was born on July 29, 1933, in Touvois, then part of Brittany, in northwest France. From childhood he was determined to become a priest, studying in minor seminaries in Legé (1945–1949) and Rezé (1949–1953), and then in the major seminary in Nantes (1953–1957).[35]

From 1957 to 1959 Célestin completed his military service, arriving in Oran, Algeria, with an infantry regiment in September 1957, assigned to a health service. One experience remained with him for life, helped to shape his vocation, and revealed the commitment to mercy and justice that he embodied throughout his life. In February 1958 he had cared for an intelligence officer with the FLN, Si Ahmed Hallouz, who had been seriously wounded and taken prisoner. Célestin advocated for the postponement of Ahmed's execution every year until Ahmed's release was secured by Archbishop Duval in 1962.[36] In 1984, Célestin received a phone call from Ahmed's eldest son, who was completing studies in Versailles. Ahmed had three times traveled to France in search of Célestin, without success. Célestin and he corresponded, and the two were reunited at Algiers airport on September 13, 1986, the day of Célestin's return to Algeria to join the community of

34 Moines de Tibhirine, *Heureux ceux qui espèrent*, 169–70.
35 Moines de Tibhirine, *Heureux ceux qui espèrent*, 258.
36 Moines de Tibhirine, *Heureux ceux qui espèrent*, 258–59.

Notre-Dame de l'Atlas. For Célestin this reunion was "One of the most powerful moments of my life!"[37]

From 1963 to 1975 Célestin worked in the parish of Saint-Dominique, located in a poor neighborhood in Nantes. There he found his place beyond regular churchgoers, visiting families in poor housing estates and working with those on the margins, who were often struggling with addictions. These eleven years proved transformative. Célestin's spirituality was one of rolled-up sleeves, of presence, underpinned by his understanding of the incarnation: Christ, in his total offering of himself, the radical sign of God's solidarity with humanity.[38]

Leaving diocesan employment, Célestin continued to work as a street educator, living in a rented apartment and employed by a center working with released prisoners. He also continued to support the work of the *Vie Libre* (Free Life) movement with recovering alcoholics. Célestin himself took on voluntary life-long abstinence from alcohol in 1967.[39] His commitment to living "in friendship and solidarity" with those whose lives were controlled by addictions and poverty was unwavering—but this way of life was costly. From Easter 1976 Célestin began to retreat three or four times a year to Bellefontaine, where he found refreshment and a place to unburden his immense pastoral load.

Nonetheless, his demanding ministry took him steadily toward burnout. One tragic event took him over the line. At midnight on May 4, 1982, Célestin responded to a call for help, but by the time he arrived at the apartment block the young man had thrown himself out of a window on the sixteenth floor to his death.[40] The distress Célestin experienced did not diminish over the following months, and he was eventually hospitalized. Amidst this crisis he had also heard a clear call to monastic life, and while on extended sick leave he began to

[37] Moines de Tibhirine, *Heureux ceux qui espèrent*, 279, 284–85, 288.

[38] Moines de Tibhirine, *Heureux ceux qui espèrent*, 259–62.

[39] Moines de Tibhirine, *Heureux ceux qui espèrent*, 297.

[40] Moines de Tibhirine, *Heureux ceux qui espèrent*, 274.

explore the possibility of becoming a postulant at Bellefontaine.

Célestin was received as a postulant there in July 1983 and as a novice on September 8. He had spent twenty years working with the poor and marginalized in Nantes, and now, at the age of fifty, he began a new journey, to become a monk. The following year, along with Michel and Bruno, he felt prompted to respond to the needs of the small Atlas community, a call that was confirmed by the renewed connection with Algeria following the unexpected contact made by Hallouz's son. Sensibly, given his recent entry into monastic life, Célestin was not sent to Tibhirine with Michel and Bruno. However, the sense of a call remained, and in September 1986, a year after Célestin had made his temporary vows, he departed for Tibhirine.[41]

Célestin settled happily into life at Tibhirine, though his extroverted nature and exuberance did not fit the usual profile of a monk—there needed to be adaptations on both sides. A gifted musician, he was soon appointed sub-cantor. In 1988, on the fifth anniversary of his entry into the novitiate, he change his stability to Atlas, and on May 1, 1989 (the day designated for the Feast of Our Lady of Africa in that year), made his solemn profession with two hundred and fifty people from near and far, including a dozen young neighbors and a local imam, crushed into the monastery chapel—a sign of support not only for Célestin, but for the monastery itself.[42]

From 1990 on Célestin faced increasingly serious health issues, culminating in major heart-bypass surgery in 1994, after which he spent some months recovering at Bellefontaine. The deteriorating situation in Algeria took a significant toll on his physical and mental health. He suffered from insomnia, which left him exhausted and fragile. Yet he found grace in his experience of being hospitalized in Médéa in 1994. He was in awe of the medical staff working in conditions of extreme

[41] Moines de Tibhirine, *Heureux ceux qui espèrent*, 280–84.

[42] Moines de Tibhirine, *Heureux ceux qui espèrent*, 286–93.

poverty, and he embraced the opportunity to relate to staff, visitors, and fellow patients. He continued to compose music, sing, and pray alongside Muslim brothers, who shared verses of the Qur'an and Hadith with him: "A very rich, albeit painful, moment, a unique moment that God has given me to live since 1986 . . . ."[43] Célestin remained at Tibhirine alongside his brother monks through their last hard years, sustained by his singing heart. In early 1996, ten years after Célestin's arrival in Algeria, Christian remarked to Dom Emmanuel Coutant, the former abbot of Bellefontaine, that "Célestin had found an equanimity that I admire."[44]

Paul Favre-Miville 1939–1996

Brother Paul is perhaps the least well-known of the brothers, at risk of being overlooked. However, his modesty, his gentle humor, his capacity to live in and contribute to community, and his very practical skill as a former tradesman made him a crucial member of the Atlas community.

Paul Favre-Miville was born on April 17, 1939, in Vinzier, Haute-Savoie, near the French-Swiss border. He lived for more than forty years in the same region with his parents in the village of Bonnevaux, where his father was a blacksmith and farrier and his mother ran a café and tobacconist shop, the hub of the local community. Paul left school at the age of fifteen, with only an elementary education, working at his father's forge. At the age of twenty he was enlisted into the 8th Marine Infantry Parachute Regiment, serving for twenty-seven months. As was the case for others of his generation, Paul spent part of his military service in Algeria during the War of Independence.

On his return to Bonnevaux, Paul trained as a plumber and heating engineer, working in this trade from 1967 until he entered the Cistercian monastery of Notre-Dame de Tamié in

[43] Moines de Tibhirine, *Heureux ceux qui espèrent*, 300.

[44] Moines de Tibhirine, *Heureux ceux qui espèrent*, 301.

1984. Later, his skills as a tradesman and practical problem solver were well used and deeply appreciated by the small community at Tibhirine. During his adolescence Paul, with his three sisters, was involved in a Catholic youth organization, the *Jeunesse agricole catholique*, and he sang in the parish choir. As an adult he contributed to civic life as a municipal counselor (eventually as deputy mayor) and as a volunteer fire fighter as well as serving in other community organizations.[45]

At the age of thirty-four "an encounter with the Living Jesus" led Paul to a deeper conversion.[46] His faith was nourished by reading and by annual pilgrimages (including volunteering at Lourdes), but not until his father's death in 1981 did he feel able to explore a vocation to monastic life. Paul entered Tamié as a postulant on August 20, 1984, the feast of Saint Bernard of Clairvaux. Aged forty-four, he was considered at the time a "late vocation" to religious life, but he entered with a level of Christian maturity and a clear sense of the long road ahead. He was formally welcomed into the novitiate on Christmas Eve 1984, and two years later, in December 1986, he took the first, temporary, vows of monastic profession.[47]

It is not clear just when Paul began to sense a call to join Notre-Dame de l'Atlas, but the desire surfaced again in early 1988 with the visit of Christian de Chergé, seeking recruits for the small community. By late 1988 this conviction had firmed, and in March 1989 Paul wrote to Christian seeking to join the Atlas community. He was by no means unhappy at Tamié—on the contrary, to leave meant relinquishing "a second family"—but his longstanding "solidarity with the poor" and concern for the "Third World" had converged with Christian's pleas for assistance. Algeria was already part of Paul's story, and while he acknowledged that much had changed, he understood the need to "maintain a Christian presence there that bears witness in simplicity to the current reality of the body

[45] Moines de Tibhirine, *Heureux ceux qui espèrent*, 50–52.

[46] Moines de Tibhirine, *Heureux ceux qui espèrent*, 67.

[47] Moines de Tibhirine, *Heureux ceux qui espèrent*, 50–58.

of Christ." His request was greeted with joy by the Atlas community.[48]

Paul joined the community at Tibhirine on December 29, 1989, arriving in time for Christophe's ordination as a priest on January 1. Paul was a good fit and settled in quickly. He worked with Christophe in the garden and was soon given the job of guestmaster. His skill as a plumber enabled him to improve the much-needed irrigation systems in the gardens. He was unquestionably the community handyman.

At the end of his first year at Tibhirine, on December 23, 1990, Paul formally changed his stability to Atlas, and in the following year, on August 20, 1991, seven years to the day after entering Tamié as a postulant, he made his solemn profession.

Family was foundational to Paul's life, and the warmth and security that he had experienced in his birth family enabled him to embrace relationships in every community in which he lived: initially "the valley" where he spent most of his life, and later the monastic communities of Tamié and Atlas. He never abandoned any of these valued relationships. Indeed, he simply embraced the brothers at Tibhirine as extended family. This sense of familial relatedness is reflected in the message Christian sent to Paul's mother after Paul's solemn profession: "We would like you to consider yourself a bit like the mother of all Paul's brothers!"[49]

Paul remained at Tibhirine, knowing, in the final years, the probable cost. On March 26, 1996, after visiting family in France, he returned to Tibhirine. That night he was abducted from the monastery with six of his brother monks.

Bruno (Christian) Lemarchand 1930–1996

Bruno's inclusion among the seven monks kidnapped from the monastery at Tibhirine in the early hours of March 27, 1996, was in a way accidental. Bruno was the leader of the Atlas

[48] Moines de Tibhirine, *Heureux ceux qui espèrent*, 60–61.

[49] Moines de Tibhirine, *Heureux ceux qui espèrent*, 73.

community's small annex at Fez in Morocco, where he had lived since 1990. He had traveled to Tibhirine on March 18 for the election of a prior, scheduled for March 31. But if his presence at Tibhirine on that night seems a matter of chance, his being a member of the monastic community of Notre-Dame de l'Atlas was not. Bruno's story is of a long, sometimes painful journey to "Nazareth," a place of hiddenness, simplicity, and peace. In his last years, while living this hiddenness in the tiny annex of Fez, he regularly hosted his brother monks from Tibhirine as they sought, and found, refuge and refreshment from the turmoil and violence of Algeria.

Born on March 1, 1930, in Saint-Maixent, in western France, Bruno (baptized Christian) spent much of his childhood overseas. His father was a professional soldier whose career took the small family on postings to Aleppo, Syria; to Langson, Tonkin (northern Vietnam) in French Indochina; and to Orléansville (now Ech-Cheliff), Algeria. Bruno celebrated the milestones of first communion, first confession, and confirmation in Algeria, in the fourth-century basilica of Peter and Paul (destroyed in the 1980 earthquake). After the death of his older sister, the family returned to France in 1939, settling in Castelnaudary, in southwest France. Bruno's faith was nurtured by involvement in a youth club run by the Sisters of Marie-Auxiliatrice, associated with the *Cœurs vaillants de France*, founded in the 1920s to provide recreational activities and Catholic formation for children. Sister Marie Josépha, the director, was a "spiritual mother" to Bruno until her death in 1980, and he traced his priestly vocation to her influence in his life.[50]

Bruno began his studies for the priesthood in 1949 at the major seminary of Poitiers. He completed his military service between 1951 and 1953, serving in logistics and then in an infantry regiment. Seventeen months in Algeria left him with memories of the "African sun" and the "warm camaraderie" of the young conscripts with whom he served. He returned to the seminary with a firm sense of his call to the priesthood.

[50] Moines de Tibhirine, *Heureux ceux qui espèrent*, 183–85, 192–93, 223.

However, after the death of his mother in 1954, he confided to his bishop that he had felt drawn since the age of fifteen to monastic life. The bishop's response—that he should test this desire by completing his studies and undertaking a ministry for five years—was the first in a line of postponements that prevented Bruno from exploring this vocation until 1961.[51]

After his ordination as a priest in 1956 and a brief temporary parish placement, Bruno was appointed to the Collège Saint-Charles in Thouars—a ministry that consisted of teaching and catechesis, preparing children for the sacraments.[52] Apart from a brief period in 1961–1962, he remained at Saint-Charles as a teacher, and from August 1965 as superior, until he entered the monastery of Bellefontaine in 1980.

In 1961 Bruno was finally given permission to explore his call to monastic life, and on September 23 he entered the Benedictine monastery at Ligugé. But his stay lasted only a month, and the experience left him doubtful about his vocation and fearful of future failure.[53]

During his time at Saint-Charles, Bruno joined a fraternity of priests, Jésus Caritas, which drew inspiration from Charles de Foucauld. It offered additional structure and support for his day-to-day ministry, and it was through the fraternity that he first came in contact with the Cistercian community of Bellefontaine and began to visit regularly for retreat. He finally joined the community in September 1980.[54] Six months later he formally entered Bellefontaine as a postulant, and on April 2, 1981, the twenty-fifth anniversary of his ordination to the priesthood, he was admitted to the novitiate, taking on his new name, Br. Bruno.[55]

Early in his novitiate Bruno sensed a call to join the Atlas community, and along with Michel, he was sent in August 1984 for a year's trial. While Michel settled quickly, Bruno did not,

[51] Moines de Tibhirine, *Heureux ceux qui espèrent*, 185–90.
[52] Moines de Tibhirine, *Heureux ceux qui espèrent*, 207–8.
[53] Moines de Tibhirine, *Heureux ceux qui espèrent*, 200–202.
[54] Moines de Tibhirine, *Heureux ceux qui espèrent*, 202–9.
[55] Presumably after the founder of the Carthusians.

returning a year later to Bellefontaine, where he was given responsibility for the busy guesthouse. Nonetheless the call to the Atlas community persisted. However, if Bruno had hoped for a speedy return, his stay at Tibhirine had brought to the surface an underlying fragility in need of careful attention and healing. In the years that followed he undertook an important spiritual and psychological journey, working with Fr. Robert Neau, a doctor and priest working for the diocese of Poitiers. [56]

Bruno returned to Tibhirine in April 1989, making his solemn profession on March 21, 1990—nine years after he had first entered Bellefontaine. His commitment to Atlas soon took him to the small annex at Fez, where he had been impressed by the "simple and hidden form of life" that he had tasted there—just three brothers living on the edge of a city of 600,000 people—and at Christian's request in October 1989, Bruno became the fourth brother, initially on a two-year mission. A year later he formally became the leader of the tiny community. He remained content in the place that had become his Nazareth, a place of hiddenness, where he was simply called to live "every day in the spirit of Mary, Joseph, and Jesus." Nazareth had been part of his spiritual imagination since his youth. He speaks often of this place of hiddenness in his late letters: "Before the roads of the Gospel, there were thirty years of Nazareth and I think that we, we'll stop there. And our part is the most beautiful: 'to abide' is a key word in monastic life, in contemplation."[57]

[56] Moines de Tibhirine, *Heureux ceux qui espèrent*, 213–37.
[57] Moines de Tibhirine, *Heureux ceux qui espèrent*, 250.

Chronology

1830 French occupation of Algeria begins

1843 Cistercian foundation established at Staouëli, near Algiers

1904 Monastery at Staouëli sold, community relocated to northern Italy

1934 Refoundation in Atlas Mountains (at Ouled-Triff, then Ben-Chicao)

1938 Notre-Dame de l'Atlas canonically established and settled at Tibhirine

1954 November 1: Front de Libération Nationale (FLN) announces struggle for independence from France, military operations begin

1959 November 8: Murder of Mohammed (Cheikh Benmechay) after he defends Christian de Chergé

1962 July 5: Algeria officially declares independence (132 years after the fall of Algiers)

1971 Arrival of Christian de Chergé at Notre-Dame de l'Atlas, Tibhirine

1976 Solemn profession of Christian de Chergé

1979 Foundation of Ribât es-Salâm (*Lien de la Paix*, Bond of Peace)

1984 Election of Christian de Chergé as prior

1988 Establishment of annex at Fez, Morocco

1990 First free elections after independence
June: Front Islamique du Salut (FIS) wins majority of seats in municipal elections

1991 December 26: FIS wins majority of seats in national election

1992 Elections canceled, National Assembly dissolved, High Council of State created, Mohammed Boudiaf appointed president (assassinated June 29)

1993 October 30: Groupe Islamic Armé (GIA) ultimatum to foreigners to leave

December 14: Assassination of twelve Croatian workers at Tamesguida

December 24: Visit of Sayah Attiya and armed men to the Tibhirine monastery

1994 May 8: Assassination of Br. Henri Vergès and Sr. Paul-Hélène Saint Raymonde

October 23: Assassination of Srs. Caridad María Álvarez and Esther Paniagua Alonso

December 27: Assassination of Père Blancs: Jean Chevillard, Christian Chessel, Alain Dieulangard, and Charles Deckers

1995 September 3: Assassination of Srs. Bibiane (Denise) Leclerc and Angèle-Marie (Jeanne) Littlejohn

November 10: Assassination of Sr. Odette Prévost; wounding of Sr. Chantal Galichet

1996 March 26–27: Abduction of seven monks from the monastery at Tibhirine

May 21: Death of monks announced by GIA communiqué no. 44

May 25: Monks' remains found near Médéa

June 2: Funeral Mass for Cardinal Duval and the seven monks, Algiers

June 4: Burial of the monks in the cemetery of Notre-Dame de l'Atlas, Tibhirine

August 1: Assassination of Pierre Claverie, bishop of Oran

2018 December 8: Beatification of nineteen Algerian martyrs, including the seven Tibhirine monks

Bibliography

Primary Sources (The Monks)

Chenu, Bruno, ed. *Sept vies pour Dieu et l'Algérie*. 2nd ed. Paris: Bayard, 1996.

Chergé, Christian de. "Chapter Talks on the Psalms." CSQ 51, no. 1 (2016): 93–119.

Chergé, Christian de. *Christian de Chergé: Spiritual Writings.* Edited and Translated by Christian Krokus and Habib Zanzana. Modern Spiritual Masters series. Maryknoll, NY: Orbis Books, 2025.

Chergé, Christian de. *Dieu pour tout jour: chapitres de Père Christian de Chergé à la communauté de Tibhirine (1985–1996).* 2nd ed. Montjoyer: Abbaye Notre-Dame d'Aiguebelle, 2006.

Chergé, Christian de. *God for All Days: The Final Monastic Chapters of Christian de Chergé.* Translated by Jennifer Rushworth. Edited by Matthew Cheung Salisbury. MW 73. Collegeville, MN: Cistercian Publications, 2025.

Chergé, Christian de. *L'AUTRE que nous attendons: homélies de Père Christian de Chergé (1970–1996).* Montjoyer: Abbaye Notre-Dame d'Aiguebelle, 2006.

Chergé, Christian de. "L'échelle mystique du dialogue." *Islamochristiana* 23 (1997): 1–26.

Chergé, Christian de. *Lettres à un ami fraternel: Correspondance avec Maurice Borrmans.* Paris: Bayard, 2015.

Chergé, Christian de. *L'invincible espérance.* Edited by Bruno Chenu. Paris: Bayard, 2010.

Chergé, Christian de. "Prier en Église à l'écoute de l'Islam (1982)." *Chemins de dialogue* 27 (2009): 17–24.

Chergé, Christian de. *Retraite sur le Cantique des cantiques.* Edited by Christian Salenson. Spiritualité. Bruyères-le-Châtel: Nouvelle Cité, 2013.

Lebreton, Christophe. *Born from the Gaze of God: The Tibhirine Journal of a Martyr Monk (1993–1996).* Translated by Mette Louise Nygård and Edith Scholl. MW 37. Collegeville, MN: Cistercian Publications, 2014.

Lebreton, Christophe. *Le souffle du don: Journal de Frère Christophe, moine de Tibhirine, 8 août 1993–19 mars 1996.* Paris: Bayard Centurion, 1999.

Luc, Frère. *Tu verras éclater le printemps: Lettres de Tibhirine.* Les Écrits de Tibhirine - Lettres 1. Paris: Bayard-Cerf-Bellefontaine, 2021.

Moines de Tibhirine. *Heureux ceux qui accueillent: vivre l'hospitalité.* Edited by Marie-Dominique Minassian. Les écrits de Tibhirine 4. Paris: Bayard-Cerf-Bellefontaine, 2023.

Moines de Tibhirine. *Heureux ceux qui espèrent: Autobiographies spirituelles.* Edited by Marie-Dominique Minassian. Les écrits de Tibhirine 1. Paris: Bayard-Cerf-Bellefontaine, 2018.

Moines de Tibhirine. *Heureux ceux qui osent la rencontre: des moines en pays d'Islam.* Edited by Marie-Dominique Minassian. Les écrits de Tibhirine 3. Paris: Bayard-Cerf-Bellefontaine, 2022.

Moines de Tibhirine. *Heureux ceux qui prient: maison de prière pour toutes les nations.* Edited by Marie-Dominique Minassian. Les écrits de Tibhirine 5. Paris: Bayard-Cerf-Bellefontaine, 2024.

Moines de Tibhirine. *Heureux ceux qui se donnent: la vie donnée plus forte que la mort.* Edited by Marie-Dominique Minassian. Les écrits de Tibhirine 2. Paris: Bayard-Cerf-Bellefontaine, 2020.

Olivera, Bernardo. *How Far to Follow: The Martyrs of Atlas.* CS 197. Kalamazoo, MI: Cistercian Publications, 1997.

Schumacher, Jean-Paul. "Les frères de Notre-Dame de l'Atlas dans la societé algérienne, à Tibhirine." In *Heureux ceux qui espèrent: Autobiographies spirituelles,* edited by Marie-Dominique Minassian. Les Écrits de Tibhirine 1. Paris: Bayard-Cerf-Bellefontaine, 2018. 17–25.

Other Primary Sources

Bernard of Clairvaux. *The Letters of St. Bernard of Clairvaux.* Translated by Bruno Scott James. Stroud, UK: Sutton Publishing, 1953. Repr., Kalamazoo, MI: Cistercian Publications, 1998.

Bonhoeffer, Dietrich. *Letters and Papers from Prison.* Edited by John W. De Gruchy. Minneapolis: Fortress Press, 2010.

Fry, Timothy, ed. *RB 1980: The Rule of St. Benedict in Latin and English with Notes.* Collegeville, MN: Liturgical Press, 1981.

Silvas, Anna. *The Asketikon of St Basil the Great.* Oxford Early Christian Studies. Oxford: Oxford University Press, 2005.

William of Saint-Thierry, Arnold of Bonneval, and Geoffrey of Auxerre. *The First Life of Bernard of Clairvaux.* Translated by Hilary Costello. CF 69. Collegeville, MN: Cistercian Publications, 2015.

Secondary Sources

Barton, John. *The Word: On the Translation of the Bible.* London: Allen Lane, 2022.

Béthune, Pierre-François de. *Welcoming Other Religions: A New Dimension of the Christian Faith.* Translated by William Skudlarek. Monastic Interreligious Dialogue. Collegeville, MN: Liturgical Press, 2016.

Bingemer, Maria Clara. *Mysticism and Witness in Koinonia: Inspiration from the Martyrdom of Two Twentieth-Century Communities.* Translated by Suzana Regina Moreira. Eugene, OR: Cascade Books, 2023.

Bosch, David J. *Transforming Mission: Paradigm Shifts in Theology of Mission.* Maryknoll, NY: Orbis, 1991.

Bourdeau, Victor. *Vingt ans après le Concile Vatican II ou vingt années de vie liturgique à Tamié (1965–1985).* 1985, Revised 2003. https://www.abbaye-tamie.com/archives/la_communaute/la_liturgie/etudes_documents/la-reforme-liturgique-a-tamie.

Burghardt, Walter J. "Contemplation: A Long Loving Look at the Real." In *An Ignatian Spirituality Reader*, edited by George W. Traub. Chicago: Loyola Press, 2008. 89–98.

Casey, Michael. *The Art of Sacred Reading.* North Blackburn, Victoria, Australia: Dove, HarperCollins, 1995.

Cowdell, Scott. *Why Church? Christianity as It Was Meant to Be.* New York: Church Publishing, 2024.

Derwahl, Freddy. *The Last Monk of Tibhirine: A True Story of Martyrdom, Faith, and Survival.* Brewster, MA: Paraclete Press, 2013.

Evans, Martin, and John Phillips. *Algeria: Anger of the Dispossessed.* New Haven, CT: Yale University Press, 2007.

Foulcher, Jane. "Living Hope: The Witness of the Tibhirine Monks." *St Mark's Review* no. 266 (December 2024): 58–68.

Foulcher, Jane. "A Monastic School of Peace in Post-colonial Algeria: Christophe Lebreton's Tibhirine Journal." *Spiritus: A Journal of Christian Spirituality* 24, no. 1 (2024): 24–46.

Foulcher, Jane. "Nuit de feu: Christian de Chergé and Prayer with the Other." *Spiritus: A Journal of Christian Spirituality* 18, no. 2 (2018): 218–30.

Foulcher, Jane. *Reclaiming Humility: Four Studies in the Monastic Tradition.* CS 255. Collegeville, MN: Cistercian Publications, 2015.

Garda, Claude. "Les monastères cisterciens d'Algérie: Notre-Dame de Staouëli—Notre-Dame de l'Atlas." *Collectanea Cisterciensia* 58 (1996): 201–16.

Georgeon, Thomas, and Françoise Vayne. *Simply Christians: The Life and Message of the Blessed Martyrs of Tibhirine.* Translated by Daniel B. Gallagher. Huntington, IN: Our Sunday Visitor, 2020.

Gilmore, Peter. "Atlas: Reawakened Memories and Present-Day Reflections." CSQ 35, no. 2 (2000): 231–38.

Hémon, Philippe. "An En-Visaged Good-By-E." CSQ 34, no. 2 (1999): 203–18.

Kavanagh, Aidan. *Elements of Rite: A Handbook of Liturgical Style.* New York: Pueblo Publishing Company, 1982.

Kiser, John W. *The Monks of Tibhirine: Faith, Love, and Terror in Algeria.* New York: St Martin's Griffin, 2002.

Krokus, Christian. "Healing and Creating in Christian-Muslim History: Charles de Foucauld, Louis Massignon, Christian de Chergé." *Theological Studies* 85, no. 3 (2024): 439–63.

Louf, André. *The Cistercian Way.* Translated by Nivard Kinsella. CS 76. Kalamazoo, MI: Cistercian Publications, 1983.

Louf, André. *La voie cistercienne: à l'école de l'amour.* Paris: Desclée de Brouwer, 1991.

Louf, André. *A l'école de la contemplation.* Paris: P. Lethielleux, 2003.

Louf, André. *In the School of Contemplation.* Translated by Paul Rowe. MW 48. Collegeville, MN: Cistercian Publications, 2015.

Louth, Andrew. *The Origins of the Christian Mystical Tradition: From Plato to Denys.* 2nd ed. Oxford: Oxford University Press, 2007.

McGlynn, Donald. "Atlas Martyrs." CSQ 32, no. 2 (1997): 149–94.

Naylor, Phillip Chiviges. *Historical Dictionary of Algeria.* Historical Dictionaries of Africa. 4th ed. Lanham, MD: Rowman & Littlefield Publishers, 2015.

Olivera, Bernardo. *How Far to Follow: The Martyrs of Atlas.* CS 197. Kalamazoo, MI: Cistercian Publications, 1997.

Olivera, Bernardo. "Monk, Martyr, and Mystic: Christian de Chergé (1937–1996)." CSQ 34, no. 3 (1999): 321–38.

Olivera, Bernardo. "Tibhirine Today: Circular Letter to the Members of the Order on the 10th Anniversary of the Passage of Our Brothers of Our Lady of Atlas." *Ordo Cisterciensis S.O.*, no. Prot. No.01/AG/06 (May 21, 2006).

Pickard, Stephen. *Seeking the Church: An Introduction to Ecclesiology.* London: SCM Press, 2012.

Ray, Marie-Christine. *Christian de Chergé, prieur de Tibhirine.* 2nd ed. Paris: Bayard, 1998.

Salenson, Christian. *Christian de Chergé: A Theology of Hope.* Translated by Nada Conic. CS 247. Kalamazoo, MI: Cistercian Publications, 2012.

Salenson, Christian. "Monastic Life, Interreligious Dialogue, and Openness to the Ultimate: A Reflection on the Tibhirine Monks' Experience." *The Way* 45, no. 3 (2006): 23–37.

São José, Nuno de "Notre-Dame de l'Atlas, mystère d'une secrète fécondité: histoire de la communauté depuis sa fondation jusqu'en 1996." *Collectanea Cisterciensia* 83 (2021): 271–306.

Scholl, Edith. "Christian de Chergé on Humility." CSQ 41, no. 2 (2006): 193–215.

Sessions, Jennifer E. *By Sword and Plow: France and the Conquest of Algeria.* Ithaca, NY: Cornell University Press, 2011. doi:10.7591/9780801454479.

Tacey, David. "Contemporary Spirituality." In *Oxford Textbook of Spirituality in Healthcare,* edited by Mark Cobb, Christina M. Puchalski, and Bruce D. Rumbold. Oxford: Oxford University Press, 2012. 473–79.

Taylor, Charles. *A Secular Age.* Cambridge, MA: Belknap Press, 2007.

Teissier, Henri. "Le monastère de Tibhirine et l'Église d'Algérie." In *Heureux ceux qui espèrent: Autobiographies spirituelles,* edited by Marie-Dominique Minassian. Les Écrits de Tibhirine 1. Paris: Bayard-Cerf-Bellefontaine, 2018. 27–38.

Teissier, Henri, and Jean-Jacques Pérennès. Introduction to *Heureux ceux qui osent la rencontre: des moines en pays d'Islam,* edited by Marie-Dominique Minassian. Les écrits de Tibhirine. Paris: Bayard-Cerf-Bellefontaine, 2022.

Vandermarliere, Sébastien. "Les abbayes de l'Ordre de Cîteaux (Stricte Observance): Sainte Marie de Maguzzano." *Collectanea Cisterciensia* 4 (1936): 218–23.

Veilleux, Armand. "Le contexte communautaire de Notre-Dame de l'Atlas." In *Heureux ceux qui espèrent: Autobiographies spirituelles*, edited by Marie-Dominique Minassian. Les Écrits de Tibhirine. Paris: Bayard-Cerf-Bellefontaine, 2018. 39–42.

Veilleux, Armand. "The Witness of the Tibhirine Martyrs." *Spiritus: A Journal of Christian Spirituality* 1, no. 2 (2001): 205–16.

Wells, Samuel. *A Nazareth Manifesto: Being with God*. Chichester, UK: Wiley Blackwell, 2015.

Wright, Timothy. *No Peace Without Prayer: Encouraging Muslims and Christians to Pray Together. A Benedictine Approach*. Monastic Interreligious Dialogue. Collegeville, MN: Liturgical Press, 2013.